D0585142

Forbidden Forward

The Justin Fashanu Story

Forbidden Forward

The Justin Fashanu Story

Nick Baker

Reid Publishing

A CIP catalogue record for this title is available from the British Library

Book Design by Andrew Searle

Cover Design by Tony Rose

Cover photo courtesy of Dick and Olive Mills

Published by Reid Publishing

53 Church Gate, Loughborough, Leicestershire, LE11 1UE

Tel: 07974 304022 Email: reidpublishing@fsmail.net

Printed and bound in India

Contents

To Junmin and Dorothy

Acknowledgements

ALL TOLD, it's taken the best part of two years to research and write this book, and it would not have been possible without the assistance of a multitude of people. Firstly, I'd like to say a big thank you to the man who shared my faith in *The Justin Fashanu Story*, Dave McVay from Reid Publishing. His expert eye, experience and assistance have been invaluable and greatly appreciated.

The aim of this book has always been to gain a unique insight into Justin Fashanu. Away from the football pitch, and underneath the bravado he so often displayed, who was he really? It's a great question, and one that can only be answered by the people who knew him. The following are some of those very people and I thank them from the bottom of my heart for the time they so generously sacrificed: family, friends, players, coaches, managers and journalists:

Colin Slater, Edward and Rachel Jackson, Susan Anderson, Les Hammond, Dave Bennett, John Bond, Ken Brown, Alastair Aitken, Martin Staines, Mark Woodrow, Mark Overton, John Lund, Graham Shurey, Ernest Cashmore, Alf Fincham, Pete Venables, Graham Morgan, John Banbury, Jeremy Smith, Gordon Holmes, Stephanie Brooks, Terry Reeve, Paul Cheston, Rik Cheston, Mark Barham, Phil Hoadley, Chris Roberts, Malcolm Robertson, Mick Dennis, Mel Richards, Joe Royle, Roger Haywood, John Barnes, Karl Tuttle, Brian Harvey, Glenn Hoy, Les King, Neil Giles, Kevan Platt, John Lawson, Keith Lennox, Peter Ward, Ian Wallace, Terry Carpenter, J. John, Nick Brotherwood, Ronnie Fenton, Duncan Hamilton, Ross Smith, Mark Smalley, Calvin Plummer, Mark Proctor, Peter Tatchell, Nick Brotherwood, Lawrie McMenemy, Les Cleevely, Nick Holmes, Steve Williams, David Puckett, Malcolm Waldron, Trevor Frecknall, Howard Wilkinson, Trevor Christie, Iain McCulloch, Ian McParland, Dave Watson, Mick Leonard, Graham Daniels, Malcolm Doney, Larry Lloyd, Neil Slawson, Chris Cattlin, Keiran O'Regan, Tony Millard, John Vinicombe, Mike Yaxley, Kevin Weaver, Clive Brewster, John Britton, Bobby Ammann, Sherri Howard, A.J. Ali, Mel Kowalchuk, Len Vickery, Gregor Young, Ambrose Mendy, Frank Clark, Bill Songhurst, John McGrane, Allan Hall, Terry Deal, Brett Gordon, Mike Bateson, Sue Bateson, Paul Compton, David Thomas, Alan Quick, John McVeigh,

George Peat, Alex Dowdalls, Kenny Black, David McCarthy, Sandy Clark, Hugh McCann, Nick Mills, Gina Mills, Grant Stantiall, Bruce Holloway, Anton Hysen, Nick London.

I'd also like to thank a host of other people who gave me their time and own insights. These also include people who helped with my research and others who connected me with valuable contacts:

Tony Campbell, Peter Sanderson, Steve Long, Craig Spafford, Edward Couzens-Lake, Duncan Holley, Sharon Ferguson, David Thomas (the other one!), Jas Baines, Norman Keen, Brian Deer, Juliet Jacques, Jason Hall, Scott Lawson, Nick London, Marcia Dixon, Peter Walsh, Ian Clarke, Debbie Hancox, Mary Bissell, David Cuffley and Rosemary Dixon from Archant Media, Craig Goldthorpe from J. Press, Andy Naylor from The Argus, Michael Grant from the Sunday Herald, Peter Steward from Line One, Colin Mitchell from *Shoot!*, Nicola Douglas from Barnardo's, Gary Newbon from Prime Ticket UK, Craig Sackfield from Centric Sports, Barrie Williams, Ralph Shepherd and Brian Bates from Notts County, Keith Daniel and Liz Stenner from The Media Group, Mick Holland from the Nottingham Post Group, Dan Tester from Stripe Publishing, Paul Berry from Wolves, Camilla Lawrence from the Metropolitan Police Department, Keith Jeffrey from East Sussex Cricket League, Simon Heggie from Manchester City FC, Paul Camillin at Brighton and Hove Albion FC, Geraint Parry from Wrexham FC, Vicky Owens from BBC Press Office, Brian Papworth from SCOA Officials, Ciaran McMahon from Coastal FC, Graham Bell from Middlesbrough FC, Pamela Claire from Ashram Housing Association, David Napier, Neil Kaufman, Peter Cresswell, Tony Green from the London Gay Men's Chorus, Alan Burrows from Motherwell FC, Claire Huggins from West Bromwich Albion FC, Matt Horner from Seaview Media, Mike Young from Coventry City FC, Richard Elliott from Lawrie McMenemy Centre for Football Research, Sam Dick from Stonewall, Hester Brierley from English Institute of Sport, Andrew Barringer from Luton Town FC, Lynn Harris from Leyton Orient FC, Bernadette Ocampo from Philo Trust, Sarah Smellie from the Christian Centre, Debbie Hancox, Malcolm Stuart, Maureen Havers from Charley Heritage Group, Frank Spilak from Holy Trinity High School, Danny Lynch from Kick it Out, David Edgley from Nottingham's Rainbow Heritage, Jason Longshore from Soccer Streets, Peter Neal and Jon Dennis from Attleborough Amateur Boxing Club, Diana Van Bunnens from John

Holmes Media, Jeffrey Kamis from Tampa Bay FC, Lorraine Sass from Blue Yonder, Andrew Wenley, Denis Harlow from the FFSA and Jeanne Upchurch from Harrison County Police Department.

Hundreds of people from Norwich contacted me after journalist, Peter Walsh, published an article about my proposed book in the Norwich Evening News back in 2011 (thanks again Peter.) As such, I'd like to express my gratitude to all the people who took the time to contact me.

Stacey Mickelbart took on the unenviable task of editing my manuscript, and that takes courage and patience. Sentence fragments are the bain of her literary existence, and I apologise for my past addiction. Thanks to her, I have finally managed to kick the habit. Thanks, Stacey, for all your hard work and professionalism. Much appreciated.

I can't exit this portion of the book without saying thanks to my boss, Lynn Booth. Along with my wife, she's also relieved I completed this project so I can regain focus on my main day job. (Note to self: burning the candle at both ends does not always endear you with one's boss.) Lynn - thank you for not firing me.

Finally, I'd like to extend my greatest thanks and love to my family. Firstly, my wife Junmin, who never complained once when I refused to budge from the computer, often late at night, and got used to the fact that evening dinner often involved eating at the computer desk and multi-tasking (eating, typing and, sometimes, cursing). She is a godsend. Thanks to my parents, Janice and Terry Baker, who helped with my research back in the UK and are just all round-incredible people.

A huge thanks to my brother Simon in New York, who has helped me in more ways than he knows. A good footballer in his own right, Simon played for the Notts County youth team in the mid-Eighties before winning a soccer scholarship to a prestigious college in New York state. After hanging up his boots, he now runs his own successful investment firm from New York city. He is a great inspiration.

Lastly, a shout out of love and gratitude to my extended family: Ed and Gemma Thompson, Steve Rigby, Lyn Smith-Dennis and Yvonne Wysall.

Girls were made to love and kiss
And who am I to interfere with this?
Am I ashamed to follow nature's way?
Can I be blamed if God has made me gay?

Paganini (Franz Lehár, 1925)

Foreword

by Robbie Rogers

WHEN I was first approached to write the foreword for this book my initial thought was, 'No way'. I asked myself: who am I to write about a man I never knew? Sure, Justin Fashanu and I had a lot in common; we were both professional footballers and gay men, but Justin was a true pioneer. He was the first professional footballer to announce to the world he was gay, the first one to bravely beat a path so that others could follow.

I obviously didn't know Justin when he was alive, but his actions along with others made my openness today possible. As such, I am incredibly humbled to be able to write about him now and thankful for the opportunity. I first heard about Justin's story when I was very much struggling with my own sexuality back in early 2012. At the time, I was playing for Leeds United and no one in football circles knew that I was gay. I remember hearing the lads talking about Justin while I was in the changing rooms at Leeds. When I heard briefly about his life, naturally, I was curious but I remember distinctly avoiding taking part in the conversation. Back then, whenever the topic of homosexuality was brought up by anyone I always avoided talking about it. I didn't want anyone to suspect that I was actually hiding the same secret that Justin had once hidden himself. However, as soon as I got back home later that day I couldn't wait to find out more about this man. I immediately switched on my computer and checked out Justin's story online. If I'm being honest, as I read about Justin's life my immediate reaction was sadness, quickly followed by a little shame. Here was a man who not only broke down the race barrier by being the first million pound black footballer, but here was someone who was also brave enough to share his innermost secret with his loved ones and the public, many of whom weren't ready to accept him. The fall out he subsequently received was horrific. By comparison, I felt embarrassed and a coward compared to him.

In recent years, various athletes from different sports have followed Justin's lead and revealed that they are gay themselves. To me, each and every one of these athletes is a role model and hero. They are taking a stand and showing people that it's okay to be true with who you really are. I understand that in a macho sport like American football it is incredibly difficult to take such a brave stand, but it is possible. Sadly, I believe that society is still incredibly close-minded and fearful of the issue of homophobia generally. Sure, slowly and surely, society is finally taking small steps forward in this regard, but there is still a long way to go. Naturally, the ultimate goal is total acceptance of who you are regardless of your sexuality.

Every time an athlete comes out publicly, the debate about 'who' was the first openly gay athlete always arises. Of course, it is Justin Fashanu's name that is, invariably, mentioned and, in my opinion, rightly so. Justin was a leader, a man ahead of his time. His story is important because it not only unites gay footballers, but connects people from all walks of life who struggle with the feeling of being an outcast themselves. In the end, we are all different but being different is what makes us so special. Ultimately, we should never feel forced to hide who we truly are.

Preface

WE'LL NEVER know exactly what was going through Justin Fashanu's mind in the early evening of Friday May 1st 1998, but one can imagine his thoughts were desperate and bleak. It was certainly far different from his glory years where the footballer had once enjoyed being one of the most popular and celebrated players in England. Sometimes, there's no telling how life turns out.

After leaving a gay sauna in Shoreditch, east London where he'd spent the afternoon, Justin crossed the street and walked a short distance down the road. Turning into a dimly lit alley, the footballer walked up to an empty building at the very end. During the day the space served as a car park, but at night it was vacant with no one in sight. It was perfect for what Justin had in mind. However, there was one small problem. For his plan to work the footballer needed to break inside. At the front of the building two crude doors of rusty corrugated iron sheets were chained together concealing a small entrance. As he surveyed the building, Justin spotted a small gap between the top of the doors and an arch just above it. It would be a tight squeeze getting through the opening, but the footballer knew he could just about manage it. Throwing his bag over his back, Justin gripped the top of the iron sheets and hauled himself up. If he made any noise, no one heard. Scaling the entrance was no easy task for someone of Justin's bulk but, still in excellent shape, it was no problem for the agile footballer. As he clambered over the top and down the other side, jagged shards of metal cut into his hands.

The interior of the car park was dark save for a few glints of light that shone though the small archway he'd just climbed through. It would have taken a few seconds for the footballer's eyes to adjust to the surroundings, and as he stood there breathing in the dust there was still time to change his mind. Alas, it wasn't to be. Justin always had been stubbornly determined and now would be no different. Exploring the car park, Justin spied a mirror on a wall. Knocking it loose, he walked into a bathroom at the back of the building and placed the mirror on top of the sink. No one knows why but maybe he wanted to look at himself one final time. Rolling up his sleeves, Justin picked up something sharp and slashed his right wrist three times. The pain from the symbolic act was nothing compared to the torment he felt inside.

Pulling a handful of paper towels from a nearby dispenser, Justin wrapped them tightly around his wrist that was bleeding on to the floor. Once the bleeding had stopped he took his Filofax and a pen from his bag, wrote a short note to family and friends then placed it on the toilet seat. His dark rhetoric said it all. The Filofax contained the names and numbers of hundreds of the footballer's friends. They were people who cared about him and if Justin had simply called one of them then maybe they'd have persuaded him to stop the madness. But none of them would receive a call. Not that night or ever again.

Walking out the bathroom the footballer grabbed four large car wheels that were scattered about the warehouse and piled them one on top of the other. It was no coincidence they were stacked directly below a metal beam. In another corner, Justin saw an electrical flex cord. It certainly looked long enough but would it hold his weight? There was only one way to find out. Making a small noose with one end Justin climbed on to the tyres, threw the other end of the cord around the beam and secured it. It was almost time.

As a practising Christian, it's likely the footballer said one final prayer before placing his neck inside the noose, tightening it and taking a deep breath. There was just one more challenge to complete before Justin could finally feel peace. To make his plan work he needed to kick off the top tyre he was standing on. The tyre, complete with metal rim, was exceptionally heavy and no easy task but, somehow, he managed it. The footballer always had excelled at challenges. Seconds later, Justin Fashanu was dead and the world of sport would soon be in mourning.

Lost and Found

WHEN IT comes to football, retired teacher John Lund will never forget one game as long as he lives. It was 1975 when Lund was a PE teacher at Attleborough Secondary Modern School in Norfolk and his under-14 side was playing a rival school from Thetford whose players were renowned for being mean and playing dirty. They were also big and Lund was outraged that his players were getting kicked and punched like it was a UFC bout, never mind a football match. To make matters worse the referee was doing nothing about the rash challenges and off-the-ball elbows. It was frustrating to watch. As the skies darkened overhead and it started to rain Lund wondered if the day could get any more miserable. His question was soon answered as Thetford began scoring.

But Attleborough's opponents hadn't counted on one person in Lund's team who was getting just as annoyed as his teacher. The boy's name was Justin Fashanu, and although he was only 14 he stood almost six feet tall and had the frame of a man five years his senior. With an ability and confidence just as big, the precocious striker wasn't about to sit back and let his teammates get kicked around. When the referee blew his whistle to commence the second half it was time for a little payback. Slowly but surely the young Fashanu 'sorted out' the Thetford players one by one, including a rival who had been picking on his kid brother John the whole game. After conceding a foul against the boy Justin offered him his hand and as he pulled him off the ground whispered: 'Pack it in with my little brother or the next time I will really do ya.' Lund, who was standing nearby, heard the comment and something told him his striker wasn't kidding. The smouldering look in Justin's eye showed he meant business. Apparently, the Thetford player believed it too because for the rest of the game he kept a safe distance and the extra space enabled Justin to break away and fire four goals past a helpless Thetford keeper. Incredibly, Attleborough went on to win the game and for Lund, Justin Fashanu was the hero of the day. The teacher may have been soaked to the bone but he couldn't have been any happier. In time he would soon discover that Fashanu's skill and athleticism were not only reserved for football. The teacher was supervising a badminton lesson in the gym one lunchtime when Justin popped his head through the door and asked if he could join in. Despite never playing the sport competitively before he went on to thrash the school's best player. Once again, Lund was astounded.

While a natural affinity for sports seemed to come easy for Justin, his early childhood had been anything but a breeze. 'Justinus Soni Fashanu' was born on 19th February 1961 in Hackney, east London. His father Patrick was a law student and his mother Pearl a nurse from Guyana. The couple were new to London and had moved to the capital city in order for Patrick to continue his law studies. Justin was the third oldest of four children that included Dawn, the eldest, Phillip and then John who was 19 months younger than Justin. While Pearl looked after the little ones her husband studied full-time. Money was tight and East London rents were high even back in the Sixties, so the family of six had to contend with being crammed inside a small terraced house. There were no luxuries with every spare penny going towards the bare essentials like food and clothing.

In 1963, Justin's life took a dramatic turn when his father announced that he was travelling back to Nigeria. Patrick believed there were more opportunities for lawyers in his home country, and despite having a family he felt staying in England was not an option. Unwilling to leave London where her mother and brother lived, Pearl told her husband that she and the children would not be joining him. The decision would have devastating consequences. Unable to look after four kids alone, Pearl made the painful decision to give up her youngest two to a children's home.

Justin was three and John two when their tearful mother handed them to a representative from Dr Barnardo's. Understandably, Pearl would reveal that waving goodbye to her children was the lowest and hardest day of her life but there was no other option. As Justin and John were being driven away she wiped away her tears and promised she would visit. Scared and confused, the Fashanu brothers could do little but accept their fate. Leaving the security of the only life they knew was, obviously, terrifying. The Fashanus' new home was a Victorian orphanage in Wood Green, London. The institution was old and grey, the stuff of a Charles Dickens novel. To the young Fashanus it must have looked like a prison. As the eldest of the two siblings Justin knew he had to be strong. It was his first big test in life and he needed to be resilient for the sake of his brother. The agony of being separated from the rest of his family was hard to comprehend but taught him an important lesson in life: there was only one person you could count on and that was yourself. Believing that he and John had, essentially, been abandoned by their parents forced Justin to grow up quickly. The experience would have significant ramifications for his relationships in the future.

While Pearl made every effort to visit her two children each weekend, the shock of being parted from his mother greatly affected John in particular. Not as strong as his brother, he spoke in a baby language that only Justin could understand, and the eldest Fashanu became his protector. Being thrust into an unfamiliar world created a strong bond between the siblings, their brotherhood a gleam of light in an uncertain future. Thankfully, their time at Wood Green was short-lived. After two years, salvation arrived in the form of an elderly white couple named Alf and Betty Jackson. Alf and Betty were from Norfolk and were visiting the institution with an eye to fostering one child. The moment they walked over to the Fashanus is one John will never forget: 'I was looking at them all the time and my eyes were saying: "Choose me, please, choose me."'[1] His prayers were, ultimately, answered because a few days later the couple returned and told the boys to pack their bags. They were leaving for a new home in the country. It marked the end of a dark chapter for the two brothers and the start of a much happier one.

Initially, Alf and Betty had only wanted to adopt one child, but when they discovered that Justin and John were going to be split up and sent to separate foster homes they couldn't bear the thought. The Jacksons lived in a little village called Shropham in rural Norfolk, about eighteen miles outside of Norwich. With a population of less than 600, Shropham's main attractions were a post office, historic pub and church. It's not much different today. Alf and Betty were originally from London and had moved east a couple of years earlier for a quieter life. If the Wood Green orphanage felt like a prison to the Fashanu brothers, the Jackson's home must have seemed like paradise. The picture postcard Flint House was an old brick lodge located at the bottom of a small, muddy lane. Surrounded by bramble bushes and fields, there were acres of land for the boys to explore. At the back of the house was a massive orchard with a bucolic array of trees and wild flowers. There was also a small chicken coop that Betty raided every morning for eggs.

At the front of the property was a shed that Alf had converted into a small factory. Alf's business was precision engineering and he made his living producing miniature components for model trains and railways. Jackson was a well-known name amongst model railway enthusiasts all over the world with Alf sending his specialist parts as far away as Australia. It was a niche market and one that enabled Alf to make a comfortable living from. Flint House was also full of character on the inside with low ceilings, creaky stairs and old fireplaces. Justin and John were given their own bedrooms in the top of the attic. Once Justin had settled in he stuck a black and white photograph of his mother above his bed. Pearl might have been out of sight but she was never out of mind. Down below a magnificent grand piano had pride of place in the drawing room. Unlike the Dickensian children's home, Flint House would have featured nicely in a Jane Austen book.

The boys' foster mum was a talented pianist who played the organ at a local 13th century church. Betty regularly hosted private piano lessons at Flint House and was also a part-time piano teacher at nearby Wymondham College. Once a year, Betty held a popular recital in the elegant setting of Kimberly Hall in Shropham. Her pupils played a variety of pieces on a Steinway grand piano in front of an admiring audience of parents and friends. After each recital, Betty rewarded everyone with a bounty of strawberries and cream. She was well regarded in the local community.

Alf and Betty also had two children of their own: a daughter Susan, who had already left Flint House by the time the young Fashanus arrived, and a son Edward. While Susan had inherited her mother's musical talents and was an accomplished singer, Edward had followed his father into the engineering game. He would later make a name for himself by inventing a machine that produced paint rollers. There were also two other additions to the Jackson clan: Labrador Cross dogs that Justin came to adore. Edward Jackson was 20 when he first met Justin and John following a trip to Italy: 'My parents had just been to pick them up from London and as you might expect they were both very nervous. They'd only been at Flint House a day or two before I met them. They had quite deep-rooted problems in the beginning. Their mother had abandoned them and that must have been a real blow to their self-confidence,' Jackson says.

Justin never forgot the day he first arrived at Flint House. His nostrils were greeted by a strange, distinctive smell that Alf explained was good ol' country air. After unpacking their bags the Fashanus were led out into the backyard where they fed the chickens and explored the garden. In the evening, Susan presented a lavish meal. Despite toiling over a new recipe all afternoon, she wasn't a bit offended when Justin took one small mouthful before spitting it out on the table in disgust. It would take a while before he got used to good ol' country cuisine too.

It's widely believed that Alf and Betty Jackson adopted Justin and John Fashanu, but that isn't the case. The Jacksons fostered the boys and, according to Edward, it was initially only supposed to be for a couple of years. Justin and John ended up staying at Flint House until they became young men, but that wasn't the original plan. Because the boys were being fostered a representative from Dr Barnardo's named Mr Scott visited the family every few months to check up on things. Alf and Betty also welcomed the boys' mother Pearl to visit Flint House whenever she liked. Pearl would shortly remarry and give birth to another son, Nicklaus.

Back in the Sixties, there were hardly any black people in the whole of Norfolk therefore the arrival of Justin and John caused quite a stir. Many folks in Shropham and the surrounding villages had never even seen a black face before. The fact a middle class white couple were fostering two minority children was, therefore, quite revolutionary. In an interview with a local reporter a few years later Betty said: 'I had my doubts whether I could take care of a little black boy but the rest of the family thought it would be okay, so we went to see them and got to know them and decided to have them.'[2] Betty revealed that only one person told them they were making a mistake.

One man who knew the young Justin better than most was Les Hammond. Born and bred in Norfolk, Hammond worked for Alf as an apprentice engineer. In the mid-Sixties, when Justin and John first arrived in Shropham, Hammond had just turned 16 and was at the house the day the boys arrived. In time, Hammond would become like a big brother to the two lads. Since Alf's workshop was attached to Flint House he saw them almost every day. Hammond also had another connection with the Fashanus. Like them, he'd also spent time in a children's home. The first few months in Flint House must have been an incredibly surreal experience for the Fashanu brothers, but Justin settled in to his new surroundings a lot quicker than John. Justin acted as a big brother in every respect with John refusing to go anywhere unless he was with him. As the months passed, John started clinging to Betty who he would come to affectionately call 'a lovely big, fat English lady.'

Justin and John went through more than their average share of trauma for children so young, but Justin seemed determined to put the past behind him. One of the first opportunities he grabbed with both hands (and feet) was football. Alf constructed a small wooden goalpost in the middle of the orchard, and when he presented Justin with a leather ball it hardly left the youngster's feet. It was love at first kick. Hammond recalls that every day the boys' morning routine was the same. After scrambling out of bed they threw on their clothes, forgot to brush their teeth, bolted down the stairs, burst out the back door and into the orchard where the football was waiting to be kicked. Never mind breakfast. When Hammond arrived for work in the morning the first thing he always heard was a ball being kicked, accompanied by laughter. It was obvious right away that Justin had a natural affinity for the game. It wasn't long before he was able to keep the ball in the air with both feet and his head. He also had a powerful right foot as John learned to his detriment after going in goal. The Jacksons found out too after one of Justin's shots smashed through the kitchen window. The goals were hastily relocated. Betty described the boys as 'naughty but nice' and whenever they got into trouble it was usually left to Alf to tell them off. The two Fashanus breathed new life into Flint House, characterised by laughter and smiles.

Football wasn't the only sport that Justin embraced. Inside the family garage was an old ping-pong table that Alf had bought Edward several years earlier. Now it was all Justin's. He quickly became a proficient player and his opponent was usually Hammond. Whenever Alf disappeared to London to visit a distributor, no sooner had his car left the driveway Justin would run into the workshop, tug on Hammond's overalls and shout: 'Come on, switch them machines off and let's get into that garage for a game!' When the boys were a little older Hammond made the Fashanus a punch bag out of an old Hessian sack stuffed with straw. Hammond had no idea just how significant that simple act would be. Justin was soon spending just as much time hitting it as kicking a ball around and it wasn't long before the straw needed replacing. What impressed Hammond was how dedicated Justin was. He had never seen such focus in someone so young.

As an adult, Justin revealed that his formative years at Flint House were the best days of his life. For a child, there was never a dull moment and the Fashanus could always find some kind of mischief to get up to. Justin said that he and John had been given another chance because of Alf and Betty. If you consider love and encouragement the ideal foundations for any child then Justin and John had those in abundance. Alf and Betty Jackson had high standards that they instilled in the two Fashanus from the moment they arrived in Shropham. Respect and manners were mandatory. Despite the challenges they had faced early in their life, both boys responded well and did not appear bitter at what had happened to them. When the boys told Betty they wished they were white like everyone else their foster mum said: 'You're black, you're going to stay black and you're to be proud of being black.'[3] Occasionally, Justin suffered from nightmares where he lashed out in his sleep. One time, he smashed his fist clean through his bedroom door. It made a change from the punching bag. Apart from those odd nightmares, life at Flint House looked normal. At least on the surface.

According to Hammond, when Justin was around nine he was forced to have his legs put in plaster. Doctors were concerned that the muscles around the youngster's knees were not developing as fast as the other muscles in his legs. Wearing plaster was the only way to ensure he didn't kick a football around, enabling his legs to get some rest. Of course, it didn't stop him from heading the ball.

In light of the physical reputation Justin would earn as a professional footballer, it's hard to imagine him wearing a cassock and singing in a church choir. But that's exactly what he did at eight, taking part in a carol service alongside his brother at Norwich Cathedral with Alf and Betty watching proudly. The following year the siblings swapped the cassocks for rags when they played street urchins in an *Oliver Twist* performance at the Theatre Royal. Justin's career as an actor was strictly one-off, just like a pony-riding lesson Betty took him to. The instructor Margaret Leeder remembers that Justin spent most of the lesson hiding behind Betty whenever a pony so much as glanced at him. Justin's fear of most things, however, would be short-lived.

At five, the Jacksons enrolled Justin at Attleborough Primary School. Attleborough was a little market town about five miles from Shropham. Justin started school in 1966, a memorable year for English football. While the nation was celebrating England's success in the World Cup finals, young Fashanu was getting his first taste of competitive football. His new school encouraged the sport and organised regular matches against other teams. With an obvious flair for the game, he was immediately selected for the team where he stood head and shoulders above everyone else, both in size and skill. His schoolyard teammate Alistair Aitken said that in one match Attleborough conceded an early goal only for Justin to equalise from the centre spot. No sooner had his teammate nudged the ball to him to restart the game, Justin saw the keeper was off his line and chipped the ball right over him. Everyone on the field, the referee included, stood there in shock and awe. In a simple gesture that would come to define his modesty, the young striker simply shrugged his shoulders. With such talent at his disposal, it wasn't long before his PE teacher Mr Claxton was selecting Justin to play with the senior team. The decision didn't go down well with some of the older players, but Justin let his feet do the talking. Even though he was a few years younger he outshone everyone.

Justin's natural athletic ability was not the only thing that began to develop, so too had his bubbly personality. Friends recall that he was forever smiling, incredibly cheeky and unfailingly polite. When John started at the same school two years later he was a lot more quiet and broody. Still in protective mode, Justin looked out for his brother as best he could and made sure he settled in. It's not surprising that John described Justin as his shining light and someone whom he idolised when he was young. Unfortunately, that would change in time.

As primary school progressed Justin forged a close friendship with his fellow teammate, Alastair Aitken. Aitken believes they were naturally drawn to each other because they were different from other children. While his friend was the sole black boy at the school (before John started) Alastair was the only deaf boy. Other people at school remember Justin as someone who was already displaying an incredibly competitive spirit. Martin Staines who was in the same class says Justin would normally win every athletic race he entered, but if he was lagging behind he would deliberately trip himself up to avoid finishing. He didn't like to lose. Staines and Justin both attended a church club on Sundays at the local vicarage. One time they were playing rounders in the rain when Justin went in to bat. As he struck the ball the wet bat slipped out of his hands and broke Staine's nose. As he writhed on the ground in agony, Staines could hear a strange squawk in the background. That famous Fashanu giggle was already developing.

Justin's school grades were less of a laughing matter. His teacher at Attleborough Primary School Mrs Blanch made the following comments about the six year old in his 1967 summer term report:

> *Justin is a lively member of the class. In a general discussion he shows keen interest and enquiring mind and makes one feel teaching is worthwhile. He is capable of appreciating adult humour and has a good sense of humour himself. Sometimes Justin's work is good and careful. Other times it is sloppy and full of careless mistakes which I think is due to a lack of concentration. This is a set back to his progress.*

Perhaps, not surprisingly, he got top marks in physical education but in the same report didn't fare quite so well in arts and crafts.

Outside of primary school Justin's best friend was Mark Woodrow. Woodrow went to a different school in Norfolk and met Justin through cycling around the local villages. Justin didn't own his own bicycle and used to borrow Betty's, an old fashioned clunker with a large metal basket on the front. Woodrow's father owned a farm and Justin was delighted when he discovered a five-a-side football pitch in one of the fields. No matter that the nets were made out of old nylon and there were no proper markings, Fashanu and Woodrow kicked a football around on that pitch for hours. Everyone in the area was welcome to join in and there was enough space for two teams. The two boys also etched out a tennis court in a garden behind Woodrow's house. Cutting the grass short with a mower and using an old net, tennis became another sport at which Justin excelled. With his power and a keen eye Woodrow never had a hope. At the end of the summer, Woodrow's father admonished both children when he saw how much they'd worn down his prized grass.

One summer day in the late Sixties, Woodrow asked Justin and John whether they were interested in earning some fast cash. It was the first time the Fashanus had been given the opportunity to make their own pocket money and they didn't need to be asked twice. A friend of Mr Woodrow needed help harvesting sugar beets and removing the weeds. It wasn't a glamorous job but it paid cash. There were thousands of beets to harvest so the farmer hired about twenty pickers. He divided the workers into separate lines, with Justin placed in one and John in the other. As everyone started picking the beets and progressed slowly forward it quickly became apparent that Justin and John were racing each other. Soon, they were metres in front of everyone else. Unhappy that the boys had forged ahead an older man shouted: 'Hey Sambo, get back in bloody line.' Woodrow will never forget the look in Justin's eyes. Although Woodrow was a good twenty yards away he could see his friend's pupils widen as he gave the man who made the comment a long, intense look. Justin was obviously hurt because he never went back.

On another occasion, Woodrow invited Justin to an event being staged by his local scout group. An affable old vicar named Reverend Staines who had the unfortunate habit of calling his young scouts 'nig-nogs' ran the pack. Rarely spoken today, the phrase was mainly used to describe someone being silly but also, occasionally, used to describe someone with black skin. It's doubtful the vicar knew just how offensive he was being but Justin certainly did. When Fashanu was called a nig-nog himself he gave the reverend a murderous look and never returned to scouts again.

Justin realised from an early age that when it came to his skin colour he was different to other people in Norfolk. Although he adapted well to his white foster parents and colour was not an issue for him personally, he was learning that not everyone shared his sentiments. When he started senior school in 1972, apart from one mixed race pupil, Justin was the only black boy there until his brother started a year later. John Lund was not only Justin's PE teacher at Attleborough Secondary Modern but also his form tutor, so he got to know young Fashanu well. Lund said Justin could not have been more popular and his colour was never an issue, at least not at his own school. Lund recounts one story of a local dignitary who once paid a visit. It was a few years after Justin had started playing football and news of his skills on the field had already filtered beyond the school gates. When the dignitary arrived at the school at break time he asked a pupil if he could point out Justin Fashanu. Lund smiled when he heard the boy say: 'That's him over there, sir, the one with the blue sweater and white trainers.' The other children didn't view Justin's colour as a defining characteristic at all.

Mark Overton was a friend of Justin's at secondary school and was also on the school team. As a midfielder, Overton loved playing with Justin because the striker always made him look good. Overton knew that all he had to do was slot the ball past the four opposing defenders for his teammate to run on to. Thanks to his speed, Justin was always the first to get to the ball and usually ended up scoring. Overton was quite happy with an assist. While most games ended with an Attleborough win, things didn't always work out that way. On one occasion, Attleborough were playing their bitter rivals Thetford in a hellish match that eventually had to be abandoned. As the only black player on the pitch, Justin was being mercilessly heckled and hacked by the opposing team. Racist comments were directed at him the entire game and when a Thetford player bit him on the shoulder it was as much as Lund could take. He immediately ordered his players off the pitch. When Fashanu took off his shirt in the minibus a trickle of blood oozed from a gaping wound on his shoulder. Rather than condemning the perpetrator, Justin apologised to the other players and told them he felt bad that the game had been cancelled because of him. His teammates quickly explained that he wasn't to blame at all and that they were just as angry as Lund at what had happened. It was an early lesson for Justin that football isn't always the beautiful game it's made out to be. It wouldn't be the last time Justin suffered such open hostility because of his colour.

Born to Play

WITH A hunger to play more football, Justin hadn't been at Attleborough Secondary Modern long before he was looking for games outside the school gates. As it happens, he didn't have to search far because the father of one of his friends coached a local youth team in Attleborough. Alf Fincham had started the team two years earlier after being approached by several boys who were fed up with friendly kickarounds on the Rec and wanted to play competitive football. Fincham duly obliged and in June 1971, Attleborough Town Youth FC was created. Two years later, his son turned up at the house one evening with a petulant 12-year-old called Justin. After asking for a biscuit, Fashanu asked whether he could play on Fincham's team. 'Justin was literally begging me! The problem was he was too young to play in the side at that stage so I really had to restrain him. It took some work though as he was so enthusiastic,' Fincham says.

Not yet a teenager, Justin was already displaying the persistence that would serve him well in the future. He continued to badger Fincham until the coach could take no more and finally agreed. The Attleborough coach would not regret it. Despite being younger than all the other players, Fincham allowed Justin to train with the Under-13 team. Realising that he was more skilled than the other players Justin was soon in the side. He made an immediate impact. One advantage was his size. He was head and shoulders above most of his opponents. Defenders quickly discovered that with two gangly arms like scythes, it was almost impossible to get near him. Naturally, Fincham was delighted and even more so when the young Fashanu began to perfect his aim. With a formidable right foot he was a natural striker, slotting in goals from all angles. In one game, Attleborough were three players short but still managed to win and it was mostly down to Justin. Playing a lone wolf position up front he picked off the defenders with precision scoring four goals.

When Fashanu first joined Attleborough Youth, Justin was fortunate to be part of a team that gelled. He wasn't the only handy player and it was as if the side had been playing with each other for years. For a coach they were a dream to manage, and it stayed that way the whole time Fashanu was with them. From 1973-77, while Justin was with the club, his teams he won a stack of trophies, including the Norfolk County Shield, League Shield and much-coveted Norfolk County Cup. In the 1974/75 season, when Justin was 13, Attleborough managed to get two youth teams into the county finals: the Under-14 and Under-18 teams. Fashanu was playing for the Under-14 team despite being a year younger. In one memorable tie Attleborough battered rivals Diss 10-1, with Fashanu and his school friend Mark Overton getting several goals between them. It's clear that Fashanu was perfecting a move that would define his play when he turned professional. A journalist from a local newspaper reported: 'Andrew Reed floated over a beautifully placed cross to leave the keeper stranded and allow Fashanu to sail in and put the ball away with his head to wrap the game up.'[4]

Lurking at the far post and running on to a floating ball was a skill that Fashanu would become a master at. If the ball connected with his head then it usually ended up in the back of the net. It wasn't just his strength that was impressive but also his speed. For someone so tall and gangly he was surprisingly quick. In an interview he gave a few years later for a book called *Black Sportsmen* Fashanu told writer Ernest Cashmore: 'The reason I became a footballer was simple. I could run faster than anybody else. I could run with the ball and hold it. I think blacks were designed to use our speed and agility. Blacks start off with an added advantage of being able to move so you've got a good start over whites. I thought I'd got the initial start and I wanted to keep ahead all the time.'[5]

When Justin was a teenager, Alf or Betty usually dropped him off at matches but if they were busy then old faithful Les Hammond would drive him instead. Hammond watched the game if he could and was proud to see how much he'd developed. While Justin was honing his football skills his mischievous personality was also developing. He was a born entertainer who felt right at home being in the spotlight. Fincham believed the reason Fashanu chose to play as a striker was so that he could score and take all the glory. He was probably right. In the Seventies, Attleborough's youth teams trained every Wednesday at the local recreation ground. In the winter, Justin often turned up wearing a bright red woolly hat and matching mittens that Betty had made for him. Despite Fincham's objections that he looked stupid Justin insisted on wearing them for games, but it was the defenders not him who ended up looking like clowns after he'd finished with them.

Fincham wasn't the only coach who had to accept Justin's off beat accessories. Graham Morgan who coached the Norfolk Schools county team was also forced to let Justin play in a bobble hat. This time around Betty had knitted him a nice purple woolly number that could only be described as garish. Of course, it wasn't just the hat Morgan noticed when he first saw Justin play in a trial match. It was the young striker's abundance of raw talent. Fashanu turned up by himself for a day of trials that Morgan and his assistant John Waters had organised. Morgan was blown away by Fashanu's speed and his ability to control the ball. They were important but rare assets in one so young. He was also difficult to read because he was so gangly which made him a menace to mark. It didn't take Morgan long to realise he had a new striker at his disposal. Both he and Waters were excited at the enormous potential Fashanu had to offer county football.

As it turns out, the Norfolk coach would be good for Fashanu, too. Before Justin joined the team, Morgan had only been running the Norfolk Schools operation for a year. At 24, he was the youngest person in the country to have a full FA coaching badge. When he'd first taken over the system was in a shambles. The kit was in such disarray that the team looked like a bunch of cattle rustlers. There were more holes in the jerseys than an old Stilton cheese and their odour was just as bad. Fortunately for Morgan, the wealthy parents of one of his players offered to buy the team a new kit and a year later, when Justin joined the fold, the players looked much more professional. Morgan believed in mentoring his players whether the subject was about football or not. Respected by the team, he always made sure he had time to listen. He was the kind of manager Justin Fashanu worked well under: firm but fair and not afraid to dish out criticism and compliments in equal measure. Fashanu was 15 when he first started playing county football in late 1976. When Morgan selected him for the Under-19 team it caused quite a stir. Previously, only sixth formers had been allowed to play. Morgan changed that allowing fifth formers to be included in the selection process too, and as a fifth former himself it meant that Fashanu got the opportunity to play county football a year earlier.

At the time, Norfolk played in the South East Senior Schools league that included the Home Counties, Suffolk, Middlesex, Inner London and Essex. The league was split into two groups with the winners of each playing against each other in the finals. The team that won the final went on to play in the national finals. At the end of the season the English Schools FA held a national football week in Skegness. While the players likely never saw much sun in Skeggy, the trip away did give them the opportunity to play teams from other parts of the country. 'We all loved it when Justin turned up because you never knew what you were going to get. Was he going to be wearing a bobble hat? He was like a cartoon character but we all had a soft spot for him. Justin gave our team of quiet Norfolk boys some character and personality. You sometimes think of the people you have met in your life who were really special and he was definitely one of them,' Morgan says.

Even though Justin would let Morgan down in later years when the striker was going through a dark period in his life, the Norfolk coach still looks back at him with fondness. Fashanu's captain in the county team was Jeremy Smith. Today, Smith is Director of the Center for Molecular Biophysics in Tennessee but in the mid-Seventies he was also clever with his feet. As a defender, he had the unenviable task of marking Fashanu in practice games.

'I remember trying in vain to mark him and he just popped out of nowhere, stuck a foot out and the ball was suddenly in the net. He was that quick you never knew it had happened. In winter games it appeared the football pitch was the last place Justin wanted to be as he'd be standing around with his arms folded and legs crossed. Of course, the next thing you know is he'd scored. It was like he played in a different dimension and I got ripped by Graham Morgan for not being able to keep up with him. Morgan knew what talent he had and let the rest of us lesser mortals know it,' says Smith.

Smith was fortunate that he only had to mark Fashanu in scrimmage games. John Banbury, a young centre half in the county team, had not been so lucky a year earlier when he and Fashanu had played on opposing teams. Banbury still recalls how bruised his body felt the morning after the game. Marking Justin had proved extremely challenging and the striker's elbows had left their mark. Being on the same side was a bonus. One county game he and Justin played in together still sticks in Banbury's mind, for all the wrong reasons. The Under-15s were playing Essex and got hopelessly whipped 6-1. Fashanu was the lone scorer for Norwich and the opposing Essex striker, some young upstart called Clive Allen, claimed a hat trick. Allen would go on to carve out an illustrious career with clubs like Queens Park Rangers and Tottenham Hotspurs. He'd also win several England caps.

Justin Fashanu wasn't the only talented player in Morgan's outfit. Other great players included Dale Gordon, who would go on to play for Rangers, Steve Goble, who'd be picked up by Manchester City, and Clive Baker, Jeremy Goss, Peter Mountford and Peter Mendham who would all forge successful careers with Norwich City at Carrow Road. Over the nine years Morgan was in charge of Norfolk county football, seven players went on to represent their country.

With so many great players at his disposal, Morgan was able to try out a number of different tactics against opposing teams. In one game, the coach opted to play a 4-4-2 formation with the two men up front essentially playing wide on each wing. Justin was placed on the right and Goble on the left. With no centre forwards for the central defenders to mark they were totally confused. Norwich won the game 1-0 after Goble broke down the left wing and delivered a perfect cross to the far post that Fashanu powered home with his head. It was textbook stuff.

Justin might have looked good on the football field but he was equally stylish off it. As soon as he hit adolescence fashion became an important focus for the young maestro, and any pocket money that came his way was lavished on designer clothes. Armed at all times with a comb for his burgeoning afro, Justin could often be spotted grooving down the school corridors singing the Aretha Franklin classic: *Young, Gifted and Black*. He didn't know it at the time but his silken tones would be required a few years later after he landed himself a record deal. With an energising personality to match his sartorial style, it's perhaps not surprising that Justin was a real hit with the ladies. There was never any shortage of girls hanging around him with one in particular, Donna Friend, often on his arm. Donna would scoop the coveted 'Miss Attleborough' title in 1978 and was Justin's main girlfriend while he was at school. Another of Justin's fans Sarah Sterman was the daughter of the school woodwork teacher.

1977 was an important milestone in Justin's life because he turned 16 which meant he was finally old enough to leave school. But turning 16 was also significant in another way, and when Fashanu began to have the first real suspicion that he might be gay. Years later, Justin would tell a friend that while the feelings weren't strong, there was no denying they were there and he was attracted to men. Rather than act on them, his immediate reaction was to suppress his feelings, but as Justin got older they would only get stronger.

As teenagers, Fashanu and his friends hung out at a local disco on Connaught Road called The Tin Hut. Graeme Shurey, a close friend, says Fashanu loved dancing and was always the last person on the dance floor to strut his stuff even after the music had stopped. Another local haunt was a pub called the White Lodge that the footballer continued to frequent after he'd become a celebrity. Sometimes, he headed into Norwich for some fun and it was there that he first encountered out and out racist name-calling. Fashanu ignored the comments but it made him even more aware that being black was going to be an issue with some people. When he had a spare hour or two, Justin enjoyed watching movies with his brother at the Regal Cinema in Wymondham. Les King owned the movie theatre and says the brothers were so tall they'd have to sit at the back. King also knew the Fashanus from a local boxing club where Justin had recently started training. Boxing was yet another thing he excelled at and his passion for the sport would soon lead to an agonising choice.

Watton Warrior

WHILE LOTS of people are aware that Justin boxed in his younger years, many don't realise just how good he was. According to his former trainer Gordon Holmes, Fash was outstanding. Holmes has trained some of the country's finest British amateur boxers and is convinced his young protégé would have been a successful pro himself if he hadn't chosen football instead.

The Londoner Holmes is proud of his connection to the name 'Justin Fashanu', and there's a nostalgic glint in his eye as he recounts how they first met. Holmes was running an amateur boxing club in Watton, a small Norfolk market town, when Justin dropped in one night. The 13-year-old had just finished playing football and tagged along with a friend who was a member. As a boxing club, Watton's was a pretty standard affair with old school boxing posters stuck on peeling beige walls. There was one solitary ring in the corner of the gym and a smell of stale sweat hung in the air. Fashanu told Holmes he wanted to try his hand in the ring himself. The trainer laughs as he remembers the first time Justin strapped on a pair of gloves and stepped through the ropes to spar: 'He was like a big floppy dog to start with, all feet and hands. You know what kids are like. Coordination is absolutely key to most sports like boxing and you have to keep well balanced. But after a while I could see that he seemed to have this natural ability to move around and I thought: "You know what? This kid could just do things,'" Holmes says.

The trainer was experienced enough to see that the floppy dog in front of him had teeth and wasn't afraid to bare them. Impressed, he invited the youngster to join him for a proper training session the following week. From that moment on, Justin was hooked and he was soon a regular fixture at the gym. Holmes says most teenagers who start boxing quickly lose interest when they realise the commitment required, but Fashanu was different. The harder his training became the more he relished the challenge. His dedication was unfailing, especially when you consider that he was still playing regular football too. If there was no one to spar with he hit a punch bag until it came time for the club to close. He would have stayed all night if he'd had the chance. Fashanu would maintain this impressive work ethic throughout his professional football career, and it is something that set him apart from most others.

Something else that stood Fashanu apart was confidence. It didn't matter who his opponent was in training, he went on the offensive from the second the bell sounded and his punches were powerful and well placed. Stepping up his training regime to three sessions a week, he continued to juggle boxing with football. While other kids his age were down the arcade or hanging out on street corners smoking, Fashanu was perfecting his punch and smoking opponents. His boxing skills would actually turn out to be useful outside the ring in later years after he found himself in a few ugly situations. Holmes soon recognised he had a potential champion on his hands. Fashanu developed a close relationship with Holmes whom he looked up to as a father figure. While he was close to his foster dad, Alf Jackson was never really interested in sports and Justin had a better connection with Holmes. Sometimes after a training session, the trainer invited him back to his house for dinner where Holmes' wife was happy to set an extra place at the table. Fashanu was soon helping himself to milk from the fridge and putting his feet on the sofa but Holmes didn't mind. He had a soft spot for Justin, especially considering what the boy had been through in his early years.

Just seven months after first taking up the sport, Holmes believed Fashanu was finally ready to fight competitive bouts. The floppy dog had been transformed into a Rottweiler and was eager to be unleashed.

The 14-year-old didn't disappoint. Justin won his debut fight in December 1975 in spectacular fashion. The fight didn't last the first round after a right hook left his opponent face down on the canvas. Justin went on to fight in 22 amateur contests, winning 18 of them. Incredibly, 14 were inside the distance and the other nine knockouts in the very first round. It wasn't bad for a kid who'd only gone to the gym for a laugh.

Les Hammond, the man who'd made Justin's first punching bag, often watched him in action and also helped with training. Not stupid enough to offer himself as a spar, Hammond rode his moped in front of the young boxer when he went for late night runs. With the moped's lights switched on full beam, he could light the dark country lanes perfectly. Hammond said Justin was so fit that he almost outran the lightweight scooter whenever they encountered a hill. Alf also supported the cause by driving his foster son to fights in his vintage Morris Minor Estate. Sometimes, he'd stay and watch from the back of the ring. Betty, however, refused. The thought of seeing Justin get hurt was too much to bear.

Justin wasn't the only good boxer in the Fashanu clan. His brother was also good with his fists. In John's short amateur career he won 12 out of 16 contests, many of his opponents from top clubs around the country. Justin made it to two national finals in his own illustrious amateur boxing career: the British Schoolboys Boxing Championships in 1977 and the Junior ABA Championships later the same year. Terry Reeve, a reporter for the *Thetford and Brandon Times*, watched both fights. Reeve says that Fashanu was one of the most personable young men he's ever met, but once the youngster stepped inside the ring it was a classic case of Jekyll and Hyde. Mr Nice disappeared and in his place was a ruthless predator that showed no mercy. The Watton Warrior fought his first final at the not-so-glamorous Pontin's Holiday Camp in Blackpool on March 26th, 1977 and there was a lot riding on it. The winner would walk away with the prestigious Schoolboy Heavyweight Champion of Britain title. By now, Justin was 16 and stood six feet tall. Weighing in at 11 stone, he cut an impressive figure. His opponent was a more experienced Irish boxer called Liam Coleman who lived in Leeds. Coleman had represented England and won the British Schoolboys Championship title twice already. With four times as many fights under his belt than Justin, the Irish lad would not be easy to beat.

Even though he was the underdog, Fashanu went on the offensive right from the bell forcing Coleman into the corner. As punches rained down on him, there was little the Irish lad could do by way of reply. Surprisingly, Fashanu won the first round with relative ease but the second was a different story with Coleman now going on the attack. This time it was Fashanu who found himself against the ropes and Coleman ended up taking the points. With only three rounds in total, both fighters had everything to fight for going into the final round.

Reeve described the third round in the *Thetford and Brandon Times* as a real 'ding dong affair.' He wasn't joking. One minute Fashanu would be on the attack only for Coleman to unleash a volley of blows himself. 'Fashanu started it brilliantly, banging away at Coleman's face. However, Coleman came back showing his experience towards the climax, though no one in the audience could have confidently predicted the judges' verdict,'[6] wrote Reeve. When the final bell sounded there was a huge roar from the crowd. A large contingent of fans had travelled from Norwich to support Fashanu and they were adamant their man had won. Holmes was also convinced of it. But in a controversial decision, the judges disagreed and Coleman was deemed the winner. As the Norfolk supporters booed, Fashanu and his trainer were both visibly gutted. But all was not lost, as they would get a chance of revenge. Two months later, Fashanu and Coleman were scheduled to meet each other again, this time in the Junior ABA Championships Final in London.

According to Hammond and Holmes, Justin trained so hard for his next fight that he made Rocky Balboa look like a part-timer. 'The rematch is the best thing that has happened to me since I was born. He just shaved me out last time but this time I'll beat him,'[7] Justin promised a reporter for *Diss Express*. Unlike the previous fight, the three-round contest was scheduled to take place at the fashionable Bloomsbury Hotel in London. By now, news of Fashanu's skills had spread throughout East Anglia and so even more journalists from Norwich were planning to travel to the capital to watch. A few days before the fight was scheduled to take place it was almost cancelled when Justin got injured. He'd been playing in a charity football match when a dubious tackle left him with a swollen ankle. While most people would have bowed out, Fashanu refused. He told Reeve there was no way he was going to miss his chance at glory. After applying ice the swelling subsided and the Norwich boxer was deemed fit with just one day to go. It was a close call but it seemed the fight would go on.

When the battle finally commenced on May 20th, 1977, it was Fashanu who took first blood, and the round, after an impressive display of combination boxing. That would change in the second. Pinned into a corner, Fashanu lost his balance and fell through the ropes and on to a chair below. Dazed and confused, it looked as if the fight might be over. Even though Coleman had not actually connected with a punch, the referee started a count anyway thus preventing an exasperated Holmes from helping Justin to his feet. As the count increased, Fashanu obviously realised the gravity of situation because he suddenly shook his head and pushed himself up. Diving headfirst back through the ropes, the fighter rolled to his feet just as the referee counted to ten. It was sensational stuff and the whole spectacle brought the house down. Fash was safe but he would lose the round.

Despite the trauma of his fall Justin managed to regain his composure and came out fighting in the third round. Not expecting such an onslaught, Coleman was caught off kilter, as powerful left and right hooks battered him. The Leeds fighter managed to land a few punches himself, but only a few were on target. Fashanu was merciless and gave the performance of his life. The Norwich youth was confident he'd won when the final bell sounded. He wasn't the only one. Holmes was also sure of victory and had never seen an amateur fight quite like it. But in a cruel twist of fate that definitely would not have happened to Rocky, Coleman was again deemed the winner. Holmes was outraged: 'Its disgusting, absolute robbery! Those scores are cock-eyed by any standard and to my mind it makes the judges all look idiots,'[8] he spat at a reporter. It seemed that Coleman agreed. Right after the verdict he shook Fashanu's hand and apologised saying that he was ashamed of the decision. A howl of boos and jeers rained down on the judges as they exited the arena. Paul Cheston, the reporter covering the fight for the Norwich based *Diss Express*, was so disgusted at the decision that he headlined his report 'ROBBED!'[9] the following day. Tragically, Coleman went on to become a professional boxer but would die in a horrific car accident in the mid-Eighties. His death would leave a dark hole in the boxing community.

The defeat in London was Fashanu's final fight, at least in the ring. The following year he'd be turning 17 so would be too old to fight as a junior. The youngster had found himself at the first real crossroads of his life. While he had a good opportunity to turn professional and make a living out of boxing, there was another sport still close to his heart. With people like Holmes calling him the hottest property in the ring it was hard to step away from boxing, but there were others who believed his destiny lay in football. It was a tough choice and the first major one he was forced to make. Fashanu's teacher at school John Lund remembers a conversation he had with Justin about the matter. Lund asked: 'If you were in a gym would you bang your head against a wall?' When Justin replied: 'No,' Lund said: 'Well, you're getting the same treatment every time you go into a ring to box.' Fashanu obviously listened because, ultimately, he chose football. In later years he revealed he also decided to play football for another reason: he could make more cash. Money was something that Justin would grow very fond of. For Holmes, it was painful to see his prized fighter walk away from the ring. In his view, he would have made a far better boxer but it wasn't to be.

While he'd been boxing, Fashanu had continued playing football for three teams: his school, Attleborough Youth FC and Norfolk Schools. So much physical activity had made him even fitter, resulting in an even higher presence in games. More presence meant more goals and his talents were soon spotted by a scout from a professional club. Ronnie Brooks was the person instrumental in bringing Justin to the attention of Norwich City Football Club. Proud of his affiliation with the Canaries, Brooks didn't mind that he wasn't paid much to look for new players. Recruiting fresh talent was something he enjoyed. Brooks was also a magistrate and would become another mentor to Justin. Graham Morgan jokes that as one of only a few black players in the whole of Norfolk, and someone whose reputation already preceded him, taking note of Fashanu wasn't unexpected. Regardless, Brooks certainly played a part in Justin's relationship with Norwich City.

Brooks first saw Fashanu play in an Under-19 county game in 1976. Two scouts from Charlton Athletic also had their eyes fixed on the striker. Hammond drove Justin to the game and was standing near them. In a not-so-subtle reference to Fashanu's skin colour, Hammond heard one say: 'At least we have no problem keeping tabs on who we're watching today.' Ultimately, the Charlton scouts would not get a chance to sign him because when the match was over Brooks beat them to it. The Norwich scout was impressed by the two goals Fashanu scored and it was obvious the striker had huge potential. Walking on to the pitch to greet the footballer after the final whistle had been blown, Brooks asked him if he wanted to try out for the Norwich City youth team. Fashanu was thrilled. As a local lad he was a huge City fan and his biggest dream was to play at Carrow Road.

In the mid-Seventies John Sainty, a former pro from London, coached Norwich City's youth team. By the time Fashanu joined the outfit his friend

John Banbury was already playing. Peter Mountford, who would go on to play professionally for City, was also in the team. Justin wasted no time impressing Sainty and in the 1976/77 season struck the net 18 times in 22 games. In two of those matches he scored a hat trick. Fashanu's form soon brought him to the attention of local newspaper reporter, Mick Dennis. Today, Dennis is a well-known football pundit for the *Daily Express* but in the mid-Seventies he was a sports reporter with the *Eastern Daily Press*. After watching Justin play, Dennis was impressed enough to interview him. Fashanu told the journalist he was determined to succeed and it wouldn't be long before he was in the Norwich first team. Dennis was bowled over by such confidence and something told him the lad wasn't bluffing.

Despite his obvious worth, Norwich were slow to offer Fashanu a contract. Whether he somehow slipped through the net or there was another oversight is unclear, but it would almost cost the club dearly. Still officially a free agent, when the young striker heard that Peterborough United were holding a weekend of trials he asked Hammond to drive him to where they were taking place. Assuming Betty and Alf knew all about it, Hammond willingly obliged. The Peterborough trials were noteworthy for two things. The first was that Justin's skill was so superior that midway through the game he started toying with defenders. At one point, he dribbled the ball up to the corner flag and proceeded to tap it against the wooden flag post. A combination of strength and gangly arms prevented anyone from getting the ball off him. According to Hammond, the small crowd who were watching cheered. The entertaining spectacle led to the second noteworthy thing: Fashanu was offered a contract with Peterborough. Dropping a jubilant Justin off at Flint House later that evening, Hammond had no idea that waiting in the kitchen was a frantic Betty wondering where the hell her foster son had been. As Hammond got an earful, Justin retired quietly (and conveniently) to his room.

Luckily for Norwich City, Fashanu had not actually signed the contract he'd been offered and when Brooks found out his star recruit was being poached it prompted immediate action: an apprentice contract was hastily drawn up. By this time, Justin had just started getting his hands dirty at a local steel plant where he'd been hired as a junior steel erector. Of course, the job didn't last long and he was soon washing his hands, picking up a pen and scribbling his signature on the bottom of an official football contract. At the tender age of 17, the chance of playing professional football was finally at his fingertips. At the time, Fashanu was only the second black footballer to sign a contract with Norwich City. The first was Johnny Miller, a right-winger who'd played at Carrow Road a few years earlier. When Justin told Betty and Alf the news his foster parents were happy, but warned him about the realities of choosing such a career. Signing as an apprentice would mean quitting school permanently and there was no guarantee he'd make the professional grade as a footballer. As people with academic backgrounds, the couple always hoped Justin would complete his studies and get some qualifications. In their eyes education was a solid foundation and should come first. Betty told a reporter: 'We're proud of him but the glamour of football is over-rated. I hope he can just keep his feet on the ground. It would have been nice if he'd been a scientist or doctor but that's just the way it goes I suppose.'[10] Justin knew the risk he was taking but was happy to take the chance. Although he wouldn't be getting paid much as an apprentice, the potential was priceless. To make life easier, the Jacksons told him he could stay at home until his future was more certain. Betty and Alf had no idea that soon there would be not one, but two, professional footballers at Flint House.

Tipped for the Top

FASHANU JOINED Norwich City at a very exciting time in the club's history. In the late Seventies, the Canaries had just regained their top-flight status after spending a year loitering in Division Two. At the club's helm was the enigmatic, cigar-chomping manager John Bond who embodied 'bling' long before the word was even invented. Bond arrived at Carrow Road in 1973 and his presence prompted an immediate change in the club's fortunes. Bond had been horrified to find that the East Anglia club didn't have an effective youth system. It was in disarray, with no real structure. Realising the importance of finding and developing home grown talent, he quickly ordered a complete overhaul. Once in place, the likes of Fashanu and Peter Mendham were soon being filtered through the system.

In 1975, Norwich City won promotion back into Division One. That same year, the team also managed to make it to the League Cup Final at Wembley. Although they ended up losing to Aston Villa, it was the start of a promising new period in the team's history. Bond renewed the fans' hope and put Norwich back on the map thanks to his huge managerial talent and those legendary, fat cigars. But there's no smoke without fire. Bond was a tough manager who expected the best from everyone, especially his players. New recruits had to prove themselves with apprentices like Fashanu expected to clean boots, muck out the dressing rooms and pick up the litter from the terraces after home games. Not that Fashanu minded. He was just happy to be there and certain his own chance would come.

Since he'd first managed the team, Bond had steered Norwich towards a more pass and move game, and to execute this style he'd hired more experienced players who weren't afraid to kick the ball around. At the top of the ladder was England hero Martin Peters who'd helped his country win the World Cup nine years earlier. Although he was almost at the end of his career, Peters was a stable force in the centre of the field. In defence was journeyman fullback John Ryan who could also switch up to midfield if required. Phil Hoadley was a reliable centre back who Bond brought in to shore up the defence. The main strike force up front was Kevin Reeves, a prolific goal scorer who was popular with fans. Reeves' style of play would complement Fashanu's perfectly.

Justin knew that if he was going to make it into the first team then he'd have to earn Bond's respect first. With that in mind, the footballer worked hard improving upon an already impressive training regime. He rarely drank and was often the last player to leave the pitch after training, usually electing to stay on for extra target practice. He was also one of the few players who trained in a private gym. Chris Roberts was the owner of Norwich Health Club on Ber Street in the late Seventies where Justin worked out.

'Back at that time there were only two types of footballers who ended up in the gym, goalkeepers and strikers, and that's because their work is so visible. Strikers, in particular, are like warriors. Fashanu used to come into my gym twice a week and we'd work a lot on physique and strength. We wanted him to look big and strong on the pitch to make opposing players feel intimidated,' Roberts says.

The trainer certainly did a good job at that. Today, additional strength training is routine for every professional footballer, but in the Seventies Fashanu was ahead of the game. His workouts were an indication of how motivated he was to obtain and maintain an edge over other footballers. He'd only been playing as an apprentice for less than a year when his hard work paid off and Bond asked him to train with the first team. Two fellow Norwich players at that time, Dave Bennett and Phil Hoadley, both remember Fashanu's commitment at Trowse training ground where the first team trained. Bennett's nose is still bent to this day after being caught by one of the striker's elbows. Impressed by what he saw, Bond offered Fashanu a professional contract.

Fashanu's big break arrived in mid-January 1979, shortly after Leicester City destroyed Norwich in an FA Cup tie. Livid at his team's performance, Bond brought in the young player to replace ex-England striker, Martin Chivers. It was a dream come true for 17-year-old Fash who, just a few years earlier, had been pleading with Alf Fincham to play him in the Attleborough youth team. Justin's first game was against West Brom at Carrow Road. Back in the late Seventies, around 18,000 fans usually turned up to watch home games at the Norwich City stadium. Located near the River Wensum and exposed to the elements, Carrow Road can sometimes be a bitter place to spend an afternoon and on the day of Fashanu's debut the temperature was hovering just above freezing. However, his performance did much to warm fans' spirits. Bond paired the striker up front with Kevin Reeves and the two forwards found an instant connection, with the new recruit able to hold the ball up and flick it on for the faster Reeves to run onto. Although the game ended in a 1-1 draw Fashanu was, surprisingly, unlucky not to get a goal after causing all kinds of problems for the West Brom defence. His youthful exuberance and speed were hard to contain.

One fan watching from the stands was Fashanu's former teacher, John Lund. His student had only finished school a few months earlier and here he was playing professional football. He'd come a long way in a short space of time. Les Hammond was also cheering, and it was a proud occasion for both men. Local reporter Malcolm Robertson interviewed Fashanu after the game. The striker joked that he was hoping his performance had earned him one of the boss's cigars and that he'd certainly be asking for a pay rise. It was cheeky yet refreshing banter, especially from someone so young. The game was recorded and replayed later that evening on *Match of the Day* and Fashanu was the main talking point. In a glowing newspaper article in the *Eastern Daily Press* a few days later, Justin was touted as a rising star and someone who was a 'genuine character' as opposed to an artificially created superstar. They were certainly positive words, but not the kind of prose that would be written about the footballer in later years.

Despite a solid debut performance, Bond didn't pick Fashanu for City's next game likely because he wanted to ease his young striker into first team football. Then again, maybe Fashanu did ask for a pay rise after all and this was his punishment! He didn't have to wait long for his next call of duty, a League Cup tie against Bolton. The game ended in a goalless draw but, again, he delivered. It was enough to convince Bond that the young player deserved more consideration.

Fashanu celebrated his first ever goal in professional football against Leeds United in March, a game that finished 2-2. A week later, he got his second. This time it was against Chelsea in front of a rapturous home crowd. Justin was proving to be far stronger than his lean frame suggested and goalkeepers messed with him at their peril. After Fashanu and the Chelsea keeper Petar Borota clashed mid-air in the penalty box, Borota had to be escorted off the pitch in a semi-conscious state. Fashanu walked away without a scratch and the game ended with Norwich winning 2-0. The striker might have been a new recruit but he wasn't about to back down. Not from anyone. Norwich winger Mark Barham discovered just that when he played with Fashanu at Old Trafford in 1979. It was Barham's debut and despite being hammered 5-0 by a superior Manchester United team, he learned an important lesson about the physical aspects of the game from his teammate.

'Back in those days it was legal to come in through the back of players, but after United's centre half had hit Justin from behind three times he'd had enough. During a corner kick for Norwich, the centre half suddenly went down with a crash and it was obvious that Justin had done him. That really woke me up to the man's side of the game,' Barham says.

Fashanu's third goal for Norwich was against Nottingham Forest at the City Ground. It was the first time that Forest manager Brian Clough and his assistant Peter Taylor saw the striker in action. They wouldn't have forgotten him either because Fashanu was the only Norwich player to score.

Away from the pitch, Fashanu was fast becoming the talk of the town. Fans related to his down-to-earth manner and his status as a local lad resulted in even more adulation. The local media adored him equally. When reporters discovered that he was, in fact, a Barnardo's boy they lapped it up. He was the ultimate rags-to-riches story: success in the face of adversity. Something else that endeared him to reporters was his willingness to give a snappy sound bite. You couldn't say that about most of his teammates. Fashanu was intelligent, witty and honest: rare ingredients for any footballer. Although he'd left school without many qualifications, he was extremely articulate. His brash honesty also added to his allure. If he'd had a bad game he wasn't afraid to admit it. Conversely, if he'd played well then he'd tell reporters he was the top dog and worth more money.

But as his popularity was growing there was one thing in Fashanu's life that was heading south: his relationship with his brother. According to John, the problems began shortly after Justin started playing regularly for City. In his opinion, Justin was starting to believe all the hype. In the past, the two siblings had been tight. The older brother had always looked out for his sibling taking on the role of protector. He'd made it clear at school that anyone caught giving John a hard time would answer to Justin. Given his boxing skills no one wanted to risk that. In his formative years, John had been firmly entrenched in his brother's shadow and not just as an athlete. Friends at school say that while Justin's bubbly personality made him popular, John was more reserved and moody. Despite being blotted out by his brother's glory, John was actually developing as a good footballer in his own right. He, too, was now playing county football and had his sights set on the professional game. The challenge was that the Fashanu benchmark had been set high, so comparisons with his brother were natural and something he was going to have to get used to. After Justin signed on as a professional footballer it must have been difficult for the younger Fashanu not to feel a little jealous. One time, Justin went ballistic after he caught John signing an autograph for a young Norwich fan outside Carrow Road. Justin told him that the boy only wanted his autograph because of Justin's own achievements and if he wanted the same recognition then he'd have to earn it first. It was tough love. One person who didn't believe all the hype, however, was the boys' foster mum. You could always rely on Betty to keep Justin's feet on the ground.

While Fashanu's relationship with his brother was being tested, the striker was making new friends in the Norwich team. One of his closest was fellow player, Dave Bennett. When Bennett had first arrived at Carrow Road, Fashanu was the first person to go up and introduce himself. 'Justin was all smiles. I knew that he'd recently broken into the first team and was going to be the next big thing. I had been looking for digs when I arrived and when Justin found out he told me I could stay with him. He said his place was just up the road but I soon discovered his idea of "just up the road" was a 17-mile drive away in the middle of nowhere,' Bennett says. It was typical of Fashanu to offer his hand and Bennett ended up staying at Flint House for three months. As a self-confessed 'Jack the lad' who was used to the big city lights of Manchester, it was a bit of a culture shock for Bennett, especially when Betty told him he had to feed the chickens. He was also instructed not to take food upstairs unless he wanted mice as company.

Bennett was gregarious and found fitting in with the rest of his Norwich teammates no problem, but he remained closest with Fashanu. Even though they possessed opposite characteristics, they clicked. Bennett would regularly drink ten pints at a nightclub every Saturday night then try to score with a girl, only to spot Fashanu across the dance floor sipping an orange juice surrounded by a horde of beauties. Justin was a natural mover in every respect. While Bennett never saw his friend actually getting physical with anyone in public, he assumed that he was more discreet. Of course, Justin knew better. By now, the young professional footballer had become even more convinced he was gay. The feelings he'd harboured as a teenager were now stronger than ever and, in time, would become impossible to ignore.

Of course, compared to nightclubs and chasing women around football was a much more serious affair. In the late Seventies, the Norwich team trained at Trowse training ground every Monday, Tuesday, Thursday and Friday. On Wednesdays, the players had the day off unless they were in Bond's bad books, in which case they'd be hauled in for extra duties. Bond usually took the sessions himself, with coaches John Sainty and Mel Machin helping him. Fashanu joined the professional football action halfway through the 1978/79 Season and hit the ground running in every respect. While many players of his age might have crumpled from the pressure, Fashanu exceeded everyone's expectations. By the end of the season, he'd managed to notch up a tally of five goals in 16 appearances: not bad for a new kid on the block. City ended up in 16th place in the First Division table, a respectable finish considering Bond hadn't exactly been given the biggest budget for purchasing new players. If Fashanu thought he was going to get some much-earned rest over the summer, he was disappointed. The Norwich players were soon on their way to Australia where a series of exhibition games awaited.

When the 1979/80 season kicked off, Fashanu was firing on all cylinders. In Norwich City's opening game against Everton he scored a goal in each half, helping his team win 4-2. In the next match, he converted another goal, picking Tottenham Hotspur's defence to pieces and helping City crush the guests 4-0. The streak continued with a goal a couple of weeks later against Nottingham Forest, a brilliant header that flew past the England keeper, Peter Shilton. City's 3-1 win ended a 12-game unbeaten run for the new European champions, so if Brian Clough had somehow forgotten Fashanu the first time he'd seen him play, then the striker was undoubtedly on the manager's radar now.

Despite his stunning performance, there was at least one downside to his job. Fashanu's first big psychological test as a professional was dealing with racism. Whereas in the past the abuse came from opponents, now it was received from so-called football fans. When thousands of people are chanting derogatory comments at just one person (you) then there's no knowing how you are going to react, at least not the first time you encounter that situation. For the most part, Fashanu ignored any chants that came his way but if the occasion warranted he cleverly turned the situation on its head. Case in point was an away game at Middlesbrough when Fashanu was being badly heckled with monkey noises. According to Rik Cheston, a childhood acquaintance of Fashanu's in the crowd, the footballer walked towards the corner of the pitch and picked up a wooden flagpole. For a split second, Cheston wondered just what the footballer had in mind, but to the crowd's amusement, instead of throwing it Fashanu held the pole above his head like a spear and struck his best Zulu stance. After a momentary pause, the jeers were replaced by cheers. It was a clever response and sometimes, regrettably, required to tame an unruly crowd. Former England ace John Barnes did the same kind of thing when he was greeted by monkey chants. If a banana was thrown on to the pitch at him then he'd pick it up and eat it. Like Fashanu, Barnes hated having to resort to such tactics and today is committed to stamping out racism in football.

Yet, as one of the few black players in the whole of East Anglia, Fashanu realised that he had a tremendous opportunity to act as a role model. In a 1981 interview for a TV programme in Norwich called *The Pace-Setters* Fashanu told the reporter that playing as an inspiration for black people was his ultimate motivation:

'The thing that spurs me on is that I am playing for other people, black people, who maybe have not had as good a life as I have had, who are living in the ghettos and have had all the prejudices poured over them all this time. I think it's good for them to know that a black person can get on. I think it's a spur for them and it's a light at the end of the tunnel and gives them hope,'[11] he said.

Fashanu was abused because of his skin colour off the pitch as well as on it. His teammate Bennett saw it first hand when he and Fashanu went to a pub following a home game. As they walked in they saw a group of skinheads perched at the bar. Fashanu ordered a round of drinks when one of the lads shouted: 'I wouldn't bother mate, we don't serve niggers in here.' Keeping his cool, Fashanu replied: 'I'll treat that remark with the contempt it deserves and say nothing more. Just enjoy your drinks gentleman.' While the comment may have been a cue for some to leave, Fashanu carried on talking to Bennett. Tugging on his friend's shirtsleeve, Bennett pointed at the exit but Fashanu told him they weren't going anywhere. Meanwhile, the comments kept flying.

After he was called a nigger for the fifth time, Fashanu turned to face the skinheads and told them: 'You really do need to open your minds gentlemen.' Shaking his head, he turned back to the bar and ordered yet another round of drinks. By this time, Bennett was starting to sweat and the two footballers stayed for another twenty minutes before finally drinking up and heading for the door. As they were about to make their way to the street two of the skinheads blocked their path. While Bennett's blood pressure hit the roof, Fashanu remained cool and told them: 'Stay where you are gents and don't come any closer. If you do come near me and my friend then I'm afraid I'm gonna have to hurt you.' Bennett could not believe what he was hearing. The two of them were clearly outnumbered, but that didn't seem to faze Fashanu at all. To Bennett's amazement and relief, the men parted allowing just enough room for the footballers to squeeze past. Once outside, two of the men followed and one of them pushed Fashanu from behind. 'See you later nigger,' he whispered. In the blink of an eye, Fashanu turned and unleashed two powerful punches knocking both skinheads to the floor. As the men ate the dust the rest of the racist crew wisely elected to stay inside the pub. Bennett had never seen anything like it and when he and Fashanu were safely around the corner his teammate apologised profusely. 'I'm sorry about that Dave. I hate having to do that, absolutely hate it, but they gave me no choice,' he said. Even though Justin was totally justified in giving the men a good hiding, he felt bad about resorting to violence. To Bennett, it only showed the measure of the man. One thing is certain: Fashanu's former boxing trainer Gordon Holmes would certainly have been proud.

The ugly face of racism reared its head again when the Norwich City team toured Florida later that summer. Fashanu was enjoying a drink next to the hotel pool one afternoon when a local redneck told him his kind were not welcome there. Enraged at the comment, the footballer walked towards the man to have a little word only for the American to slip open his jacket, revealing a handgun tucked inside a leather holster. It was enough to stop Fashanu dead in his tracks. According to Bennett, Justin was not impressed at the way he was treated by locals in Florida generally, many of whom were openly racist.

Back in Norwich, aside from Bennett, another friend of the footballer was Mel Richards who owned a local hair salon. Fashanu was by far Richard's most high maintenance client who told him he was the only hair stylist in town who could cut his hair just the way he liked it. Richards joked that Justin was more particular about his hair than any woman he knew. Like his friend, Richards had also been abandoned as a child and had spent a period of time in a children's home himself. His experience at the home had been horrific and on many occasions he'd had to fight off sexual predators. He counted himself lucky that he'd been old and strong enough to overcome them. Years later, Richards would often wonder if Fashanu had been a victim of sexual abuse himself. The footballer had been much younger than the hairstylist when he'd lived in Barnardos and would not have been able to put up such a fight. Fashanu never spoke about his own experiences preferring to change the subject if the conversation started to get too heavy. Both men were close enough that Richards didn't mind at all when the footballer borrowed his prized sports car one evening and ended up keeping it for over a month. 'That's just the way Justin was: a naughty boy but total style,' Richards says.

Richards was also a good friend of Bennett's and the trio often hung out together. Over the years he knew him, Richards witnessed Fashanu hook up with a variety of beautiful women and, today, believes the footballer was bisexual. Back then, of course, he was not aware that in private, Justin was actually trying to come to terms with his sexuality. While the footballer may well have been attracted to women, he was attracted to men too. In later years, Fashanu would reveal that not being able to tell anyone about his conflict was a terrible burden. What made the situation worse was the macho profession that he worked in. Football was hardly a sport where gay players were prevalent. At the time, there was not even one official professional gay footballer in the world, never mind England. Fashanu believed his one and only option was to suppress his secret and stay silent. It wasn't easy.

When he first started playing regularly for the Norwich first team, Fashanu was reportedly earning around £500 a week. That was big bucks for an 18-year-old. With that kind of cash flowing into his pockets, it wasn't long before he moved out of Flint House and rented a small apartment in the centre of town. The newfound freedom suited him. With more money than he'd ever possessed before, Fashanu decked out his wardrobe with an array of designer clothes and as soon as he'd passed his driving test bought a sports car. Les Hammond says the footballer looked extremely proud the day he rolled up to Flint House in a gleaming, spanking new orange MGB GT. When Hammond asked Fashanu to take him for a spin, however, he would live to regret it. As they were speeding down a country lane half an hour later, one of Fashanu's Cuban heels got stuck under the accelerator. As the car hurtled towards a sharp bend in the road, only quick thinking from Hammond prevented the car, and perhaps its passengers, from being obliterated. Yanking on the hand brake and pulling the keys from the ignition, the car came to a stop just in the nick of time. Hammond soon discovered that Fashanu's driving skills were definitely not on par with his football ones and the MGB was soon covered with all kinds of dents. Fashanu blamed other drivers but Hammond knew better.

Fashanu also seemed to have a problem with parking tickets. In short, he never paid them. The footballer seemed to believe that because he was now a local celebrity he could park his car wherever he liked. As the tickets started piling up, only a few choice words from Fashanu's mentor Ronnie Brooks seemed to get through to him and he finally paid up. As someone who was renowned for being polite and respectful his compulsion to disregard the law seems at odds with his character. Like many young people who come into money, Fashanu was only having a good time with it but along with that he adopted a level of irresponsibility. Parking fines and refusing to pay them is something that would hound him for the rest of his life and it shows the complexity of his character. Money and holding on to it is something else that would cause him strife.

Brooks was not only a football scout but also a local magistrate, and one of the few people who Justin listened to. After Fashanu signed for Norwich City the two became instantly close and Fashanu regularly turned up at the Brooks' house unannounced. Ronnie's wife Stephanie didn't mind. She adored Fashanu just as much as her husband. Brooks was one of a number of men in Justin's lives who would become a father figure of sorts. Before Brooks it had been Gordon Holmes. Brooks understood football inside out and realised the pressures Fashanu faced. He was often a good sounding board in times of stress. The same service was extended to John Fashanu who was also close to him. Despite having a loving foster family, it seems that Justin was not able to get over his own father leaving. Looking for a figure to replace his dad would be a re-occurring theme throughout his life.

Failure to comply with the country's parking regulations is not the only thing Brooks assisted the footballer with. Training was another area. He regularly volunteered his time to help Fashanu practise his shooting skills, but if the striker was late for a session then Brooks went ballistic. He dedicated hours of his time throwing footballs over Justin's shoulder and getting the striker to turn and volley them against the gym wall with both feet. There's no doubt that these sessions really helped the footballer develop. Fashanu was naturally right-footed but was soon equally proficient with his left. Brooks acknowledged: 'Justin was the biggest find of my life. One can't hope that that type of youngster will come again in a lifetime.' No kidding.

John Bond didn't know it but while Fashanu was signed as a Canary he sometimes played club cricket too, Les Hammond first introducing him to the game. Hammond played for Attleborough Cricket Club and if he ever found himself short of players then he'd ask Fashanu to make up the numbers. Contractually, as a Norwich City player, Justin was banned from taking part in any other sports, but he always did Hammond this favour provided no photographs were taken. The last thing he needed was for Bond to see him in a local newspaper holding a bat. Not that he had much impact on the cricket field, however. It was the one sport where his skills were greatly lacking, his versatility with his feet failing to translate well into cricket. Whenever Fashanu was placed near the boundary, instead of stopping the ball with his hands and throwing it directly to the wicket keeper he'd stop the ball with his feet and try to flick it up. Wasted seconds meant more runs for the opposition.

Like all good amateur cricket teams, Attleborough usually started every game by warming up with a pint or three at the local pub. One Sunday morning the team was playing an away match at a small village just outside Norwich. As Hammond ordered a round of drinks at the bar he heard loud giggles coming from the adjoining room. Going in to investigate there was a group of people standing around Fashanu who was flicking pickled onions off the bar with his foot and catching them on the back of his head. As usual, the youngster was revelling in the attention.

Indeed, bizarre incidents seemed to follow Fashanu wherever he played cricket, like the time he and Hammond were on the way to a match in Felthorpe. The two men were being driven by a teammate in an old Vauxhall Viva van when they got hopelessly lost. Spotting an elderly couple at the side of the country lane ahead, Hammond instructed Fashanu to ask them for directions. Once the van had stopped the footballer thrust open the rear doors and jumped out. But before he could utter a word the couple had turned on their heels and ran. In quiet, rural and mostly white Felthorpe, the older couple didn't recognise one of the UK's rising football stars, thinking instead they were about to be abducted by a large black man. True to form, Fashanu thought it was hilarious. But Hammond's favourite cricket story by far is when Justin was 14 and he joined the team for a game at Costessey just outside Norwich. As he was fielding near the boundary two young gypsies sitting on a fence nearby started making racist remarks. Fashanu gave them two or three chances to stop their abusive talk, but when they didn't it became apparent that more drastic action was required. Walking up to the fence, Justin grabbed the biggest boy, threw him over his shoulder and carried him to a nearby trough where he dumped him head first into the dirty water. In shock, the boys beat a hasty exit, only to re-appear half an hour later with their burly fathers and a dozen other bruisers. The travellers invaded the pitch and reaped havoc, causing the game to be abandoned. On the ride back to Shropham, Justin was not a popular man.

A Shot at Destiny

NORWICH CITY'S match against Liverpool on Saturday, February 9th 1980 is etched into the memories of thousands of Norwich City fans, and certainly in the minds of anyone who knew Justin Fashanu. The game at Carrow Road would change the course of the footballer's life and fortunes forever. If it sounds over-dramatic that's because it was. The day before the game, Fashanu and a group of friends shared a lunchtime meal and some laughs at the Pig and Whistle in the centre of Norwich. The pub was one of Justin's locals and on this particular day, Dave Bennett and Mel Richards joined him. During the course of the lunch, the discussion turned to how the striker should celebrate if he happened to score. While Bennett suggested flapping his arms out, Richards told him to simply stick his finger in the air and point to the heavens, cool as fuck. With Liverpool leading the league, no one expected for one moment that the young star would actually manage to breach the team's mighty defence and even get a chance to celebrate, but the men had a laugh imagining it.

In 1980 The Reds were the team to beat after winning the league the previous year and lifting the European Cup in 1977 and 1978. The club was at the top of its game with Kenny Dalglish, Jimmy Case and Alan Hansen just a handful of the stars in their line-up. When Liverpool travelled to Carrow

Road in February 1980, they were level with Manchester United at the top of the table. By comparison, Norwich had begun a slow descent south dropping to tenth place. With so much at stake, both teams badly needed three points so the match promised to be an entertaining spectacle.

When the next day arrived and the teams kicked off, Liverpool took instant control looking for an early lead and they almost got it, too, but after a few tense minutes for City fans it wasn't the Reds but Norwich who ended up scoring first courtesy of Martin Peters. The celebrations were cut short when Liverpool managed an equaliser from David Fairclough a short time later and the same striker then found the net again. It was turning out to be a hell of a battle. As the intensity increased so did the number of goals with Kevin Reeves restoring parity for Norwich just before the interval.

At the beginning of the second half Liverpool stepped up a gear and within a few minutes Fairclough had netted his hat trick. The young striker was having the game of his life, but no one would be talking about him at the end of the game. After Fairclough's third conversion, so started a move from Norwich City that would lead to what their fans will forever call 'that goal.' It was left back Greg Downs who initiated proceedings by taking the ball across the halfway line into Liverpool territory. As Liverpool ace Jimmy Case scuttled across the field to close him down, the Norwich defender played a quick one two with Graham Paddon before sweeping the ball wide to Kevin Bond. Bond passed to John Ryan who was just outside the penalty box, who then fed the ball to Fashanu. With his back towards the Liverpool goal, Fashanu flicked the ball up with the outside of his right foot, turned and fired it with his left. His aim could not have been more precise with the ball flying into the top left corner of the net. The Liverpool goalkeeper Ray Clemence was helpless and could do little but watch the ball as it curved past him.

As the whole of Carrow Road exploded in disbelief and delight, Fashanu lifted his right finger into the air looking every bit as surprised as everyone else that the ball had actually gone in. No one will ever know if the previous night's conversation with Bennett and Richards even registered in the striker's mind, but Richards certainly takes the credit for the one finger salute. It was a sensational goal and one that would change Justin Fashanu's fortunes forever. For better and worse. It didn't matter that Norwich went on to lose the game 5-3, Fashanu's masterpiece was the only thing people were talking about that day and for the whole week after (much to Fairclough's chagrin). *Match of the Day* cameras had recorded the game for the BBC's flagship evening sports show, so the whole country got to see the goal themselves in replays. The sensational strike would go on to be voted the BBC's 'Goal of the Season' and, in an instant, Justin Fashanu became a household name. And all this while he was still a fresh-faced 18-year-old just ten days shy of his 19th birthday.

If Fashanu was a rising star before his golden goal, it's fair to say he was exalted to hero status thereafter, at least in Norwich. Endorsements started flooding in and every reporter wanted a sound bite from the 'next big thing'. Just months earlier, Justin had been cleaning boots for Norwich and now the world's biggest sports companies were clamouring for him to wear their own boots for free. It was a surreal time for the striker who told people that he'd only been doing his job.

Fashanu's rise continued in April 1980 when the footballer was called up for international duty. He was selected to play for England's Under-21 team and found himself paired up front with Garth Crooks, some young striker from Stoke City. It was a big game: a UEFA semi-final tie against East Germany at Bramall Lane, Sheffield. Although England lost 2-1, Fashanu scored in the eighty-fifth minute thus cementing his immediate future with the England squad. He would go on to play two more games for the England team before the end of the year against Norway and Switzerland, scoring against the Swiss.

To cap Fashanu's outstanding year, at the end of the regular domestic season sports reporter Alan Parry presented him with a silver plate for winning the BBC's much-coveted Goal of the Season. The footballer received it at Flint House with Betty, Alf, and John all in attendance. The scene was filmed for *Match of the Day* and gives a wonderful snapshot of life inside the Fashanu/Jackson home. With Betty, Alf and John sitting nonchalantly around a country-style kitchen table, Justin looks almost embarrassed to accept the award. When Parry asks John what he thinks of his brother's achievement the shy teenager almost quakes in his boots. Although John was still an unknown in the football world, his fear of most things would diminish in time and he'd eventually become even more famous than his brother. For now, however, it was Justin's time in the spotlight. In one shot, the cameraman is positioned just behind the footballer's shoulder filming Fashanu's reflection in the plate. It's hard to tell if the footballer is concentrating on reading the plate's inscription or trying to recognise his own reflection. He was no longer an anonymous player from an obscure village in the Norfolk backwaters. Now he was a major player in every sense, and his life was about to get a whole lot more complicated.

Living Large

FROM THAT moment on there's no doubt that Fashanu was forced to grow up extra quickly. He'd always been mature for his age but now there were higher expectations from his coach and fans. And while he may not have been ready for the attention he gained, he certainly revelled in it. More money meant more designer clothes for the wardrobe and cars for the garage. It wasn't a bad life and not long before the footballer's MGB was traded for a sleek BMW. Much to Brooks' dismay, unpaid parking tickets also increased. It seems that Justin would never get to grips with that one.

Because Norwich was a small city, reporter Mick Dennis often bumped into Fashanu around town. Sometimes they met in nightclubs and the footballer usually had an entourage of beauties, mostly blonde, in attendance. Fashanu was always smiling and super courteous. While most footballers of that era were legendary for having an appalling dress sense, Fashanu had a sharp sense of style all his own. White suits, à la John Lennon, were a favourite. Looking back today, Dennis sometimes wonders if the image Fashanu cultivated was actually just a show and whether the footballer was trying just a little too hard. Underneath the white suit and behind that enigmatic smile, who was the real Justin Fashanu? When asked by a local TV reporter what it was like to be in his shoes the footballer gives us a hint when he replied: 'I like having the fans around most of the time, as it's nice to be wanted and loved and it's something you will miss when you are not in the limelight.'[12] His answer points to a need for affirmation and affection, likely due to the early desertions he experienced from his parents, Patrick and Pearl. Although his foster parents supported him the best way they knew how, Betty and Alf never watched Justin play the very sport that meant the most to him and that became his career. In that sense, while his surrogate family was kind in many ways, it was lacking in others. Justin was also beginning to realise he was different from other men when it came to his sexuality and that too must made him feel isolated. Craving attention was an obvious, but superficial remedy, that would eventually come back to bite him in a way he never could have possibly imagined.

Despite his newly found fame, Fashanu still made time to catch up with old friends and honour the many requests made of him. Top of the list was opening local fetes. One Saturday, Fashanu was invited to open a fundraising event at Wymondham High School by the schoolmaster, Brian Harvey. The master had known Justin since the footballer had first arrived in Norfolk thirteen years earlier and was struck by how modest he'd remained. Fashanu had also kept ties to the boxing scene and sometimes dropped into the Norwich Lad's Club on Duke Street to watch the latest talent in action and give some tips. One of the boys who met him was Karl Tuttle. Fashanu told him that he'd chosen football over boxing because it would mean a longer career with less pain. Destiny would argue differently.

Another place he and some of his other Norwich teammates hung out was the Church of England Young Man's Society in the centre of town. Their presence had nothing to do with God and everything to do with the full-sized snooker table in the corner of the hall. Glenn Hoy, a local lad, was a regular and says the players went there because they liked to play snooker religiously. Of course, Fashanu was good with a cue and very few people could beat him. No event was too insignificant for the footballer to accommodate. He and Neil Giles became friends after Fashanu presented trophies to Giles' local pub darts team following a chance meeting down his local. When Fashanu's old mate from Flint House Les Hammond asked the footballer to present prizes at the annual Attleborough Cricket Club dinner, Fashanu happily obliged. But just like old times, Hammond had to promise there would be no photographs. Fashanu had a game for Norwich City the next day and the coaching staff had told him to be in bed by nine.

Incredibly, Fashanu was also the manager of Shropham FC where his duties included taking a weekly training session, picking the team and watching their games (when time allowed). He also maintained regular contact with his old club Attleborough FC. By now his former teacher John Lund was playing for the club's seniors. When Fashanu was sidelined at Norwich City with a minor injury, he asked Lund whether he could train with the team for a couple of sessions. Surprised but delighted, Lund said yes (if Bond had found out there would have been hell to pay). At the end of each training session the Attleborough players always finished proceedings with a long run, the slower players starting out first and the faster ones at later intervals. Lund always considered himself a competent middle-distance runner and, after pairing off with Fashanu, wondered if the footballer would be able to keep up. Half a mile into the run and it was Lund who was struggling to keep up with Fashanu himself. As they neared the clubhouse his partner suddenly switched things up a gear leaving him to eat dust. The teacher learned two important lessons that day: he wasn't a good runner after all and never underestimate the fitness of a pro footballer.

As if Fashanu wasn't a natural at most things already, he was also handy when it came to good old-fashioned communications. His outgoing personality gave him some natural skills, but he was quite capable of making naive mistakes, understandable for someone of his age. His more polished media performances came about after a discussion with Norwich businessman Roger Haywood, who he had met several times at the gym where they both trained. Haywood was a high-flying PR professional with his own offices in Norwich, Peterborough and London and had recently moved to the sticks from the 'Smoke'. Haywood was a Norwich City fan and had watched Fashanu's progress with interest. In one conversation after a gym training session, he asked the footballer about a particularly tough interview where Justin had got flustered. Haywood had recently developed the technique of issue management and explained a few pointers about working with the media. He was amazed when he discovered the footballer didn't have an agent. After explaining how Fashanu could benefit by being more savvy and confident, the footballer asked Haywood to manage his affairs. It would prove to be an interesting partnership.

The two got on well and after a few training sessions Fashanu's media performances became more assured and he learned how to control discussions in a more informal way. Journalists began to realise he had a bigger story to tell. After these early times together, one of the first national activities Haywood arranged to broaden Justin's profile into something approaching a rising young personality was a double page fashion spread in *The Sun* newspaper. The next activity was to put out a record with Fashanu on vocals. Recorded in a London studio in early 1980, the footballer's unusually high-pitched voice sounds as if his briefs may have been on the tight side. The 12-inch single was called *Do it 'Cos You Like It!* with Haywood on sax. The most interesting thing about the record, by far, is the cover design featuring Fashanu flashing his million-dollar smile and wearing a bright red leather jump suit borrowed from the newspaper photo shoot. Whether Justin's manager was trying to capitalise on a good looking black footballer who could move just as gracefully off the pitch as on it, as some claimed, Haywood won't deny. However, the confidential truth between the two was that Fashanu recognised that he had limited capabilities in football and a professional career in that sector could be short-lived. He took to the public attention and wanted to broaden his career opportunities. As for his record, what Fashanu did was to kick-start a new trend of professional footballers who picked up a mic themselves and kicked it. Who can forget John Barnes' impressive vocals on New Order's classic *World in Motion* record a decade later? Thankfully, Fashanu's own cut was strictly a one-off with him and Haywood agreeing that the young footballer's talents lay elsewhere.

Another gig Haywood arranged for Fashanu was a guest presenter spot on a local BBC Radio Norwich football magazine show. Fashanu presented a weekly segment called *Fashanu Focus* where he talked about everything football related. At only 19-years-old, the footballer had the wit and confidence of someone far maturer. (Sadly, the man who would go on to become Norwich's biggest superstar, Alan Partridge, had not started working at the station yet. As such, Fashanu did not have the pleasure of meeting the great man.)

For the most part, Haywood and Fashanu's partnership was smooth sailing but that wasn't always the case. On one occasion, Haywood received a phone call from an irate Ken Brown. The assistant manager had been told that his star striker had taken part in a charity go-karting event the previous evening and was livid because Fashanu could have been seriously injured. Haywood rang the footballer immediately to check out the truth and Justin said he didn't think anyone would have noticed him. As a local celebrity who also happened to be one of the few black men in Norwich, it was quite the statement. Haywood was furious with his client and saw it as irresponsible and unprofessional. A broken leg could have had a devastating impact on his main livelihood. Though he had known nothing about it, Haywood took the heat regardless. He met up with Brown, explained the situation and gave him an assurance it would never happen again.

One real benefit that did come out of the partnership was Haywood's training for Fashanu in the art of interviewing. Considering he'd only been under the media spotlight for less than a year, Justin learned fast. One of his best performances in front of the cameras was when he was a guest on Noel Edmond's Saturday morning show *Swap Shop*. The footballer answered Edmond's questions and fielded phone calls from viewers with ease. When a caller asked him why he'd chosen professional football as a career he replied: 'It's better than working in a factory.' At least he was being honest. Fashanu brought in a variety of prizes to give away, including a signed photograph of him standing inside Mel Richard's hair salon. Richards was watching the show at home and when he saw the prize being offered he spat out his breakfast cereal. The photograph Justin was giving away happened to be his, and had mysteriously disappeared from his salon wall the week before. Now he knew where it had gone.

When it came to Fashanu's love life, the footballer began dating a friend he'd known for a couple of years in Norwich called Julie Arthurton. Although Richards never met Julie personally, Justin regularly talked about her and to all intents and purposes it seemed that the relationship was genuine. While Bennett met Julie on a couple of occasions he got the impression that Justin wanted to keep her out of the spotlight. As such, neither Bennett nor Richards can comment more on the relationship.

As far as Fashanu's main day job was concerned, at the beginning of 1980 his form was in top shape and he should have been a regular fixture in Bond's team, but his lack of discipline was holding him back. Fashanu had always been a physical player, but things he had been able to get away with in the past as an amateur were not going to wash now that he was a professional. A referee was only going to allow his elbows to come into contact with an opponent's face so many times before taking action. In Fashanu's second season as a professional he was severely rebuked by Bond after head butting Bristol City defender David Rodgers, forcing Rodgers to leave the game. It was a momentary act of recklessness that left Bond fuming. Considering the player's polite, well-mannered reputation off the pitch Fashanu's behaviour on the field is hard to reconcile. His aggression was sometimes way over the top and revealed a belligerent alter ego. In the incident against Rodgers, Bond was so incensed that he apologised to the Bristol City manager Alan Dicks at halftime. When he got back to the dressing room he completely lost it with Fashanu. Ken Brown remembers Bond's nose being inches from Fashanu's as he bawled at him and wondering if his colleague knew the striker was a handy boxer. Rather than accept Bond's words, a churlish Fashanu told reporters that the manager had been bang out of order and he was planning to lodge a complaint with the PFA, the players' union. It wasn't the best move and he was subsequently fined and dropped for City's next game against Nottingham Forest. Given his successful strike rate against Forest in the past, Clough must have been relieved when he saw the team sheet. Fashanu's reaction to Bond's attack on him, which was more than justified, shows an immaturity that would gradually fade over time, but his physical presence would only grow.

Fashanu was brought back for the last game of the season against Derby, scoring to help Norwich win 4-2. But another impulsive tackle in that game forced Bond to reprimand him again. Just like with unpaid parking tickets, it seemed the footballer was never going to learn. When a reporter asked him what he thought about his fierce reputation Fashanu denied he was aggressive and simply went in for tackles hard. Many players begged to differ, viewing Fashanu's style of play as plain dirty. By the end of the season Justin had still managed to score 11 goals in 34 league appearances plus two other goals in an FA Cup game and League Cup tie. Norwich City ended up in twelfth place.

If Fashanu thought he was going to get a summer vacation he was in for a shock. Bond had arranged for the team to play a few exhibition games in China and Hong Kong in a groundbreaking tour. At the time, City was only the second professional English club to tour East Asia. The team ended up playing four games, winning three and drawing one, but the real entertainment happened off the pitch. It was, of course, Fashanu who was centre stage. The most notable incident happened after the team bus dropped the players off at their hotel in what was then known as Peking. What should have been a relaxing couple of days turned into a 'Whodunit?' weekend after Bond's suitcase went missing. At the dinner table that night he politely asked the players if anyone had picked it up accidentally. When no one raised their hand Bond's tone changed: 'One of you cunts has taken it and when I find out you're gonna' fackin' pay,' he snapped.

Fashanu happened to be sharing a room with Peter Mendham, and as they packed up their stuff to vacate it two days later they noticed an unopened suitcase in the corner of the suite. Nervously, Fashanu asked Mendham if the suitcase was his and when Mendham shook his head a brief pause was followed by an awful realisation: it was obviously their manager's. One of them had picked it up in error, but the problem now was who was going to tell Bond. Rather than risk his wrath, Fashanu threw the suitcase into the elevator, hit the lobby button and raced back to his room. Bond was reunited with his bag as he checked out of the hotel a short time later and was, understandably, seething. Although he didn't have any direct proof who'd taken it he did have one main suspect: Dave Bennett. As such, the midfielder ended up getting the cold shoulder for the rest of the tour. It would be three years before Bennett found out the real culprit when Fashanu finally admitted it over a beer.

By the time the 1980/81 season was in full swing, Bond had recruited another experienced player into the fold. According to Joe Royle, the Norwich City manager called him out of the blue and told him he needed someone with experience to help a talented forward in the Norwich side named Justin Fashanu. Royle didn't need a description. Like the rest of the country he'd seen the striker's amazing goal against Liverpool and knew all about him. Bond brought in the mature 31-year-old to replace Kevin Reeves who he had just sold to Manchester City. Royle's debut was against Stoke City, a game that City won 5-1. Fashanu grabbed three goals within the space of just 20 minutes making it one of the fastest hat tricks in the club's history.

Despite a positive start to the season, however, the team began to falter and by the time October arrived City had only managed two wins in eight games. The results were frustrating for an in-form Fashanu who'd already added ten goals to his tally. By contrast, Royle was having problems finding his own form and was dropped. But things were only set to get worse. In mid-October Bond made a shocking announcement. After seven years in charge, the Norwich City manager declared he was leaving the club and heading to Manchester City. His resignation was immediate. Everyone was stunned, not least the players. Ken Brown told the media that he would not be following and the next day City appointed him as their new manager. For days after Bond's departure Fashanu was also the talk of the town. Rumours circulated that the new Manchester City manager was planning to take his young protégé up north with him. When that didn't materialise, there was speculation Fashanu might be heading to Leeds United instead. Brown drew a line under all the rumour-mongering when he told fans Fashanu's future remained firmly with Norwich.

Unfortunately, Norwich City's standing in the league was not quite as solid and by the time Brown officially took over in late October 1980, the club found itself sitting in the bottom half of the table. By the New Year they'd dropped even further down the rankings. Results didn't improve in 1981 and the only sure thing was that it was a dismal time to be a Canaries fan. The team looked to be in freefall.

Despite a lacklustre season domestically, Fashanu's services as a striker were required once again internationally. The England Under-21 side played a friendly against Ireland and won 1-0. But the victory for England was something Norwich City could not imitate, and more losses for the club followed. One big upset was a 4-0 pummelling at the hands of Birmingham City with all of the goals conceded in the last 15 minutes of the game. TV cameras recorded the game, and after the match Fashanu was clearly wound up.

'We've got to fight and we've got to battle. It's going to be bloody hard, if you'll excuse my French, to get off the relegation zone. I think it's about time that players in the team, and I hope the manager doesn't mind me saying, look at themselves, me included, and say, "Look we're here in the first division, we love everything that goes with it: the nice suits, the nice cars and if you get into the second division, it's gonna be a bloody hard struggle." I can't understand why we can't be ruthless. Players at this club are too nice,'[13] he said.

While passion is good, one reason you can't be ruthless is because you can get booked and sent off. Fashanu knew all about that first hand. While the footballer's statement shows he was clearly passionate about playing for his club, you can't help wondering if he was also concerned about the potential relegation of his lifestyle. Ultimately, his battle cry failed to rally the troops with Norwich continuing their losing streak. By April, the club had been sucked into the dreaded drop zone and were duly relegated at the end of the season. It was a bitter blow, especially for Fashanu who had carried on scoring despite the team's poor results. The Norwich striker had managed an impressive 19 goals in 40 league appearances, plus another three goals in six League Cup/FA Cup appearances. Of course, no one was more disappointed than Brown who suspected relegation would result in the departure of some of his best players. He was right. Whether it was an intentional move to try and keep Fashanu out of the spotlight, Brown handed Fashanu an air ticket to Australia and told him he was playing for Adelaide City over the summer. The young striker played 11 games and scored five goals.

While Fash was Down Under, his striking partner Joe Royle was still in sunny Norwich. One evening, Royle received a surprise phone call at home from the Nottingham Forest manager Brian Clough. In short, Cloughie wanted to know what he thought of Fashanu's skills. Royle gave his teammate top marks and said that he was one of the most exciting strikers he'd ever played with. Clough thanked him for his honesty and hung up. Fashanu might have been out of sight but, apparently, was not out of mind. Clough wasn't the only manager circling Fashanu. Now that he'd settled into his new job with Manchester City, Bond was keen to reunite Justin with his former striking partner, Kevin Reeves. But, ultimately, it wasn't to be. Writer and football historian Edward Couzens-Lake explains:

'Relegation and rising debts meant that Norwich had to sell Fash, with Forest ultimately making the best offer. At one point they were reported to have offered any one of their players, apart from Peter Shilton or Trevor Francis, as part of the deal, which was a testament to how much they wanted him. Other clubs were said to be interested, including Liverpool, but it was Clough's persistence and determination that won the day.'

But signing Fashanu would cost the Nottingham Forest manager dearly. In mid-August 1981, the footballer, accompanied by Ken Brown, travelled to a hotel in Peterborough where Clough and his faithful press officer John Lawson were waiting. According to Brown, when they reached the hotel Justin disappeared into a room with Clough, spent precisely thirty seconds signing his name on the Forest contract, before re-appearing. Brown hadn't even had a chance to sit down. Justin's time in Norwich was ended that quickly.

More staggering is the price that Clough had paid. Malcolm Robertson's headline in the *Eastern Daily Press* the next day said it all: 'Fashanu Makes it a Million!'[14] In a sensational move, the Nottingham Forest manager had propelled Justin Fashanu into the record books by making him the first black player in British football history to move for a million pound fee. It seemed there was no stopping his ascent. If the footballer's feet did, momentarily, leave the ground, then they hit terra firma with a bump pretty quickly once reality set in. Such a high price tag brought equally high expectations, especially where Clough was concerned. During his time with Norwich, Justin had scored a total of 40 goals in 97 appearances, and Clough expected a similar return. When Fashanu was asked what he thought about the move he told a reporter: 'I have got no apprehensions playing for Brian Clough and I know exactly what he wants. He wants to be a successful manager and I want to be a successful footballer,'[15] At least Fashanu was clear on things.

As news of the footballer's departure spread throughout East Anglia, some people wondered whether it was the right move. Reporter Mick Dennis was one of them. Although Justin was mature for an 18-year-old, he was still young in years and had never really experienced life outside of the county. In Norwich, there were people who genuinely cared about him and he had a solid support network of family and friends there. In Nottingham, he knew no one. Was he ready? Ronnie Brooks and Les Hammond also shared Dennis' concerns. While the world suddenly seemed like Fashanu's oyster, working under the controversial Clough was like swimming with sharks. The young footballer was entering uncharted waters and there was no telling what might happen.

Shattered Dreams

IF FASHANU was excited about joining Nottingham Forest, the fans themselves were absolutely jubilant. Like the rest of the country they'd seen what the striker had done for Norwich City and, like Clough, anticipated the same. Keith Lennox is a life-long Forest fan who has been watching his team since the late Seventies. Like many of his fellow supporters, Lennox relished the arrival of the country's very first million pound black player with excitement, but also realised that expectancy can sometimes turn sour: 'I've always had certain misgivings about how fickle many of my fellow supporters can be. Forest fans do seem to have more than their fair share of real curmudgeons and even Clough was sometimes critical of them. Forest fans expect a great deal from new players, especially high profile signings like Fashanu, and if a player doesn't deliver they are quickly berated. There's no mercy,' says Lennox. His words would prove portentous.

When Fashanu signed for Nottingham Forest in 1981, it seems there was one thing he didn't quite grasp. There was only one legend in Nottingham – and it wasn't Robin Hood. That honour belonged to Brian Clough, self bestowed or not. One of the manager's favourite mantras was 'All life's a game' and Justin would soon learn that the only rules Clough played by were his own. Clough was one of the most controversial managers in

English football. Loved by fans but not by the game's rulers at the Football Association and the Football League, he had a big persona and was a law unto himself. Nicknamed 'Ol' Big Ead', the Forest manager was known for being a loose cannon and if you got on his wrong side he'd let you know.

Fashanu nearly managed to draw Clough's ire before he'd even put on a Forest jersey, just ahead of the team's summer tour in Spain. With the ink still drying on his contract, he had been ordered to meet Clough and the rest of the team at Heathrow Airport. While en route from Norwich, Justin realised he'd left his passport at home. His driver that day, Kevan Platt, worked in the Commercial Department at Norwich City. Normally, Platt's regular day to day duties involved drumming up more sponsorship deals for the club but his orders that morning were to drive Fashanu to Heathrow, make sure the footballer got on the plane and return home. It had seemed a simple assignment but when Justin announced his dilemma that changed in an instant. 'I knew there was no time to drive back and retrieve the passport, so I hit the accelerator. If we could make it to Heathrow ahead of the Forest contingent then I knew there was a slim chance to save the crisis,' Platt says. In the days before global terrorism, Heathrow Airport had a small passport bureau that issued temporary visas. After reaching the airport at break-neck speed the footballer was getting one stamped just as the rest of the Forest team was checking in. Clough was never any wiser, but Platt will never forget how Fashanu's chapter at Forest almost ended before it had even begun.

Like his new protégé, Clough had been a formidable striker himself back in the Fifties. He'd scored more than 200 league goals for Middlesbrough and Sunderland before a knee injury in 1962 ended his career soon after. Hanging up his boots, Clough went into football management with Hartlepool before moving to the Baseball Ground and securing Derby County's first Championship title in 1972, all the time in partnership with Peter Taylor. After leaving the Rams acrimoniously, Clough joined Leeds United but the appointment didn't last long. After just 44 days, the players staged a public revolt against their new manager and Clough was sacked. Via Brighton, he arrived at Second Division Nottingham Forest in January 1975, steering the side to promotion in 1977 before remarkably claiming the First Division title the following season.

In February 1979, Clough created a piece of domestic football history when he signed striker Trevor Francis from Birmingham City making him

Britain's first million-pound footballer. Forest secured their second successive League Cup that season and also the European Cup, the £1 million pound man heading the winner to confirm an astonishing turn in fortunes for Forest. When the parochial East Midlands club then successfully retained the European Cup a year later in Madrid, the Forest manager achieved that legendary status. In the late Seventies and early Eighties, Forest's achievements made them the envy of Europe's finest. Yet examining the club in retrospect it's clear that when Justin joined, those fortunes had peaked and an element of decline had set in. The team of virtual unknowns that Clough had melded was falling apart. The formidable strike partnership of Tony Woodcock and Garry Birtles had departed, and the Larry Lloyd-Kenny Burns backbone had been broken at the centre of defence. To compound matters, Francis had suffered an Achilles tendon injury and suddenly Clough had found himself without an effective strike force.

To remedy the problem, Clough had brought in two new forwards: Ian Wallace from Coventry City and Peter Ward from Brighton and Hove Albion. Unfortunately, neither Wallace nor Ward was working out the way the manager had hoped. To make matters worse, Clough's own partnership with Taylor, who'd followed him to Forest, had started to sour. Things had got so bad between them that some days they weren't talking at all. To top off the chaotic scene Clough was, reportedly, hitting the bottle. When Fashanu entered the picture it wasn't an ideal environment for any footballer to be in. Duncan Hamilton, a young sports reporter in Nottingham, sympathised with Justin. He knew that while Nottingham was hardly London, it was a much bigger city than the one Fashanu had just come from. There were more bars, nightclubs, restaurants and stores than Norwich. A move to Nottingham was, therefore, a big deal for the ex-Norwich striker.

What didn't help things is that whenever Clough signed a new player he often gave the new recruit the cold shoulder when he first arrived. This is especially true if a player had cost him a lot of money. Clough's approach didn't provide the warm, welcoming environment that Fashanu was used to at Norwich City. Trevor Francis had received the same rough treatment himself when he joined Forest. To ensure that his new million-pound striker didn't get too big for his boots, Clough handed him his debut by selecting him for Forest's A Team. Peter Ward had also been on the receiving end of Clough's unpredictable behaviour himself when he'd first joined the club. Travelling back to Nottingham after an away match one evening, Ward asked the bus driver to drop him off at a service station where his car was parked. Clough, who was sitting nearby, told the driver to keep going: 'With a bit of luck the cunt will get run over,' he barked. When Ward was eventually allowed to disembark he was a mile up the road from his car and had to walk down the hard shoulder of the motorway in the dark and rain. Understandably, he was not a happy camper.

Fashanu endured the worst possible start with his new team, starting with a red card in the summer tournament in Spain as Forest eventually lost to Real Zaragoza on penalties. Fashanu's early exit was a blow. Back in England Fashanu's First Division debut was a home game against Southampton in late August. Mark Proctor, a 20-year-old midfielder, had signed for the Reds a week earlier and it was his debut too. Forest won the match 2-1, with Fashanu's striking partner Francis scoring both goals despite still carrying an injury. Clough might have expected a better return with two million-pound centre forwards playing in his side. Proctor was impressed with Fashanu's self-confidence and found the footballer affable. The same could not be said for Clough, whose mood on any given day was unpredictable.

After seven games Fashanu still hadn't scored which prompted Clough to act. Walking into the dressing room after a defeat, Clough told the striker to look closely at a framed photograph he was clutching. The black and white photo was a shot of the manager in his heyday scoring a header for Middlesbrough: 'Young man, this is what you have to do. Score goals,' he said. Fashanu bowed his head while the rest of the team sniggered. To make matters worse the club had arranged for a local car dealer to provide their star striker with a sports car. The dealer Terry Carpenter presented Fashanu with a new Toyota Celica F2 with the footballer's name boldly emblazoned on the side. As a marketing stunt, Carpenter had paid a local graphic designer to produce miniature football stickers that Fashanu could stick on the side of the car each time he scored. The stunt ended up causing a huge embarrassment when, after seven games, not one single sticker had been applied. It was another two matches before Fashanu finally found the net (against Clough's beloved Middlesbrough.)

Despite being unable to find his scoring touch, one thing Fashanu hadn't lost was his physical presence. In a game against Manchester City,

Ward was running on to a cross from Forest winger John Robertson when he heard an almighty crack behind him. Turning around, Ward saw the Manchester City centre half Tommy Caton lying on his back holding a bloodied nose. It was broken. Walking nonchalantly away from the scene was an innocent looking Fashanu. In Ward's eloquent phrasing, Fashanu had 'done him' and the Forest striker was fortunate that the referee hadn't seen. If Clough hoped his striker would start hitting the net as well as opponents he would be disappointed, however. It took another month after his first goal before Fashanu converted his second in a third round League Cup tie against Blackburn Rovers in mid-November. It was the only goal of the game and gave Forest a much-needed win. It also meant that there were now two football stickers on the side of Fashanu's car.

It wasn't only the Forest manager who was on Fashanu's back, so were the fans. In some games a small section openly jeered at him whenever he touched the ball. Never mind that he was on their team. Fashanu's old striking partner at Norwich City Joe Royle says that Justin was the sort of player who responded to positive comments and encouragement, and he didn't get either from Clough or some fans. In Royle's mind it was no surprise that he'd lost his form. When Fashanu travelled back to Norwich one weekend to see his family, he dropped round to see Ronnie Brooks. The footballer appeared despondent. Fashanu told the football scout that he couldn't seem to do anything right with Clough and that his confidence was shot. Brooks told him to stay strong, keep his head up and that goals would follow. Secretly, Brooks was concerned. He'd always worried that Justin had flown the nest at Norwich too soon and it looked as if his fears were coming true.

While Clough didn't always supervise Nottingham Forest's training sessions, when he did attend he carried a squash racket that he waved about. It became his trademark. Although he never hit anyone with it the threat was always there. Clough suffered from a heart murmur, so every few weeks he'd jet off to the warmer climes of Majorca for a weekend of rest. When he was away, Taylor and the other assistant coach Ronnie Fenton took the sessions. On some occasions, the so-called 'Blocks' (blacks and jocks) took on the rest of the team for a light-hearted scrimmage. When Clough didn't make training, most players breathed a collective sigh of relief. Hamilton says the Forest manager scared the living wits out of all the younger players, Fashanu included. A player never knew how he was going to treat them. One day Clough might be nice only for him to tear a strip out of you the next time in front of everyone. If he didn't like the way you looked at him, or thought you were getting too cocky, you were a marked man. It was very disconcerting for players and meant their guards were always raised.

On the pitch, Fashanu's frustrations continued to manifest themselves. Rather than goals, he accumulated more bookings. In December, the footballer was banned for three matches by the FA after one yellow card too many. Naturally, the ban did not go down well with Clough who criticised Fashanu in the local press.

'If results go well while Justin is out, he might just have to go in the reserves to sort himself out. I hope he spends his time out of action thinking about how to channel all his efforts into playing centre forward and how to get the goals he is capable of scoring. Justin has been booked half a dozen times, but none of them, to my knowledge, have come from getting hurt in the six-yard box,'[16] Clough said.

Like at Norwich, Fashanu didn't seem able to rein in his aggression. He never showed any belligerence or hostility off it, so it's unclear exactly why he could be such a brute. It went against the grain of his character. Like other contradictions in his life, this one was an enigma too. John Fashanu would also become an overtly physical player himself when he started playing professional football, so maybe it was in the blood.

There was at least one bit of good news in Fashanu's personal life. The footballer had finally managed to find a home in Nottingham after staying at a hotel for a few months. The footballer's house was located inside a plush, gated area called The Park in the centre of town. Once he'd settled in, Justin invited his girlfriend from Norwich to move in. Again, the status of his relationship with Julie is not exactly clear. After the footballer moved to Nottingham, Justin had seriously began questioning his sexuality.

Justin Fashanu was only 20 when he joined Forest, but in many ways he was more mature than other men his age. Being thrust into the national spotlight at 17, moving to a new city and working for a capricious manager forced him to grow up quickly. He was unique among other professional footballers in his sensitivity, but ahead of the game in terms of fitness, too. When he moved to Nottingham, he employed the services of fitness coach Osman Raif. Raif was a martial arts expert, trained masseur and nutritionist who ensured that Fashanu stayed on track. Raif's presence irritated Clough, especially when the manager learned he was Fashanu's private masseur. Fashanu was simply employing the kind of health professional that current clubs regularly use for footballers. With fitness and nutrition vital foundations for any professional footballer, it was actually a progressive move. Of course, in Clough's traditional perception, employing such a person was just ridiculous.

Fashanu might not have been in top form when it came to kicking a football but it was a different matter when it came to writing witty prose. The editor of the weekly football magazine *Shoot!* hired him to pen a column and it proved a hit with young readers. One article the footballer wrote just after Christmas looked like an entry torn right out of his personal diary. He told readers he was down in the dumps after learning he'd just been banned by the FA following one red card too many. Fashanu wrote that he was ashamed and Clough and Taylor both get an apology. The striker obviously understood that Clough was coming to the end of his tether with his poor disciplinary record: 'I can promise you that I never deliberately set out to foul another player. I go in hard, the First Division demands that, but my sole intention is to win possession, not leave a defender on his back clutching his leg in agony… From now on my behaviour will be beyond reproach. That's a promise,'[16] Justin wrote.

But Fashanu's promise turned out to be a tough one to keep, as the bookings continued. Fashanu's attitude to parking didn't ingratiate him with his manager either. As in Norwich, Fashanu left his car wherever he pleased. As the fines stacked up, Clough told Justin that unless he paid them he would give police permission to arrest the footballer. He wasn't lying. Clough was also unhappy that Fashanu sometimes threw his boots into the crowd after a game. If he'd scored more goals then he probably wouldn't have considered it a problem, but he was growing tired at what he perceived to be a petulant attitude. In February 1982, Clough told local reporters that despite Fashanu's form, the Forest manager planned to get him scoring again: 'In the football world, Justin is still a baby and I know he needs help, advice and encouragement. I'll do everything in my power to point him in the right direction,'[17] Clough said. Nothing could have been further from the truth. Within a week, Fashanu was placed on the transfer list along with Wallace and Forest captain, John McGovern.

In a surprising, but pleasant, twist the striker was selected for the England Under-21 squad in the UEFA European Championship Quarter final first leg against Poland in Warsaw. Fashanu played up front alongside West Ham's Paul Goddard and although he didn't score, England won 2-1. Fashanu's display garnered praise from the England manager, Ron Greenwood: 'For somebody who has struggled to find goals this season, I thought he did remarkably well,'[18] Greenwood said. They were welcome words for a striker who'd forgotten what a compliment sounded like.

Secrets

IT WAS a few months after he'd first arrived in Nottingham that Justin Fashanu made a courageous move away from the pitch. It had been some time since the 20-year-old first realised he was gay, but he'd never explored that side of his sexuality. He'd never so much as been to a gay bar before, never mind a nightclub. And certainly not in Norwich. Now that he was in Nottingham, however, it was a different story. Unlike Norwich, the East Midlands city had a vibrant social culture with more opportunities to discover who he really was. In the early Eighties, a club called Part Two (formerly La Chic) on Canal Street was the main centre of the local gay scene. The venue had opened in late 1980 and was run by local businessman Ross Smith. While it hadn't been easy for Smith to get permission to open his doors, it was worth the effort. The club became an instant hit with people from all over the country traveling to party there. At the time famous guests included the singer Marc Almond, ice skater John Curry and actress Barbara Windsor. The new club was large, boasting three bars, dance floor, restaurant and so-called 'quiet area'. Smith invited Fashanu to Part Two after meeting him and Julie at a party one week. The footballer told the club owner that Julie was his girlfriend, but Smith was never convinced.

'Justin was hanging around with Julie and they used to come to the club regularly. It was only after he started coming in by himself, without Julie, that the penny suddenly dropped and I figured that Justin could be a fully paid-up member of my club,' Smith says.

In later years, Fashanu would reveal that what he really wanted in life was a meaningful relationship with someone, but in the early Eighties he seemed more interested in superficial encounters. The footballer was enjoying exploring his sexuality in a way he'd never done before. Fashanu fell in love with the gay scene because it offered him a much-needed release from the pressures he was facing in his daily life at Forest. He told a friend he was attracted to the underground society because the people he met there had fun and didn't seem to care what anyone thought. The footballer related more to them and they were worlds apart from his contemporaries at Nottingham Forest.

One thing that struck Smith was Fashanu's naivety. For his birthday one year, the club owner organised a tramp's supper evening and a few hours before the party was due to start Justin called in a panic asking him how he should dress. After explaining the obvious Smith was gob smacked when Fashanu turned up wearing a brand new Armani suit that he'd slashed with scissors. Fash wasn't being flash he just didn't own any old clothes.

When Fashanu first started visiting Part Two he was always discreet with Smith letting the footballer in through the back door. But as the footballer started to become more relaxed he began to get more brazen. It wasn't long before he was driving his car right up to the entrance of the club and throwing his car keys to the doorman. 'Talk about being naïve! There he is in the public eye, and not enjoying it so much, and he's parking the only white Toyota Supra in Nottingham right outside the door of the only club in Britain licensed for gay members. He might as well have just worn a pink shirt when he played football,' Smith says. When it came to men, Fashanu liked guys his own age or slightly younger: the cute, skinny, white preppy type. Many nights Fashanu would call Smith up and ask him if there was anything in the club he might fancy. It was always one-night stands with Justin and never anything more serious.

Fashanu was soon visiting other gay clubs down in London. One of his favourites was a huge super club called Heaven, right under Charing Cross railway station. The club was so large that it was easy to get lost in the crowd and remain anonymous. During a visit to the club one Saturday, Fashanu met human rights and political campaigner Peter Tatchell who would become a close friend and confidante. At the time, Tatchell was a Labour parliamentary candidate and in the media spotlight himself. Amusingly, after a chance meeting on the dance floor neither Tatchell nor Fashanu had any idea who the other was.

'I was dancing by myself and having a good time and out of the corner of my eye I saw this guy sipping a pint of beer and looking at me quite intensely. He winked and smiled and I did likewise and then he motioned for me to come over. He introduced himself as Justin and complimented me on my dancing. I tried to get him to dance but he wouldn't. He said, "Let's chat" and we ended up talking for the next few hours,' Tatchell says.

The only thing 'Justin' revealed that night was that he worked in sport and 'Peter' was, similarly, circumspect about his own career. When he left the club at the end of the night Fashanu passed on his phone number and over the next few weeks the two men spoke regularly on the phone. It would be another six weeks before they finally discovered each other's real identities and it was a shock to both of them. Tatchell would go on to become one of the few people in Justin's life whom the footballer really confided in. The more they got to know each other the more Fashanu revealed the things that were tormenting him. Not surprisingly, the footballer was going through a great deal of angst about his career. The whole Clough episode was really affecting him psychologically and this was reflected by his performance on the pitch that was not up to what he or others expected. Fashanu didn't feel supported by his manager at all.

Tatchell claims that Fashanu first had inklings he was gay at the age of 16 but had repressed them. While he longed for a stable and loving relationship this seemed beyond the realms of possibility to him. Tatchell could tell that the footballer was experiencing a huge dilemma since other people and his belief system were telling him that his feelings were wrong. The footballer also broached his relationship with his brother. Justin adored John but felt he could not confide in him about his sexuality. He knew he would not understand. Tatchell and Fashanu continued their late night phone conversations for several more weeks, with the footballer admitting it felt good to finally be honest with someone.

A couple of months after they met, Fashanu invited Tatchell to an entertainment awards event at The Venue in Victoria, London. He insisted

Tatchell travel there with him and his mother, Pearl, and that Tatchell sit with them at his table on the main stage. At the time, Tatchell had not come out publicly, either, though some of the tabloids were already hinting he was gay. He knew that by being seen with him Fashanu was playing a dangerous game. When he told the footballer his concerns, Justin replied: 'I'm fed up of hiding. I want you to be here and I'll take the consequences, whatever they may be.' It was almost as if Fashanu wanted to be outed. While coming out publicly would certainly have offered peace of mind, Fashanu realised it would also have introduced a different kind of turmoil into his life simultaneously. Being the world's first openly gay professional footballer would bring its own set of problems. There was no knowing how people would react. Justin was already stressed about his under-par performances on the pitch and Tatchell recognised his vulnerability, fearing that coming out might compound the already considerable pressures on Fashanu. Thus Tatchell advised him to delay any public announcement until his career was a little more stable and he'd, hopefully, patched things up with Clough.

But it was really only a matter of time before word of Fashanu's late night excursions got back to Clough, himself. When they did it sparked a huge showdown. One of the manager's minions at Forest eventually shared the local gossip with Clough and Fashanu was hauled into his office. According to Clough's autobiography *Clough* the Forest manager asked Justin where he would go if he wanted a loaf of bread. When Justin replied: 'A baker's' Clough asked where he'd go if he wanted a leg of lamb. Justin answered: 'A butcher's', prompting Clough to retort: 'So why do you keep going to that bloody poof's club?'[19] It was certainly direct. The striker didn't deny it and simply shrugged. In Clough's mind the footballer's silence was confirmation and resulted in him making Fashanu's life even more difficult. Although Clough didn't know how to handle his striker, the Forest manager claimed to have him twigged after only a few weeks of meeting him: 'He was a playboy rather than a footballer. He tried to portray the macho image but he wasn't macho he was flamboyant. He tried to fool me and I saw through his make believe,'[20] Clough wrote. In years to come, other people would agree with those sentiments.

Once the rumour was heard by a few Forest players it spread like wildfire. The team was getting ready for training one afternoon when the Forest midfielder Kenny Burns surprised everyone by asking Fashanu straight out whether he was queer. 'Do you want to come here and say that right to my face?' Fashanu asked in reply. Given Justin's boxing skills, Burns wisely declined. With Fashanu's manager on his back and his fellow players talking behind it, the striker's life was becoming even more of a struggle. It wasn't like he could talk to his brother about it either. To make matters worse, Forest fans had also caught wind of the gay rumour. Although nothing had been printed in the press, fans had heard through the grapevine that Clough had caught Fashanu in a gay club and gone ballistic. For a small section of fans, Clough's anger towards Fashanu made them justified in criticising him as well and when he played many were openly hostile to him from the stands. There were catcalls and homophobic name-calling. But not all Forest fans felt the same way. Keith Lennox was one of them.

'The treatment that Brian Clough gave to Justin publicly, as well as behind closed doors, was something I found very distasteful. The rumours about Justin's sexuality made it all too easy for some Forest fans to get on his back. Many of these fans were not only homophobic but racist too. I certainly heard fans close to me using homophobic language and calling him a "poof" and "fairy",' says Lennox.

Lennox heard the news that Fashanu might be gay from a friend who worked in the music business who'd just come out himself. Lennox wondered how the macho world of football would react to such an admission from Fashanu. Football was hardly like the music industry. The rumour soon gained national attention when the tabloid newspaper the _Sunday People_ got wind of it. A reporter approached Justin before a game and asked him whether he was gay. Fashanu now had the perfect opportunity to come out publicly but, for whatever reason, he chose to deny it. The following day the paper ran the story anyway under the headline: 'Soccer Superstar Justin Fashanu Answers All the Gossips – Truth About My Love Life'.[21] Wary of libelling the footballer, the report stated that Fashanu was kicking back against the malicious gossips who were saying he was gay. But the paper wasn't cautious enough. When he saw the report Fashanu was absolutely livid and instructed a lawyer to start legal proceedings. He ended up winning substantial damages. While Justin had every right to protect his privacy he'd effectively dug himself into a hole by denying he was gay. If he revealed the truth in the future then the _Sunday People_ would have every right to sue him for lying. From now on, when it came to his private life, he'd have to tread very carefully.

With his career at an all-time low, Fashanu started splitting more of his time between Nottingham, Norwich and London. He was still in regular contact with his foster parents in East Anglia and also travelled to the capital to see his mother, brother and sister. Back in East Anglia, John Fashanu had turned professional himself and was now playing for Norwich City. Although he wasn't a regular in the first team, City would be the first of several professional clubs that he played for in his career. As for Justin, if he believed things could not get any worse in his professional and personal lives he was mistaken. First it was the death of Alf Jackson, a person who'd provided him with the chance to succeed in life. Justin travelled to Norwich for his foster dad's funeral and was, naturally, shaken by his sudden loss. But something else was about to happen that would inspire even more conflict and confusion: religion.

Twisted Faith

IN THE spring of 1982, Justin Fashanu's life looked far different than just one year earlier. Back then, the player had still been living in Norwich and was at the top his game in every respect. Revered by his manager, adored by fans, and surrounded by friends the world seemed his to take. But things had changed. A year on he was feeling the weight of the world on his shoulders. He believed he was living a lie and that lie was starting to eat at him. What didn't help is the footballer rarely discussed his feelings, choosing to bottle them up instead. When Ross Smith tried to broach any deep subject with his friend, Fashanu refused to open up. But the footballer was about to be confronted with a divine intervention that would re-shape his whole life. It all started when he dropped his car off at his local car dealership one afternoon following a minor prang (his driving had not improved since his Norfolk days). While he was waiting for a replacement vehicle the owner invited the Forest star into his office for a coffee. Terry Carpenter supplied several local footballers with cars and as he was talking to Justin he noticed the player seemed slightly down:

'Justin looked crestfallen and he seemed to be in a bit of state. I poured him a coffee and we ended up talking for more than three hours. As we were chatting I suddenly became very inspired and I put my coffee down, looked at him square in the eyes and said: "Do you know, Justin, I think

I know someone who can help you." He said: "Who's that?" I paused and said: "Jesus Christ can help you, Justin." To my amazement he said: "Tell me more,"' Carpenter says.

Carpenter drove the footballer back to his house where they continued their conversation about God. The dealer explained what religion had done in his life and what it could do for Fashanu if he accepted Jesus himself. The dealer read the footballer some passages from a Gideon Bible and then prayed for him. At the end of the afternoon, Fashanu told Carpenter that he was inspired himself: 'I want Jesus in my own life,' he proclaimed. The following Sunday Fashanu attended a service at Carpenter's Pentecostal church. According to the car dealer the footballer prayed to God and invited Him into his world. From that moment on, Fashanu had new meaning in his life. At a service a few weeks later, Justin gave a testimony:

'I was speaking to a young lad yesterday and he said: "Whenever I see things about you, it's always Fashanu. It's never God or anything like that," and I thought, "He's right." I've been playing football for Justin Fashanu, and I thought that from now on I'm going to play for Him and please Him. When I am scoring it's gonna be for God and I hope I can go on from strength to strength.'

Fashanu might have thought he'd found the answer to his problems but, in reality, he was only inviting more conflict into his life. Homosexuality is not widely accepted by the church today, and it certainly wasn't back in the Eighties. Reverend Sharon Ferguson chairs the Lesbian and Gay Christian Movement, an organisation that promotes inclusion in the church. Ferguson says that for many people being gay and being Christian are seen as opposites. This was especially true in the Eighties, when it seemed the only impression people had of gay men was the immoral, raving effeminate queen with a rampant sex life. She explains:

'The gay lifestyle was totally at odds with Christian ethics. The pressure would have been around behaving, or being perceived to behave, in keeping with the gay lifestyle in order to be accepted into the gay community or behaving as a Christian to be accepted into the faith community. This leaves a person with having to choose either, to deny a huge part of who they are, or to try to keep both aspects separate from each other.'

When it came to his own sexuality and faith it didn't take Fashanu long to realise he was at odds. As a born again Christian, he knew practising homosexuality was wrong but it was hard to ignore his true feelings.

While professing to be a Christian and celibate his true feelings remained impossible to ignore and anonymous sex, often with rent boys, continued. In an effort to find peace Fashanu spent more time at his new place of worship, a Pentecostal church in the centre of Nottingham. Preacher David Shearman, whose sermons attracted large congregations, headed the Christian Centre. In the summer of 1982, Justin was introduced to J. John, a preacher at St Nicholas' Anglican Church also in the centre of town. J. John was a self-styled religious guru who travelled extensively as a speaker all over the world. Fashanu said J. John was a comfort when it came to some of the big problems in the footballer's life like his career, offering him counsel from a religious perspective. The footballer and preacher both owned houses in The Park and as they got to know each other, they formed a close bond. Fashanu revealed how Clough didn't show him an iota of consideration and his lack of empathy was difficult for the more sensitive Fashanu to understand. Of course, because J. John didn't know that Justin was gay it meant the preacher didn't get the full picture of what was actually causing Justin the most angst. J. John didn't completely understand the hostility between the footballer and Clough. Justin kept his sexuality a secret to everyone in his church and no one there knew. Ultimately, hiding it only added to the pressure he already felt. While Justin made every effort to repress his feelings in line with the teaching of scripture it was difficult. It went against the grain of who he was. As a result, he found himself under even more strain.

At the City Ground Fashanu tried to improve the two things that really mattered: his performance on the football field and his relationship with the Forest manager off it. Neither of them got any better. By the end of April, the footballer had played 31 games for Nottingham Forest but only managed four goals and, as the end of the football season loomed, Clough had all but given up on him. He told Fashanu that he was offloading him to the reserve team. It was obviously a huge blow. Calvin Plummer, who'd joined the club as an apprentice, took Fashanu's place in the first team and says the former Norwich star could not have been any nicer about it. Rather than being bitter Fashanu told Plummer to go for it. This was typical of the way Fashanu treated the younger players in general.

At Nottingham Forest, Fashanu was forced to play out the remaining matches of the season with the reserve team. Reporter Duncan Hamilton watched a game and was amazed when Fashanu almost scored an own goal from the halfway line. He was trying to play the ball back to the goalkeeper but totally misjudged it. The move reflected just how low his confidence had sunk. The two men spoke after the game and Hamilton could sense the striker was going through the grinder: 'I like Nottingham but I don't want to stay at Forest. Not with him,' Fashanu said, referring to Clough. Peter Ward also pitied him. He'd watched the apprentices training one morning and commented to one on how bad their passing skills were. 'Yeah, we're doing it the Fashanu way,' the boy replied.

Meanwhile, Clough's own relationship with his assistant manager had deteriorated beyond all hope of salvaging it. At the end of the season, Taylor shocked fans by announcing he was retiring. He claimed his health was not good and was calling it a day. But just three months after his exit, Taylor made an astonishing recovery when he re-surfaced in the game as the new manager of Derby County. Since Derby is a fierce local rival to Forest, and given the pair's acrimonious departure from the Baseball Ground nearly a decade earlier, Clough was incensed at what he considered the ultimate betrayal. Things between the men soured even more when Taylor enticed Forest winger John Robertson to Derby while Clough was on a charity walk in the Pennines. This was more than Clough could take. The Forest manager called his former friend a rattlesnake and never spoke to him again. At the end of the 1981/82 season Forest finished in the bottom half of the First Division, their lowest position since promotion to the top flight back in 1977. Clough was unimpressed. Fashanu's fortunes didn't improve either. He suffered a fractured knuckle in a friendly game in Spain during Forest's 1982 summer tour.

After returning to England, Justin made one of the biggest decisions of his life: to reconnect with his absent father. The last time he'd seen Patrick Fashanu was almost twenty years earlier when the footballer had been a toddler. It was 1963 and Patrick left his family in London to travel back to Nigeria. The decision had enormous ramifications for the family, particularly Justin and John. The elder brother had never been quite able to get over the abandonment and spent the subsequent years of his life trying to find another father figure. According to J. John, the footballer wanted to see his estranged father to find out more about him and ask him why he had left his family.

Justin's trip to Lagos, Nigeria was no secret to local reporters who were waiting for him in arrivals at the airport. The footballer told them he had come to meet the man who he was related to by blood but knew nothing about. During the visit Justin sent a postcard to his friend Gordon Holmes and Gordon's wife Betty in Norwich.

Dear Gordon and Betty,
This is going to be a great trip. We have met our uncle and brothers
(same father but lots of wives.) We meet our father over the weekend
for the first time. Should be good. I might even stay!! The living
conditions are very good for the rich but very poor for others without
money. I hope to find out about myself and the Fashanu family over
this trip.
Lots of Love,
Justin

The content of the postcard reveals that Justin was hoping for something
positive to come out of the trip. However, it wasn't to be. The meeting
between father and son was recorded on TV by a local news station. A
reporter asked Justin whether he thought his father had abandoned him
prompting the player to reply: 'The way I look at that is my father has come
back to Nigeria. The way the press said it is that he abandoned (me), but I
have never said that.'[22] That may be what Justin said publicly but the truth
lay elsewhere. The meeting was short and obviously not as fruitful as Justin
had hoped because it would be the last time the young Fashanu saw his
father again. Justin never discussed the trip with anyone, but it was obvious
to those who knew him that he returned to England a disappointed man. As
such, the footballer's search for a replacement father figure only continued.

When Fashanu got back to Nottingham a deep sense of uncertainly was
also affecting his career. No sooner had he stepped through the gates of
the City Ground than he was summoned to the manager's office. Clough
told him to pack his bags as he was being sent to Southampton on loan.
For many Forest fans this meant only one thing: Fashanu's days at the City
Ground were as good as numbered.

No Saint

A WEEK before his meeting with Fashanu, Clough had called his friend Lawrie McMenemy, the manager of Southampton. The conversation had been short and to the point. Clough wanted to know if McMenemy could take Fashanu off his hands. The Saints manager knew that things hadn't been working out for the footballer at Forest, but taking the striker on himself was another story.

As it happened, McMenemy had a little problem of his own. His star striker Kevin Keegan had decided to leave after two years at the club to join Newcastle United. This meant McMenemy was without a striker right as the season started. The timing could not have been worse. With this in mind, McMenemy told Clough that he might be able to help him out after all, but would have to speak to his board of directors first. With the board also worried about the situation they gave their manager an immediate 'okay' to pick up Fashanu. Clough was in luck. According to McMenemy, the plan was to take the Forest forward on loan for one month and see how it worked out. McMenemy still remembers the conversation he had with Justin.

'I remember he sat in my office and I reeled off the deal and what the bonuses would be and that kind of thing. When I'd finished talking, he sat and looked at me. I said: "Well, there you go then, there's the pen. What's the problem?"

"Well, I want to know what else I'm getting," he replied.

"What else you're getting? You haven't come here to make money pal." I said.

"Well, I expected more than that."

There was a brief pause and then I said: "I tell you what. I'll just get Brian Clough on the phone and see what he's got to say shall I?"

"Give us the pen!" he snapped and quickly scribbled his name on the contract.'

Fashanu knew he needed to get away from Clough and staying at Forest was NOT an option. While he thought his contract was open for negotiation, however, McMenemy knew otherwise: 'I think in his own mind he was a star striker and thought he was coming down to Southampton to do us a big favour. I knew the set up and that he had to come because Brian had told him to,' McMenemy says.

During the meeting, McMenemy noticed that Justin didn't have a suitcase with him. The only clothes he had seemed to be the ones he was wearing. Calling in one of the apprentices, the Saints manager told him to take the striker into town and show him some stores. It would prove to be a costly mistake. A week later, a bill arrived at the club from one of Southampton's more refined tailors. Attached was a note that said Fashanu had purchased several suits and instructed them to send the invoice there. McMenemy was stunned. That would not be the only bill the Saints received for Fash. Over the next few months, parking fines also arrived by the handful.

When reporters in Nottingham found out about Fashanu's move south it prompted the following headline in the *Nottingham Evening Post*: 'Nottingham Forest's One Million Pound Misfit Joins Southampton on Month's Loan.'[23] With a headline like that it seems even local journalists believed the footballer was an oddity. Fashanu booked himself into a hotel in the centre of Southampton. There was no point selling his house in Nottingham until his future was more certain. He was only on loan and that meant anything could happen. As if to reinforce this point when the day came to take the official Southampton team photograph, one was taken with Fashanu and another without.

While Fashanu didn't get the royal treatment he'd been hoping for in terms of negotiating his contract and wages, one perk he did get was an apprentice to show him around town. 17-year-old Les Cleevely got that job that also included cleaning the new striker's boots. Cleevely says that Fashanu was far different from other footballers: polite, genuine and generous so he was happy to show him the sights. At some point while Fashanu was in Southampton, the footballer's relationship with his girlfriend Julie ended. The couple had spent close to a year living at Justin's home in The Park and after the split Julie moved back to Norwich. According to Cleevely, it was an amicable break-up and the couple remained on good terms. Like others, Cleevely does not know what the exact status of the relationship was because he never saw it firsthand.

Saints fans heard about Fashanu's appointment when an announcement was made a few days before the club's season opener in late August, 1982. The other shocker was that Forest keeper Peter Shilton had also been signed. Duncan Holley, a life-long Saints fan and author of five books on the club, says the arrival of both players came at a time when McMenemy was out of favour with a lot of fans. For one, Kevin Keegan's departure had angered a lot of people. Fashanu's debut against Coventry City in the opening game of the season did nothing to lift the fans' spirits with the Saints losing 1-0. Next, the team faced Watford at home with Elton John's beloved team battering Southampton 4-1. Things improved in the third game when Southampton beat Aston Villa 1-0 and Fashanu scored the winner, but after a whitewash at White Hart Lane (Spurs 6-0 Southampton) the Saints suddenly found themselves propping up the division.

Fashanu's Southampton teammates expressed no problems with their new striker on or off the field. It was common knowledge why he had been sent to Southampton on loan, but no one asked him about his fractious relationship with Clough directly. Most remember him as a larger-than-life character with a unique dress sense. David Puckett was astonished when Fashanu turned up at Eastleigh Airport for an away game one morning in a pair of hot pants and vest. Nick Holmes was equally surprised when the striker arrived for training sporting a pair of tight fitting pink shorts. Incredibly, Justin's eccentric and colourful taste in fashion (that screamed clichéd gay) did not lead anyone to consider that he actually might be. One can only assume that because pastels and bright colours were popular in the Eighties no one suspected a thing. Saints player Malcolm Waldron, however, always believed that the footballer's smile masked something. He often wondered what Justin was hiding. Apart from the obvious, Fashanu was actually considering coming out publicly. He told his friend Peter Tatchell that he was fed up with leading a double life. On one hand, Tatchell thought it would be good for Justin to announce the news because he'd no longer have to look over his shoulder. It would also be a positive move for the gay community. Tatchell believed that Fashanu would be an excellent role model, a high profile figure who might reduce some of the stigma of being gay. However, dealing with the impact it might have on his life was a far different matter. Tatchell was worried that his friend might not be able to cope with the consequences. On the football pitch there was no one tougher than Fashanu, either physically or mentally, but when it came to his personal life he was much more vulnerable. Tatchell presented him with both the pros and cons of coming out and, ultimately, Justin decided not to reveal his secret. At least for now.

As Fashanu was looking inwards, the Saints fans were looking at a Southampton team in disarray. The team had started the 1982 season on a losing streak and more defeats followed. What didn't help was that the club had lost two of its key players in bizarre circumstances. It happened when the side had been playing Sweden's IFK Norrkoping in a first round UEFA cup tie away, and Steve Moran had been arrested along with another England international, Mark Wright. After the game the pair had visited a nightclub, met a couple of girls and taken them back to the players' hotel. What went on wasn't clear but police had been called early in the morning and Moran and Wright were arrested for sexual assault. Both men would eventually be released without charge, but in the meantime Swedish police were holding them in a cell while they carried out an investigation. That meant McMenemy was two players down just when he needed them.

One bit of good news, at least for Fashanu, arrived in late September when the striker donned an England Under-21 jersey once again. His services were required for the European Championship final first leg match against West Germany. The game was staged at Bramall Lane, Sheffield and Fashanu hammered home a goal in the 51st minute. His conversion helped England secure a 3-1 victory. England would go on to win the tournament 5-3 on aggregate after the second leg match in West Germany. After the game, Fashanu told reporters: 'I have certainly known the highs and lows of professional football. It's nobody's fault what has happened to me in these last few months and I have no intention of shouting from the rooftops now. I am a young man who has learned a lot recently.'[24] Justin might have believed he'd seen the lowest depths of football but he hadn't experienced anything near it yet. The most painful was still to come.

Right now, however, the player's confidence level was turned to high and Fashanu's good fortunes only continued. In early October, Southampton played Notts County and McMenemy remembers the game for three reasons. The first was a 1-0 win courtesy of the second, a Justin Fashanu goal. The third was that Notts County manager Jimmy Sirrel complained after the match that he was unhappy someone from Nottingham had scored against a Nottingham team. Sirrel might not have been pleased with the result but he was impressed with Fashanu. He knew all about what had happened to the striker at Forest and had witnessed many other players come and go under Cloughie just as quickly. Unlike Clough, however, Sirrel rated Fashanu and still believed he was a good player. As such, when the manager returned to Nottingham he started making inquiries about Justin.

But Fashanu's auspicious streak was about to end. Despite scoring three goals in nine games, McMenemy told him that he could not afford to make the footballer's move permanent. Reluctantly, Justin returned to Nottingham. He was disappointed but there was nothing he could do about it. No sooner had Fashanu walked through the gates of the City Ground than he was summoned to Clough's office and informed he was being sent to Derby County. This time, Fashanu wasn't going anywhere and he told Clough as much. The Forest manager didn't like dissent from his players at the best of times and was absolutely seething. When Fashanu turned up for training the next day he entered the dressing room to find the new assistant coach Ron Fenton waiting for him. 'Fash, you're out of here,' Fenton said. 'The boss says you've got to go home. You're suspended on full pay.' A defiant Fashanu told Fenton otherwise: 'I'm training. Make me,' were his exact words. With that, the footballer walked out of the dressing room and headed towards the training ground. In the Eighties, Forest trained on a field next to the River Trent, a two-minute walk from the City Ground. After Fashanu arrived there with the other players and started warming up, he could never have guessed what would happen next. Back at the ground, Fenton had informed Clough what was going down and the Forest manager had called the police. Ten minutes later, Clough and two uniformed officers arrived at the training ground where the irate manager instructed Fashanu to leave. When the footballer refused to comply Clough reportedly yelled: 'If you don't get off this training pitch then I am going to kick you in the calf!' In a surreal scene that would have made a good Monty Python sketch had it not been so serious, Fashanu was escorted off the pitch by the two officers then banned from the ground. It was a horrible incident made worse by the fact that it happened in front of the other players.

Duncan Hamilton first heard about it when he got a frantic call from his news editor. Someone had called the *Nottingham Evening Post* with a tip-off. Grabbing his notebook and pen, the reporter scrambled out the door and rushed straight to the ground. There were looks of bemusement and shock on all the faces of the Forest players he met. None of them could quite believe what had just happened. Hamilton managed to catch up with Fashanu at the player's home a little later, where the despondent footballer told him that he planned to contact the Professional Footballers' Association (PFA) to lodge a complaint. Justin was, naturally, distraught and still shell-shocked. He vowed to keep away from the City Ground to allow all parties a 'cooling off' period.

It seemed that things had come to an impossible impasse between Fashanu and Clough. Justin had learned the hard way that no one messed with the Forest manager and got away without at least a scratch. In Justin's case, it was more like broken bones. While many Forest fans were outraged and embarrassed at the way their manager had treated Fashanu, the feeling on the terraces was a different story. Die-hard followers wanted him gone. In the letters pages of the *Evening Post* and *Football Post* opinion was pro-Clough with most people saying the manager had been totally justified in his actions. Hamilton says that Justin didn't help matters by failing to explain himself. He didn't do a good job of getting his side of the story across and, as such, didn't win public opinion. In comparison, Clough was a master at conveying his point of view. Just as he'd promised, Fashanu contacted the PFA, whose Secretary, Gordon Taylor, was as outraged as Fashanu at the way Clough had handled things and told the player that the union would be backing him all the way. In a subsequent appeal, the panel ruled in the striker's favour and ordered Clough to allow Fashanu back at the City Ground. Clough's response was short but definitely not sweet: 'Justin Fashanu has no future at this club,' he snapped.

Behind the scenes, Clough was now making every effort to offload his troublesome striker. He didn't have to look far. Sirrel hadn't forgotten Fashanu's amazing goal against County when they'd played Southampton the previous month. Despite the fractious relationship Fashanu shared with Clough, Sirrel really wanted him for Notts. But Jack Dunnett MP, the club chairman and owner, was the person who held the purse strings at Notts and it was he who had the final say on whether the club could afford him. Dunnett phoned Clough to find out how much he wanted to part with his estranged striker and was pleasantly surprised at a quote of £150,000. For a player Forest had shelled out £1million for just a year earlier, it seemed a hell of a bargain. But there was still one more obstacle to overcome before any champagne corks could be popped. Would Fashanu want to play for Notts County? More to the point, would he want to stay in a city where he'd practically been dragged to hell and back?

With his relationship with Clough at a stalemate, Fashanu said he was interested in joining Notts provided the price was right and he agreed to meet Sirrel and his assistant Howard Wilkinson to talk about terms. After several phone calls and more meetings, Dunnett was close to signing the striker but still hadn't met all of Fashanu's financial demands. He still wanted more money. It seems incredible that after being thrown a lifeline, Fashanu was reluctant to grab hold of it. Considering his form with Forest, he was hardly in a good position to ask for more cash yet this didn't seem to faze him.

Turning to an unlikely source for help, Dunnett contacted the *Nottingham Evening Post* sports editor, Trevor Frecknall. The call interrupted Frecknall's teatime dinner but Dunnett got right to the point. If Frecknall could pay Fashanu to write a weekly column for the local newspaper then it might be enough to persuade the footballer to sign for Notts. Frecknall thought about it for a second before replying: 'Well Jack, I can't really afford to pay more than £50 a week.' Before he could say another word, Dunnett interjected: 'That will do. Thanks,' before slamming the phone down. When Frecknall regained his composure he called the Notts County Secretary Dennis Marshall. 'Do I take it that you've got a new centre forward?' he inquired. Marshall told Frecknall to keep the news under his bonnet until the next day and, in return, he would make sure the *Post* got an exclusive.

Marshall was true to his word and on December 10th 1982, the *Nottingham Evening Post* was the first to announce that Notts County had just purchased Justin Fashanu. Frecknall reported that the player's new wage would be fifty per cent less than what he earned at Forest earning the following quote from Dunnett: 'It shows the lad is not entirely a money grabber!' Given Fashanu's demands for a higher wage during the negotiation phase, we know that wasn't exactly true so it was obviously good PR on Dunnett's part. An extra fifty pounds a week sounds like loose change to a professional footballer but it meant that Fashanu was able to continue writing, something he enjoyed. Clough also made the paper, saying he was glad the matter was finally over and that it had dragged on long enough. Surprisingly, given what had happened, his last words were: 'I wish him all the best.' After the news broke, it was revealed that John Bond had also tried to secure Fashanu but by the time he'd found out the player was for sale Notts County had already sealed the deal. Bond was livid. As for Fashanu, he was actually happy to stay in Nottingham where his luxury home was located.

The news of Notts' new signing was no real surprise to Forest supporters, the majority of whom supported Clough's view that the Fashanu affair had dragged on long enough. By now, Keith Lennox was one of them: 'Like most fans, I felt more concerned that the club had suffered and now that these off field distractions were removed the club's form and fortunes might improve. The old adage "the club is bigger than the individual" probably affected my thinking at the time,' Lennox says. For Notts County supporters the signing was a complete shock. History had shown that footballers who went from one Nottingham team to the other rarely did well at their new club. To many fans, Fashanu had proved a disaster for Forest and cost them dearly. Why should he fare any better at County, they reasoned? The footballer had a great deal of proving to do and the pressure was building once again.

Resurrection

WHILE BRIAN Clough was glad to see the back of his flamboyant striker, Jimmy Sirrel was rubbing his hands. The diminutive Scot knew that with the right kind of environment and mentoring, Fashanu could easily recapture the kind of form that had brought him to Nottingham in the first place. As managers, Sirrel and Clough had one thing in common: both were successful, but in most other aspects they could not have been more different. Raised in one of the toughest areas of Glasgow, Sirrel had been forced to think on his feet from an early age. It was a skill he'd continued to nurture when he was older as a professional footballer and then as a manager with great success. At the home he shared with his wife Cathy, the couple often hosted newly signed apprentices and sometimes older, more experienced players to help them settle in. Many of them came to look at him as a father figure. Sirrel had two children of his own, but viewed his players as an extension of his own family. In these respects, he was just the kind of manager Fashanu needed. The *Nottingham Evening Post*'s Trevor Frecknall suspected that Sirrel had a sneaking admiration for Fashanu's willingness to rebuild his career in the same city where it had almost been shattered. Not many people could do likewise and this was testament to the footballer's inner strength.

In many regards, Notts County was similar to Norwich City. It was a smaller, warmer, more family-friendly kind of club and a better fit for Fashanu all round. Compared to Nottingham Forest, however, County was definitely the poorer relation failing to match the type of success that its neighbouring team enjoyed. But it has to be added that while Forest had become the toast of Europe, Notts joined them in the First Division in 1981, after being absent from the top-flight for 55-years. It was the club's third promotion success achieved under Sirrel, proof of his quality as a manager. The oldest professional football club in the world was playing in the big league. The question now was could Fashanu help them stay there?

When Fashanu joined Notts, Howard Wilkinson was in charge of the team after Sirrel had moved upstairs as General Manager. Sirrel had hand-plucked the then little known Wilkinson from Conference side Boston United two years earlier, and the partnership had proved fruitful. Wilkinson was a former teacher and his disciplined approach was one Fashanu responded well to. The manager delivered stern talks, pen and clipboard in hand. Backing him up, Sirrel would restrict himself to a few words. After Wilkinson finished giving his team talk Sirrel would then turn to the players and say: 'Great. Now let's get stuck into the bastards!' Wilkinson knew that Fashanu had talent because he'd coached the England Under-21 team when the striker had played for his side. His power made an impression on him that hadn't faded. Wilkinson didn't give a damn what Clough thought about the footballer. Like Sirrel, instinct told him Fashanu could do well at Notts. Wilkinson still remembers the cold, December morning Fashanu signed for the club. As soon as the formalities were over, he dragged the footballer out the door for a long run along the River Trent. He was relieved to see the striker was still fit.

Fashanu joined the Magpies as the 1982/83 season was already in full swing and things had not started well. The team had won only nine out of 19 games and Wilkinson was beginning to fret. In one game Ipswich Town hammered Notts 6-0, and the team was getting a similar battering in the press. Fashanu's debut was a home tie in December against West Ham United. Notts lost 2-1 but Fashanu did enough to warrant the manager's praise.

In late December, Wilkinson got a lucky break. Wintry conditions forced Notts' next few fixtures to be cancelled, opening up a brief window to change the team's tactics. Wilkinson was a hard taskmaster who frequently made his team train twice a day, and with Notts on a losing streak additional sessions were scheduled. A strict training regime suited Fashanu. Even though he'd only played a few games for the Saints he'd maintained a high level of fitness. As usual, his loyal personal trainer Osman Raif was by his side making sure he stayed on track. Wilkinson's new strategy depended on Notts maintaining possession and getting the ball wide in the opponent's half and across into the penalty box for Fashanu to run on to. Notts were blessed with two exceptional wingers, Iain McCulloch and John Chiedozie, to carry out this role.

While Fashanu had felt like an outcast at Forest, he received a warm welcome at Meadow Lane from the County players. There was friendly banter in the dressing room and no sign of the cliques that had developed over the River Trent. Fellow striker Trevor Christie will never forget the first time he saw Justin in the dressing room. Not only did the new striker have an incredible physique, but also an impressive range of creams and lotions to go with it. After every shower, Fashanu took at least 45 minutes to apply all his different creams on to his body. There was a cream for his face, another for his legs and a different one again for his feet. While Christie never actually saw a lotion for Fashanu's balls, he suspected there might have been one for those too. As you'd expect in a macho dressing room, Justin received a well-earned ribbing for his vanity, but in time things changed. After Fashanu's teammates began to notice just how smooth and healthy his skin looked, they were soon asking him for the lotions themselves.

It was well known amongst the Notts County players that Justin might be gay. When you're football club is virtually a stone's throw from your nearest rivals, rumours abound. The one concerning Justin's sexuality had not escaped the players' notice, but none of them were bothered by what they heard. The only thing that mattered was that Fashanu scored goals. Who he scored with off the pitch was his concern. The only person who didn't seem to know about the rumours was Wilkinson, who claimed he was shocked when the revelations about Fashanu eventually made national headlines. Wilkinson was not homophobic and didn't mind at all, just surprised no one had told him.

On 1st January 1983, Notts could not have asked for a tougher tie to ring in the New Year as the club faced Liverpool, the top team in the league, at Meadow Lane. Notts lost the game 5-1, but it was Fashanu who scored for

Paradise Found: Justin (left), John and Bubbles in the back garden of Flint House.
(Just out of shot is a rickety wooden goalpost that Alf built. Alf had no idea how
significant his construction would prove in both boys' destinies.)
Credit: Jackson family

Smiles Apart: Justin (left)
and John at primary school.
Credit: Jackson family

Life's a beach (at least in Justin's early years. Later in life, Justin would be plagued by many demons).
Credit: Jackson family

The Fashanu brothers explore the Norfolk countryside with a friend.
Credit: Jackson family

It seems hard to believe this innocent looking cherub would carve out a fierce reputation as one of professional football's toughest players.
Credit: Jackson family

The Fashanu brothers with foster dad, Alf Jackson, at Flint House. It's John who has the gun drawn.
Credit: Jackson family

Summertime at Flint House. Justin was a natural at football, but also handy with a racket. *Credit: Martin Staines*

Can't see the Fash for the trees. An energetic Justin aged six. *Credit: Jackson family*

Dressed up for Sunday Service. Christianity would feature strongly throughout Justin's life, for better and worse.
Credit: Jackson family

At fourteen years of age Justin stands head and shoulders above his brother. It's not just his stature but also his football skills that overshadow his brother, but these will be reversed in later years.
Credit: Jackson family

Above: 1975: The Fashanus display their very best behaviour (and 70s suits) for a family wedding.

Below: Alf Jackson (and his two foster sons) wondering where the hell he's left the car. *Credit: Jackson family*

Growing up fast: Justin and John displaying the cutting edge of fashion. Note the large collection of football trophies on far shelves.
Credit: Jackson family

A great shot of John with his wonderful foster parents, Alf and Betty Jackson.
Credit: Jackson family

Captain and top goal scorer Justin Fashanu with Attleborough Secondary Modern Senior Football Team. Mark Overton is 2nd from left, bottom row. (1976/77)
Credit: Jackson family

Wearing one of Les Hammond's old cricket jumpers to keep warm, this official school photo shows young Fash was an excellent badminton player.
Credit: Jackson family

Barnardo's

Dr. Barnardo's London Divisional Office,
Tanners Lane, Barkingside, Ilford, Essex. IG6 1QG
Telephone 01-551 0011

TW/DVM/PS.

16th October, 1980.

Mr. & Mrs. A.G. Jackson,
Flint House,
Shropham,
Attleborough,
Norfolk.

Dear Mr. & Mrs. Jackson,

As you know, now that John is 18 he passes out of our care, and
therefore you are no longer officially foster parents for us.

I feel that I cannot let this time pass without writing to express
on behalf of us all in Barnardo's, our thanks for all that you have
done for Justin and John over the years. We know that as with being
ordinary parents, being foster parents is not an easy task, and that
there are painful and worrying times, just as there are happy and
enjoyable ones, and the former could be less bearable when you are
bringing up someone else's children; because of this we hope that
we do not undervalue foster parents, and I feel that praise for
their efforts cannot be too high, especially when the end products
are as Justin and John.

Although I have never had the pleasure of meeting yourselves or either
of the lads, I have, as you can imagine, heard much from Mr. Scott and
especially in the case of Justin, from "other sources".

Please accept our most grateful thanks for the splendid work that you
have done for these two young men.

With every good wish for the future.

Yours sincerely,

D.V. MANN.
PROJECT LEADER.

Dr. Barnardo's (a Company Limited by guarantee)
Reg. Office: Tanners Lane, Barkingside, Ilford, Essex. IG6 1QG
Reg. No. 61625 England

Job Well Done: A touching letter from a Barnardo's representative
to Alf and Betty Jackson. *Credit: Jackson family*

Boxing Smart: Justin smiles proudly for the camera after winning
a competitive fight in the junior division, 1977.

Below: Justin's boxing trainer Gordon Holmes honing a young maestro's skills.
Holmes was one of several men in Justin's life who became a father figure.
Credit: Gordon Holmes

John was also a good boxer in his own right. The skills he learned in the ring would be put to good use when he eventually joined Wimbledon FC (a.k.a. the 'Crazy Gang').
Credit: Gordon Holmes

Ronnie Brooks: one of the men responsible for bringing Justin to the attention of Norwich FC. Brooks was a football scout and close to both Fashanu brothers.
Credit: Stephanie Brooks

Above: All smiles and a little bit a' bling on show at Trowse, Norwich.
Trowse is a small village where Norwich City used to train.

Below: A young Canary fan has his day officially made with a photo next to his
hero. Fash signed for Norwich as a professional in 1978 and spent three
successful seasons with the club. *Credit: Andrew Wenley*

Norwich City player, Dave Bennett. The midfielder was Justin's best friend when the two men played together in the late 70s/early 80s.
Credit: Dave Bennett

Bennett scoring a sensational (and rare!) goal with his head, with some predatory striker lurking, open mouthed, at the far post. *Credit: Dave Bennett*

Bennett, Fashanu and another friend pose for the camera
at a fancy dress party in Norwich, 1979.
Credit: Dave Bennett

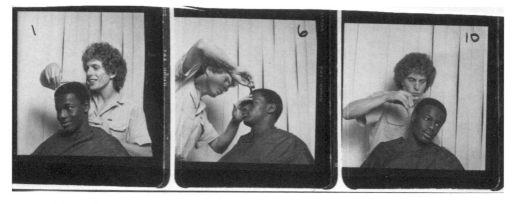

A Cut Above: Justin was always very particular about how he wanted his hair styled.
Luckily for him one his best friends in Norwich, Mel Richards, owned a hair studio.
Here's Mel in action. *Credit: Mel Richards*

Do it because it's your duty, because it's your responsibility. Do it for the sake of your country, for the honour of your parents, for the love of sweet Jesus. Do it for peace, the environment, eternal love. Do it because you feel the need, the urge, the desire. Do it because you have to, because a man must do what a man's gotta do. But, above all, **do it 'cos you like it!**

Justin Fashanu

Don't let the red jumpsuit fool you. Justin's vocal talents for his 1980 vinyl release: Do It 'Cos You Like It! was not on a par with his footballing skills. As such, the record was strictly a one-off. *Credit: Roger Haywood*

A jubilant Justin shortly after joining the mighty Nottingham Forest in 1981. Sadly, the smiles would soon be wiped off the footballer's face by erratic manager Brian Clough. (Who knows what Cloughie made of that nail varnish?)
Credit: John Lawson

Thumbs up after his Forest debut... the optimism would turn to despair.

the Magpies. It was his first goal for the club, a wonderful strike inside the box that left the Liverpool goalkeeper Bruce Grobbelaar standing. In the next ten matches, the striker would score four more times prompting the question: could the Fashanu of old be back? It certainly appeared that way.

Tactically, Wilkinson put the 6ft 2in striker up front as the target man and pulled back his forward partner Christie slightly to play more of a supporting role. In the wings were the supporting cast of McCulloch, Ian McParland and Chiedozie. McCulloch liked Fash, but there was one thing about him that sometimes irked the fiery Scot: the striker's attitude on the pitch. 'I had one or two fall-outs with Fashanu because he could sometimes be lazy and not work. I'm the complete opposite and sometimes that caused problems,' McCulloch says. In one game, Notts were playing Southampton when McCulloch shouted at the striker to sprint across the pitch and close down the advancing full back. 'Fash just stood there and looked at me as if to say: "Why should I do that?"' McCulloch says. After the ball went out of play, the Scot sprinted up to Justin himself and called him a few choice words right in front of the dugout. In fairness to Fashanu, when the game was over he apologised. McCulloch admits that although the striker could be stubborn he was never afraid to face up to his faults and say sorry. Not many other players did the same. Despite their occasional differences, McCulloch really liked Justin and when he broke his leg the following season Fashanu was one of only two Notts players who visited him at his home. The Scot could tell Justin was a good egg he just needed more discipline sometimes.

When you consider that Fashanu had just started at a new club with a lot to prove, the stakes were high. His lack of discipline on the pitch, therefore, is something that leaves you scratching your head. Whether the footballer believed he had so much talent that he believed he could slack off sometimes, or just refused to chase balls that were not passed directly to his feet because of a star ego, we'll never know. It's another example of the multi-faceted enigma that was Justin Fashanu.

Away from football, Fashanu seemed more contented overall. One barometer of his happiness was his level of socialising. At Forest, the footballer had rarely ventured out with his colleagues preferring to keep to himself, but at Notts it was a different story. While Justin was still frequenting Part Two, his favourite hangout, he was also mixing socially with his new teammates. Notts County keeper Mick Leonard was the closest to Justin and often asked the striker to join him and his friends for drinks. At the beginning of his tenure at Notts, Justin had been hesitant. He knew he was still an enemy to many Forest fans and often received verbal abuse when he was out in town. After a few reassuring words from his new keeper, however, Justin started loosening up.

On one occasion, Leonard arranged to meet Fashanu at the striker's house in The Park. When the keeper arrived, he was surprised to see former tennis player and TV sports presenter Sue Barker sitting on the sofa. Leonard had heard Justin was handy with a racket and now he knew why. Later that night, as they were having drinks at a local pub, Fashanu asked him what he was up to the next day. The keeper said that he was heading up to Yorkshire for the night to enjoy himself and told Fashanu he was welcome to tag along: 'No one gives a fuck who you are up there and they certainly won't recognise you,' he said. Fashanu surprised him by saying he'd tag along. The next day Fashanu picked Leonard up in his car and they made their way up north. But halfway into the journey they became hopelessly lost in the middle of the moors. When a farmer appeared on the road ahead of them surrounded by 200 sheep they had to laugh. It didn't look like they were going anywhere for a while. As the farmer walked past the car a short time later Fashanu wound down his window to ask for directions. 'Aye Fash, no problem at all,' the man replied. 'You need to go down this road, take a left, go over a small bridge and you'll see the sign for the motorway ahead. Good luck mate.' So much for Leonard's comment about not getting recognised!

An hour later, Fashanu finally pulled up outside the pub they'd been heading to. Located in the pretty village of Ripponden, The Old Bridge Inn was run by an eccentric gay landlord. The establishment was well known in the area for attracting gay clientele as well as the region's jet set. Manchester United players could often be seen rubbing shoulders with pop stars like Mick Hucknall from Simply Red. Fashanu might not have been as big a star himself but he certainly had fun that night. When the landlord eventually called last orders, Leonard was informed that a wealthy businessman was hosting a party at his mansion just down the road and the goalkeeper asked Fashanu if he wanted to go.

'I said to Justin, "Listen mate, we've been invited to this house party and it'll probably be good, but there will be lots of gay people there. The reason I'm telling you is that you need to know that I'm not setting you up. I'm not bothered, either way, but I've heard about the rumours about you and this party will be packed with gay people. If someone sees you there then there may be some negative press for you if word got out,'" Leonard said. Fashanu's response was short and to the point: 'I'm not bothered.' 'Good man,' replied Leonard. 'Then let's get out of here and have some fun.'

When the two footballers turned up at the house party it was already in full swing. Now that he knew Fashanu was cool with everything, Leonard's next priority was sealing the deal with an attractive blonde he'd met the last time he was in the area and who happened to be at the party. Things seemed to be going well on that front until halfway through the night she disappeared. Leonard eventually spotted her an hour later in an adjacent room, cuddling and smooching with none other than… Justin Fashanu. To Leonard, Fashanu's manoeuvres were an obvious indication that the footballer was bisexual (much to the goalkeeper's dismay!).

Back home in Nottingham the young apprentice Fashanu had met in Southampton, Les Cleevely, contacted the Notts County striker with some news. Things hadn't worked out for him with the Saints and he needed a move. He asked Justin if he'd heard of anything. Fashanu said he'd ask around and get back to him. Within 24 hours Fashanu called Cleevely back and told him to pack his bags: the player had cleared it with Wilkinson for the apprentice to train with the Notts team and his first training session was scheduled first thing the next morning. Cleevely was speechless. He'd spoken to several other people to ask them if they could help him out and Justin was the only one who'd even got back to him. To cap it all, the Notts striker told Cleevely he could stay at his house for free. It actually turned out to be a perfect move for the keeper. After benefiting from the expertise of County's coaching staff, Cleevely went on to secure a contract at Crystal Palace and he's never forgotten who made it all happen. Like the other players at Notts County, Cleevely had also heard the rumours about Fashanu's sexuality but never discussed the subject directly with his friend. During the time he stayed with him, Cleevely never witnessed anything to suggest that Fashanu was gay. The Notts striker regularly spoke on the phone to his ex-girlfriend Julie in Norwich. Cleevely's own friends often probed him about the subject and Cleevely's reply was always the same: 'Look, I can't tell you anything because I haven't seen any signs, okay?' As far as Cleevely was concerned, the jury was still out regarding Fashanu's sexuality anyway. When they'd lived in Southampton the two of them had gone clubbing one night and decided to visit the local red light district after closing time. The plan for a bit of late night action was scuppered, however, when they both bottled it at the last moment and headed home instead. To Cleevely, if Justin did like men he also liked women too.

Towards the end of the 1982/83 season, Fashanu received another unexpected call, this time from his former teammate at Norwich City, Dave Bennett. The Norwich player informed him that the Canaries were travelling to Nottingham to play Justin's former club Forest the following week, and he wanted to catch up. Knowing how badly Clough had treated Fashanu, Bennett told his friend he'd make Clough pay by scoring.

Incredibly, Bennett actually went on to convert not one but two goals for City in a thrilling encounter that eventually ended 2-2. One of the conversions was an overhead kick and the other a rocket blaster from 25 yards out. What made it even more remarkable is that Bennett hardly ever scored. Sadly, Fashanu wasn't at the game to witness the goals personally because he still felt uncomfortable with how things had ended at his old club. However, he reluctantly agreed to meet Bennett in the players' lounge after the match was over. Naturally, Bennett was in exuberant spirits and when he spotted Fashanu he ran up and gave the striker a big hug. 'Those two goals were for you mate,' he proudly announced. Though it was obvious Fashanu was uncomfortable, Bennett was disappointed when Justin suggested they finish their drinks quickly and exit the lounge. It wasn't quite the welcome Bennett had been expecting, especially after his killer performance. He could understand how his friend might be feeling but a warmer reception would have been nice. Fashanu's older brother Phillip accompanied the two friends and after Bennett finished his pint the trio headed back to Justin's place. It was the first time Bennett had met Phillip and he was struck by how nice and polite he seemed, much like his brother. Phillip worked in the business world and was something of an entrepreneur. Justin was not as close to Phillip as he was to John but tried to catch up with him as often as he could. As far as John Fashanu's own fortunes were concerned his contract at Norwich City had now ended and he was playing for Crystal Palace on loan. His career was gradually picking up speed.

Back at Fashanu's house Bennett announced he was taking a quick bath and then the three of them were heading out for a night of celebration. It wasn't every day he scored, especially not two such spectacular goals. What the Norwich player really wanted next was to drink more beers then get laid, and was determined not to let Fashanu's apathy spoil the party. No sooner had Bennett started soaking in the bath suds Justin knocked on the door and asked if he could come in.

'He perched himself on the toilet seat and told me he'd found something wonderful in his life that he wanted to share: God. I couldn't believe it! There I am, trying to soak up the day's events and how incredible it had all been when Justin starts talking about religion. He's telling me how it had changed his life and that he'd spoken in tongues when he'd been worshipping and had finally seen the light. He was really trying to instill the God thing in me. Halfway through his spiel I said: "Listen Fash, in all fairness, I have just scored two of the biggest goals of my career and all I want to do tonight is go shagging and drinking. This is not the right time to try and convert me to God." There was a slight pause before Fash got up, winked and smiled. "I didn't think it was but I thought I'd give it a try," he said. Unbelievable!' says Bennett.

As Fashanu closed the bathroom door behind him, the Norwich player could not help thinking how much his friend had changed. 'Fun Fash' had disappeared and in his place was someone the Norwich player hardly recognised.

Later that night when they hit the town, Bennett noticed the dirty looks Fashanu was getting. Whenever the group entered a bar people literally nudged each other and pointed. Bennett said it felt as if the footballer was Public Enemy Number One in the East Midlands city. It was a far cry from Fashanu's days back in Norwich where everyone still treated him like a hero. Now Bennett understood why Fashanu was reluctant to go out in public. Later that evening, Fashanu arranged for them all to get into a nightclub where Bennett was pleased to bump into his teammate Martin O'Neill. O'Neill, a former Forest player himself, was now playing for Norwich City but enjoying being back on his old stomping ground, a place he'd lived for more than a decade. Half an hour later, Phillip informed Bennett that Justin had left.

' Phillip said that Justin wasn't feeling comfortable inside the club so had decided to leave and go to a late night prayer meeting. I'd had a few glasses of champagne by then, and I told Phillip I was extremely disappointed. I'd been looking forward to catching up with Justin and had even scored two goals for him but, apparently, he couldn't be bothered to hang around,' Bennett says.

Ever since that night he's wondered if Fashanu really did go to a prayer meeting. After all, Part Two was only around the corner. Bennett was right in his assumption that Justin had changed. The last time the two men had hung out seriously with each other was in Norwich. Back then, Justin was at the top of his game and not struggling as much with his sexuality. Religion had also been absent from his life. The new Fashanu had a lot more stress in both his personal and professional lives and it was beginning to show. The confident young man of old had been replaced by someone far more insecure. The biggest pressure Justin still faced was keeping his sexuality a secret, but as rumours about him being gay kept resurfacing they were becoming more difficult to contain. When Bennett returned to Fashanu's place the next morning, the Notts County striker wasn't around. Still upset, Bennett wrote Fash a terse note that read: 'I thought you could have stayed out, thanks a lot.' Thereafter, Bennett would hear or see very little of Fashanu. When a serious injury forced the Norwich player to take early retirement from football a couple of years later Bennett moved to Spain and the two men lost touch. 'I decided to open a bar and blow my insurance money in spectacular fashion, but I'd often think about Justin. We didn't have a massive falling out or anything but we just seemed to go our separate ways,' Bennett says.

A few years later, Bennett would be having a drink at a bar in London with Justin's former teammate from Nottingham Forest, Viv Anderson. When Fashanu's name was mentioned in passing, Anderson said how bad he'd felt for him when he was at Forest. He added: 'You do know he's gay don't you?' It was news to Bennett. Justin Fashanu gay? No way. If he were then he'd have known about and he told Anderson as much. Anderson told him he was wrong and they ended up betting each other a hundred pounds over it. It would be Bennett who'd end up paying.

While no one knows for sure if Fashanu did go to a prayer meeting the night his former Norwich teammate was in Nottingham, it's clear that Justin's faith was important to him. BBC Radio Nottingham sports commentator Colin Slater is a practising Christian himself, and he and Fashanu once attended a seminar together organised by Christians in Sport. Slater is a legend in Nottingham and is often called the 'Voice of Notts County' having covered some 2000 County games. His successful 2011 memoir *Tied Up With Notts* documents his days covering the Magpies, and while Fashanu was playing for Notts Slater got to know the footballer.

'I picked up Justin from his home and when I saw his apartment I couldn't help observing he lived in some style. We drove the short distance to where the event was being held and I could tell that Justin was seriously inquiring into the Christian faith. At the forum, people from a range of sports talked about their faith and when Justin was introduced he stood up and thanked everyone for inviting him. He was very genial and humble. On our journey home, we talked about some of the things that had been raised. It seemed to me that Justin was definitely looking for God. At the time, there were all sorts of rumours about his sexuality but that never came into any conversations that we had. I think between his faith and his sexuality he was in a lot of turmoil,' Slater says.

Over time, Fashanu became more involved with the Christians in Sport movement. Former professional footballer Graham Daniels is general director of the organisation today and met the Notts striker at a CIS-related event in Cambridge in the mid-Eighties. Daniels was playing for Cambridge United at the time and invited him to a dinner party he was hosting for other Christians. According to Daniels, Fashanu was completely comfortable evangelising and sharing the story of his own faith.

Malcolm Doney, a freelance writer and practising Christian, also talked in depth with Fashanu about his faith. Over the summer of 1983, Doney was commissioned to put together a book of interviews with Christian celebrities and travelled to Nottingham to interview Fashanu. The book was being produced by fellow Christian, Nick Beggs, bass player with the pop group Kajagoogoo. In his interview Justin told Doney: 'I reckoned that since God was my father and protector, he would be a kind of insurance policy against problems and hardships. But I've come to realise that I still face problems.' Justin's comments show an obvious naivety. If he really believed God would protect him from the harsh realities of life then he was learning the hard way that the universe does not operate that way. Despite his realisation, Doney says Fashanu appeared very excited about having God in his life and said being a Christian had given him a new purpose. The writer would meet the footballer again a few years later, but in very different circumstances.

In 1983, Fashanu had his own writing interests himself. As per his contract with Notts County, one of his duties was to write a weekly column for the local newspaper the *Nottingham Evening Post*. The column was simply called 'Fash' and the person who actually wrote it was local sports editor, Trevor Frecknall. Every Wednesday at 10am, Frecknall visited Fashanu at the footballer's home to discuss the upcoming column. The footballer always trained at 10:30am so the visits were brief, but Frecknall will never forget the first time he turned up at his apartment:

'When I knocked on the door a fit, muscular man greeted me and bid me enter. I thought I was going into Madame Pompadour's boudoir. Justin was lying in tight, white briefs on a massage bed, his black body glistening. He explained to me that the tall, handsome gentleman who had opened the door was not his butler but his private masseur,' Frecknall says.

The masseur, of course, was Osman Raif and according to people like Les Cleevely the relationship between Raif and Fashanu was purely professional. As for his column, Fashanu always had an idea of what he wanted to write about each week and discussed it with Frecknall who then returned to the office to write it up. Over the years the reporter had the same deal with other footballers like Neil Webb, Nigel Clough and Notts defender Brian Kilcline, but Fashanu always gave the impression that he put more into the task. Frecknall always appreciated that. The more Frecknall got to know Justin the more he got the impression that the older Raif was a father figure. Like Gordon Holmes and Ronnie Brooks, Raif was sometimes strict with Fashanu which is exactly what the footballer needed and responded to.

Ultimately, Fashanu's first season with Notts County proved well worth the money the club spent on him, with the striker scoring seven goals in 15 matches. It wasn't a bad return on someone Clough had labelled a misfit. At the end of the 1982/83 season, Notts finished in 15th place with the unstoppable Liverpool scooping top League honours. With runs to the fourth rounds in both the FA and League Cups (Fashanu scored twice in FA cup games), Howard Wilkinson was happy with the club's performance. Considering how the team had started the season, the manager had done a stellar job. But success would not come without a price, at least for Notts County. When the season eventually finished, Sheffield Wednesday enticed Wilkinson away from Meadow Lane with a lucrative offer he couldn't refuse. With the new season less than two months away, Jimmy Sirrel suddenly found his ship without a rudder.

A Rollercoaster Year

AS THE start of the new 1983/84 season loomed, the last thing Jimmy Sirrel either wanted or needed was to take hold of the managerial reins once again. He'd only just settled into his new position upstairs as general manager and coaching the first team had not been on his agenda. The departure of Howard Wilkinson was a bitter blow, but Sirrel was old and wise enough to know that in football nothing is ever permanent. Justin Fashanu was also sorry to see Wilkinson leave. The 22-year-old striker had blossomed under the former manager's strict, but fair, rules of employment. It had been a good chapter in his life. The same cannot be said about the next one. In July 1983, Notts County chairman Jack Dunnett announced that the club had found a replacement for Wilkinson. In a surprise move, former Nottingham Forest legend Larry Lloyd was named manager. It seemed that Sirrel was off the hook.

After a big money move to Liverpool from Bristol Rovers, Lloyd's own career as a professional player was on the wane when Nottingham Forest picked him up from Coventry City. The burly defender was rebellious and rumour had it that while he was with Clough's team he was forced to pay hundreds of pounds in fines. Clough and Lloyd were two strong personalities who invariably clashed, though it was Lloyd who always came off second best.

As a defender, Lloyd had been notorious for leaving his mark on opposing forwards too. In the late Seventies, one of those strikers had been a fresh-faced Justin Fashanu after he'd just signed for Norwich City. The two players had battled it out then and it would be no different now. Some people, including sports commentator Colin Slater, seriously doubted whether Lloyd was the right person for the manager's job at Meadow Lane. His experience was limited to previously managing Wigan Athletic, and Slater believed the club needed someone with more experience.

Fashanu and his new manager clashed right from the start. One thing that annoyed Lloyd was that Justin never called him 'boss.' Fashanu always insisted on calling him 'Larry' and that irritated the manager no end. Like Clough, Lloyd found Fashanu to be an enigma and unlike anyone he'd dealt with before. Lloyd has lots of examples of Justin's bizarre behaviour, like the day the striker dropped by his office to chat about the team's performance. At the time, Notts were languishing near the bottom of the league table and struggling. As Fashanu left the office his parting wisdom was: 'Larry, just remember that it took the Israelites two thousand years to come out of the wilderness.' Lloyd was left scratching his head. Another time, the Notts manager was reading a newspaper when he spotted an article about Fashanu and religion. The footballer was talking about his faith and how he would score 25 goals for God. Since Fashanu had only managed to score twice for Notts County for Lloyd, the manager was left fuming. He immediately called Fashanu and told him: 'If you can score 25 goals for God then how about scoring 25 goals for me? God can get another job, I bloody can't!' When reflecting about Fashanu today Lloyd still scratches his head: 'Of all the players I have managed in my career, Justin was probably the most difficult. He was very single-minded and very difficult to manage. Many better managers than me have failed in that respect. He had his own ideas about life and things and he just went about it.'

After the new season had kicked off, Notts actually came out of the starting blocks at a fair pace, beating Leicester City and Birmingham in quick succession. Fashanu claimed his first goal of the season against Coventry City the following week, a game that Notts ended up losing and which marked the start of a losing streak that extended through December. One notable defeat was a drubbing from arch rivals Nottingham Forest. Before and during the game, Fashanu was mercilessly heckled by Forest fans who shouted: 'We're sick and tired of you Fash-anu.' He was also targeted on the field by the

Forest defenders who were keen to exploit the frustration the striker was undoubtedly feeling. The challenges came in hard. As the game intensified, so did Fashanu's blood pressure and it was only a matter of time before he reacted. The breaking point came midway through the second half. After conceding a foul near the touchline, Fashanu shouted a volley of abuse at the linesman who'd flagged him that resulted in the striker's immediate dismissal. It was a dreadful day for him and also his team, which ended up getting hammered 3-1.

As if the match results weren't bad enough as they stood, the team was also notching up a large tally of bookings. In one game alone the referee waved nine cards at different Notts players. When a reporter asked the Notts manager for a comment after the game he replied: 'Well, I'd have to question the commitment of the other two.' It was classic Lloyd.

But it wasn't all bad. According to Slater, Fashanu delivered his best performance for Notts in a game against Manchester United at Old Trafford a few days after Christmas. Slater witnessed it first hand as he commentated live from the press box. With just ten minutes remaining, Notts were trailing 3-1 when Fashanu tied things up with two goals in the dying minutes. It was an incredible climax and the first time the Magpies had gained a point at Old Trafford since the 1940s. The celebrations extended well beyond that night, with Fashanu touted a hero for his killer performance.

With just a few days remaining before the end of the year, it appeared as if Notts were finally turning the corner and the next twelve months promised to be a thrilling instalment. Fashanu had got his mojo back. But destiny would, ultimately, spoil everyone's party. What should have been the start of a fairy tale instead turned into a horror story when, on the very last day of the year, Fashanu suffered a life-altering injury. Notts were hosting Ipswich Town at Meadow Lane when, midway through the second half, Fashanu's right knee was caught by Ipswich defender Russell Osman's stud. Although it didn't look serious from the sidelines, the gash was so deep that it required three or four stitches. The cut, in itself, wasn't a problem but the stitches were. It seemed the needle used hadn't been properly sterilised, causing an infection to set in. A few days later, Fashanu's knee gave him such agony that he was forced to call a doctor to his home in the middle of the night. By the time specialists looked at the knee, the infection had already wreaked extensive damage and Justin was told he would likely be out for the rest of the season. He was devastated by the news. In just a matter of days, a season that had looked so full of hope was now hanging in tatters. With their star striker sidelined, Notts' own fortunes suffered a nosedive with defeat following dismal defeat.

For Fashanu, the next six months were a challenging and worrying time. Specialists informed him that what had, at first, seemed like a minor injury was much more serious. The infection had attacked the synovial membrane in his knee meaning the striker would need a series of operations. One specialist told him the injury might even be a career-finisher. With football the only way of life Fashanu knew, retiring was not an option. Resurrecting his iron resolve, the footballer worked hard to prove the specialists who doubted him wrong, but the road to recovery would not be an easy one. It would not be cheap either. Just when he felt fit to play again, Justin's knee flared up and he found himself back at square one. He soon learned that when it comes to rehab, an eagerness to push things too far only leads to frustration. Iain McCulloch witnessed Justin's exasperation first hand: 'He was a fitness freak and it was a very tough time for him. Not being able to play and get his frustrations out, I think that had a big effect on his mentality,' he says.

'Exasperating' was the same adjective used by Notts County supporters to describe their team's performances. When the 1983/84 season finally wrapped up, the Magpies had managed only a handful of wins. With a disappointing 41 points, the club finished second from the bottom in the table and automatically relegated. Birmingham City and Wolves, from the West Midlands, joined them. To add insult to injury Nottingham Forest finished third from top, two places behind Liverpool, who clinched the title.

At the beginning of the summer, Fashanu announced that he was joining his evangelical friend and mentor J. John in India to work with the philanthropist, Mother Teresa. The plan was to spend three weeks preaching the gospel and helping out in the slums. Fashanu's benevolent spirit is impressive and also extended closer to home. According to Dave Bennett, Justin sometimes invited homeless people he met in the centre of Nottingham back to his home for food. A couple of them even stayed with the footballer. While his India excursion seemed like a very worthy trip, however, it would never actually happen. Just before he was due to leave Fashanu was given the all clear by specialists to start kicking a ball around. The good news came at just the right time because the Notts County squad was about to embark on a summer tour to Africa and Fashanu was deemed fit enough to join them. Notts had been invited to play four amateur teams in Kenya to help raise money for African athletes.

Today, the tour is best remembered by what happened off the pitch than on it and centres around an incident involving Fashanu and another Notts County player. It all started one evening when a few members of the team were visiting a nightclub in Mombasa. The club called Bora-Bora was a well-known hang out for local prostitutes. Since Mombasa was one of the main epicentres of the HIV epidemic in Africa the players had been given strict instructions not to fraternise. According to Mick Leonard, towards the end of the evening he was sharing a beer at the bar with fellow teammates Ian McParland and Pedro Richards and Fashanu was on the other side of the club being chatted up by a very attractive local. The way the woman was scantily dressed in a short skirt and high heels it was obvious to the men she was a prostitute. About an hour later, Leonard noticed that as Fashanu was making a move to exit the club his Kenyan companion was none too happy about it. Storming over to the bar she asked: 'What's up with your friend? Is he married or what? Why doesn't he like me? Why won't he take me home?' Whether he'd drunk too many margaritas or simply didn't think Richards chirped: 'Oh, don't you know luv, he likes boys not girls.' Turning towards Fashanu the woman shouted: 'Is it true you like boys not girls? I want to know! Do you prefer boys to ladies? Tell me right now!' Remaining calm, given the circumstances, the striker politely asked the woman who'd told her and she pointed over at Richards. Leonard remembers Fashanu looking intensely at the midfielder for about five seconds before turning and walking out of the club. Richards' comment was a pretty big signal that most of the Notts County players believed the rumours about Justin to be true, but while most of them chose not to say anything the Notts player had taken it one step further. He would pay a painful price.

The next morning, the squad was scheduled for a training session at a field located a half-hour drive from the hotel. As the players piled on to an old bus, Fashanu sat down quietly alone near the front. The training session started with a scrimmage with Fashanu and Richards on opposing sides. From his vantage point in goal, Leonard noticed that as the game progressed Fashanu appeared to be deliberately inching closer to the County defender. He soon realised why. As Richards ran past Justin towards the end of the game, the striker suddenly unleashed a powerful upper cut that connected perfectly with the bottom of Richards' chin. The midfielder was momentarily rendered airborne before landing in a heap. Once again, Fashanu's former boxing trainer Gordon Holmes would have been impressed as it was a perfect strike. While the rest of the players looked on, Richards tried to get to his feet, but with stars in his eyes he had no chance of remaining vertical. 'You'd better stay down Ped,' instructed Rachid Harkouk, the County midfielder. 'Otherwise Fash will fucking kill you!' He sensibly complied. When Lloyd ran over and asked what the hell was happening, Fashanu said: 'Ask him. He knows,' pointing at Richards. The Notts manager shook his head and announced that training was over.

When he returned to England in June 1984, Fashanu was smacked with a reality check himself. Since his professional career had begun six years earlier, he had always played in the top division. Now that Notts had been relegated he faced the prospect of second tier football. As someone who was used to competing against the best, playing in a lower division didn't sit well. But the problem was his knee. Although it had held out on the Kenyan tour he hadn't pushed it. Playing First Division football in England was an entirely different matter. If he pressed things too hard, Fashanu knew he risked injury and losing another season. Larry Lloyd also faced his own set of challenges. His biggest one was winning and if Notts failed to perform in the first few matches of the new season then he knew the consequences. The axe was poised.

In July, Fashanu met someone in Nottingham who would become a good friend in later years. Neil Slawson was an 18-year-old college star footballer from Los Angeles who'd travelled to England to try and make it as a professional. Lloyd invited him to try out with the Notts County team and Slawson met Fashanu at a training session one morning. Although it was the first time they'd met, Slawson already knew about the striker. His famous goal against Liverpool was legendary in America and Slawson was a big fan. Ultimately, Slawson would only spend one week training with Notts before heading to Derby County but during the seven days he was at Meadow Lane Fashanu was incredibly affable. He not only offered to mentor the young American but gave him a place to stay at his home in The Park. There was just one understanding: Slawson was told he'd have to abide by Fashanu's strict rules.

'Imagine my disbelief that a superstar I had once watched on TV in high school had now offered me a place to live at his posh house! Frankly, I was in disbelief. But I didn't have time to daydream as Justin was very tough on me as a mentor. He told me he was going to teach me the ways to be a professional both on the pitch and in life,' Slawson says. Slawson's situation might have felt surreal, at first, but he was quickly slapped back into reality by a stringent regime. Fashanu was determined to teach him what it required to be a true professional footballer. Slawson's diet was closely monitored, as was his alcohol consumption, and Fashanu made sure the American was punctual for all his training sessions.

One of the first times Slawson saw the sterner side of Fashanu was when the young ace missed the last train from Derby to Nottingham one evening. He'd been on a date with a girl he'd met the previous weekend and, with no money to pay for a taxi, had been forced to sleep on a bench in the train station. When he finally made it home the next morning, Fashanu was not impressed and read the riot act. It was the one and only time Slawson saw Justin even close to mad. He did not to repeat his mistake.

A few weeks later, Slawson received a call from his anxious parents back in California. They were concerned about a rumour that they'd heard from a friend that Justin was gay. In short, they wanted to know if their son was 'okay'. Slawson told them that it was the first he'd heard about it but not to worry, everything was fine. After putting their overt concerns to rest, Slawson asked Justin about it later that day: 'Don't believe everything you read in the newspapers,' was Fashanu's reply and nothing more was ever mentioned on the subject.

Slawson ended up staying with the Notts striker for several months and he's never forgotten the valuable lessons he learned from his famous mentor. While some people might raise an eyebrow and wonder if Fashanu's intentions really were that honourable I'd argue they were. Fashanu helped Slawson out in exactly the same way that he'd helped Les Cleevely out before him. According to Slawson and Cleevely, Fashanu knew they were both heterosexual and the footballer had genuinely wanted to help their careers. Mentoring takes time and not many other professional footballers were doing the same. Once again, it shows the kinder side of Justin who was willing to teach others what he had learned himself. Slawson would return to America the following year, and the next time he and Justin met it would be Fashanu who needed guidance from Slawson.

As far as Larry Lloyd's own fortunes were concerned, when the club managed just a single win in their first nine games of the new 1984/85 season he was sacked. The former Forest player's time at Meadow Lane had not been pretty and Lloyd, for one, was not sorry to leave. 'I found with my Forest background that I wasn't accepted by the supporters and even one or two of the directors and senior management didn't want me around. I found it very difficult and when it was time to leave I was not too unhappy about leaving Notts County,' Lloyd says.

Former Notts player Richie Barker who had managed Stoke and Shrewsbury took over as manager, but a new presence in the line-up did little to reverse County's fortunes. Barker hadn't been in the job long before supporters were calling for his head too. Fashanu's performance was equally stymied. Although his knee was holding out, by November the striker had only managed two goals. When reports circulated that he was looking for a transfer it prompted a gruff response from Brian Clough in his weekly newspaper column: 'Justin is way off target if he thinks a change of team will solve all his problems. At 23 years old he's got to sort himself out in so many respects, no matter what happens. Otherwise, I fear for him.'[25] If Clough really was that concerned about Fashanu's welfare his sentiments were arriving late.

As the season progressed, Fashanu's form eventually picked up but by early 1985 so had the number of bookings. Mick Leonard says that in one game against Wolverhampton Wanderers the Wolves keeper John Burridge ended up in the back of the net, along with the ball, after a 50-50 challenge with Fashanu in the six-yard box. Burridge always fancied himself as a bit of a tough guy, but after that incident he didn't venture out from under his cross bar again for the rest of the game.

In March 1985, Fashanu made the local news headlines when he refused to play a game on the Sabbath. He told reporters he'd always been unhappy about playing on Sundays but a recent riot he'd witnessed involving Millwall fans had finally pushed him to take a stand. In short, he said the riot was a sign from God that he was angry with him: 'I prayed long and hard about pulling out. It's not a case of not being bothered. Football cannot just divorce itself from the problems of society. I realise that if I continually disobey God I will take the consequences.'[26] He didn't win himself any friends when his admirable stand was blamed for the team's loss.

In April, with Notts hovering just above the relegation zone, Barker was sacked and Sirrel reinstated as manager. Sirrel's return was an inspired move, at least for Fashanu, whose goal scoring ability magically re-appeared. It's worth mentioning here that Fashanu's form often depended on who was managing him. If the relationship with his manager was good, like with Sirrel or John Bond, then the footballer's performance blossomed. Conversely, the opposite was true. In Sirrel's case, the transformation was instantaneous with the striker scoring in Sirrel's first four games back in charge.

Notts' fourth match at Meadow Lane was a big one with the Magpies hosting Manchester City at home. Both teams had a lot at stake, with City vying for promotion and Notts trying to avoid relegation. Incredibly, by the interval, Notts were 3-0 up and Fashanu was once again on the scoring sheet. At half time the game was almost called off when the visiting City fans rioted. Realising their team would likely lose, their only hope was to try and force a replay due to 'game abandonment.' The City fans were thwarted only thanks to some effective policing from Nottinghamshire's finest. It was a nail biting second period, with Notts just managing to hold on to their lead and win the game 3-2. Fashanu played a blinder and received a standing ovation from fans. Among them was the manager of Brighton and Hove Albion, Chris Cattlin. He'd travelled up to Nottingham specifically to watch Fashanu play.

'I watched the first half from the stands and the second half from the terraces. Fashanu looked good from both angles. Mick McCarthy was playing centre half for Manchester City and, in my opinion, was the best centre half in the division at the time. Fashanu drove him absolutely mad and didn't give him a second. I have never seen McCarthy look so flustered. He was all over the place. Fashanu ripped him apart,' Cattlin says.

The Brighton manager had been looking for a big striker for months, and Fashanu was an ideal candidate. He was aggressive, a menace in the box and could actually score too. When he got back to Brighton, Cattlin spoke to Howard Wilkinson and Lawrie McMenemy for their advice. Both managers said they would hire Fashanu again in a heartbeat. Next, Cattlin spoke to former Brighton and Forest player Peter Ward who was now playing football in America. Ward said that despite finding Fashanu a little odd, he highly recommended him as a teammate. It was another tick next to the striker's name. Finally, Cattlin talked to the former Forest manager Peter Taylor who was still at Derby County. Considering Fashanu's sensational exit from Forest, Cattlin was surprised when Taylor also gave him top marks. With glowing references all round, Fashanu looked like Cattlin's man. But, for the moment, he was still at Notts County and desperately trying to help the club avoid relegation. To do so, Notts needed to win their final game of the season at Fulham and hope that Shrewsbury Town beat Middlesbrough in their last game. If all these things happened then the Magpies' fate would be determined on goal difference. But in the end, the Shrewbury Town game wouldn't matter because Notts lost to Fulham. The nightmare of playing Division Three football was now a harsh reality, though that it arrived on the same day as the Bradford Fire Disaster at Valley Parade certainly put relegation and sport in general into perspective.

Cattlin didn't know it, but as he was weighing up his options about Fashanu someone else was already making a move for the Notts striker. Joe Royle, who'd played alongside Justin at Norwich, was now managing Oldham Athletic and he needed a new forward himself. He invited Fashanu to Oldham for talks. It had been a few years since the two had last seen each other and Royle was looking forward to the reunion. When his former teammate turned up for the meeting, however, Royle was shocked by how much Justin had changed:

'We had a good chat about things and talked about his future. I said: "It ain't worked out for you Justin, come up here and enjoy yourself." He said he'd go home to think about it and I told him I'd call him early the next morning. The next day I called him but there was no reply. When I eventually got hold of him I said: "Justin where have you been? I told you I was gonna ring you." He said: "Oh was that you ringing? I'm sorry, but I have been talking with the Lord." Justin informed me that the Lord didn't think it was right for him to join Oldham and that was that. It appeared as if his life had taken on different dimensions,' Royle says.

Their meeting would be the last time that Royle would see Fashanu. The next week, Notts accepted a £100,000 transfer fee from Brighton and Fashanu headed down to the south coast for a medical. His new wage would be slightly lower than the one he received from Notts County: £45,000 per year. Despite his prior surgeries, Fashanu looked in first-class condition and was given the all clear by the club doctor who examined him. Sirrel was sorry to see Fashanu go but understood his decision. With Notts relegated, Sirrel knew the footballer wouldn't be the only player looking for the door. Nottingham had been a city of mixed fortunes for Fashanu but he'd finished on a high. Despite being told his career was finished, the footballer had managed to claw his way back from the abyss and proved he could still be a top class player. Could he maintain it? Only time would tell.

Dark Days

WHEN JUSTIN Fashanu joined the ranks of Brighton and Hove Albion the footballer's future looked promising. Considering the extent of his knee injury, his previous season at Notts County had been nothing less than phenomenal with a multitude of goals. Chris Cattlin hoped that Fashanu would not only help Albion win promotion back into the First Division, but also resurrect his England career. The striker had already earned 11 England caps with the Under-21 side and was eager to win more. The Albion manager described the player's pre-season training as all singing and dancing and the footballer looked in peak form. As the 1985/86 season was about to kick off Cattlin had high expectations. The manager was still smarting from the previous season when the club had narrowly missed out on promotion. Like the Notts County players, the Albion squad also gave Fashanu a warm reception. The midfielder Keiran O'Regan says his unassuming nature won him instant friends. Unlike more famous players who sometimes looked down on other less-well known teammates, there was no attitude from the new recruit.

Before the season started, Justin settled into a small basement flat in Regency Square. The area might have been fashionable, but the rented apartment was in stark contrast to his home in The Park. It was dark and dismal. Sadly, the footballer's latest chapter would turn out to be just the same. The first indication of trouble appeared during a pre-season friendly against Oxford United. Midway through the game, Fashanu limped off the pitch with his right knee swollen. After it subsided, Fashanu was declared fit, but two games later the problem returned. Further treatment followed and Fashanu made a determined comeback playing in Brighton's next 11 games, even scoring two goals. But the end of the line arrived in February 1986 during an FA Cup tie against Peterborough. Fashanu's knee took a knock and this time the swelling didn't go down. The striker was transferred from the treatment room to the hospital, where an arthroscopy revealed a disturbing prognosis: monoarthritis synovitis. Simply put, the infection that had first attacked the knee joint had done more damage than doctors had previously thought. A rheumatologist recommended a synovectomy: the surgical removal of a part of the membrane surrounding the joint. Doctors told Justin that if he went ahead with the operation then it might hamper his career as a professional footballer. According to the Brighton physiotherapist Michael Yaxley, Fashanu was, naturally, devastated at the news and sought an array of second opinions. They all concurred with what the previous doctors said. Not willing to risk his career by undergoing such drastic surgery, so began Justin's search for alternative treatment.

With his leg in a cast, Fashanu's Brighton career was over after just 20 games. Cattlin was gutted too. Losing his new striker was a big blow to the team but he was also concerned for Fashanu. Being told your career might be over was the worst news any professional footballer could hear. What's disappointing is that Cattlin and Brighton would have been a good fit for Fashanu. As a strict, but fair, manager who never tolerated anything less than the very best from a player, Cattlin was just the kind of manager Fashanu would have thrived under. Alas, it wasn't to be.

Unable to train, Fashanu found himself with unwanted time on his hands. Tony Millard, a Brighton reporter, often saw the footballer at the Brighton Centre watching tennis. In 1986 the Centre hosted an international women's tournament and whenever Millard reported on matches he'd spot Fashanu in the stands. The footballer seemed lost. Incapacitated and with an uncertain future, Fashanu was stuck in a new city with few friends. Writer Malcolm Doney, who'd met Fashanu in Nottingham a few years earlier, dropped in to see the ailing striker when he was driving past Brighton one weekend.

Doney was shocked to see how much the footballer's fortunes had changed. Instead of living in splendour as he had in Nottingham, Fashanu was holed up in a cold, dark flat.

'To see a former one million pound footballer living in such a damp, basement flat was really quite distressing. Justin had his leg in a cast or splint and didn't seem to have any friends. I felt very sorry for him and invited him to dinner with me and my wife. We caught up on all the news and, despite his situation, he put on a brave face,' Doney says.

While Justin's career seemed close to the rocks, his brother's own fortunes were blossoming. For the past two years John had been playing Second Division football for Millwall. In the Eighties, the south east London side was notorious for having the worst behaved fans in the Football League who were regarded as the ultimate football hooligans. In 1986, John switched allegiances and signed for the southwest London side, Wimbledon. With Wimbledon it was the players who were considered the hooligans. Dubbed 'the crazy gang' because of their eccentric and boisterous behaviour, the players regularly got into trouble on and off the pitch. The team's most notable star was midfielder Vinnie Jones who was considered one of the hardest and dirtiest men in football. John Fashanu had also forged his own reputation as a physical player so he fitted in seamlessly.

Back in Brighton, perhaps the biggest indication of just how lonely Justin felt was his friendship with Brighton student, Kevin Weaver. Weaver was walking along the seafront one day when he spotted the footballer hobbling past on crutches. As a big fan, he could not resist saying hello.

'I just started chatting to Justin and he was very approachable. Considering how famous he was, he was not arrogant at all and very down-to-earth. I was just a student with no money, so was amazed when we ended up exchanging phone numbers. I had been at Carrow Road and saw him score his Goal of the Season against Liverpool and I was in awe of him. He was my boyhood hero and I'd even painted an oil painting of him,' Weaver says.

Weaver was even more amazed a few weeks later when Fashanu called him and asked if he wanted to meet up. It would mark the beginning of a brief, but solid, friendship. The footballer first arranged to meet Weaver at the student's home. It was a surreal situation: a former million pound player sitting and drinking tea in a living room that looked like a bomb had hit it. Weaver's housemates were a bunch of hairy bikers who'd turned the home into a leather-making workshop, but Justin wasn't fazed by the mess one bit. When Weaver and his housemates hosted a house party that summer Fashanu turned up with a football. He was soon entertaining the revellers by keeping the ball up with just his head and shoulders in time with the heavy rock music that blasted out of the speakers. Weaver says the footballer had a big smile on his face the whole evening and loved the attention.

At the time, Weaver was a trendy looking twenty-one-year old who could easily have doubled for the lead singer of Depeche Mode. Sporting a blond flat top haircut and equally sharp clothes, Weaver was at the cutting edge of Eighties fashion. It's quite possible that, at first, Fashanu might have thought he was gay. The heterosexual Weaver isn't sure because the subject was never mentioned, but Weaver certainly didn't know that Justin was. In retrospect, Weaver says the only hint Fashanu might have been gay was that the footballer never shared the student's enthusiasm for women. The opposite sex was one of his favourite topics of conversation but never reciprocated by the Brighton striker.

For the next couple of months, Weaver introduced Fashanu to the highlights of student life including dodgy bars and clubs. Fashanu rarely drank. On one occasion, Weaver invited him to a nightclub called Savannah near Brighton Pier. After waiting at the back of a long line for several minutes, Weaver grew impatient. Walking up to the entrance, he informed the burly doorman that the famous footballer was in the queue and asked if they could skip it. Weaver was stunned when the doorman announced that he'd never heard of Fashanu and told him they'd have to line up like everyone else. Inside the club later that evening Justin seemed a little withdrawn. At first, Weaver thought the footballer was embarrassed at what had just happened but soon realised that he was actually quite shy.

The more he got to know Justin the more Weaver sensed that his new friend was quite lonely and seemed to be a bit of a lost soul. It's precisely because Justin felt that way that Weaver believes the footballer embraced religion so much. In fact, he seemed consumed by his faith, attending a local evangelical church in Brighton regularly. Justin often invited people he met there back to his apartment for prayer meetings. Although he is not religious himself, Weaver finally agreed to attend a prayer meeting at the footballer's place one Sunday afternoon after a great deal of insistence. Unlike other times he had met him at a bar or nightclub Justin seemed a lot more at ease and jovial.

'Justin was keen that I become involved and was at pains to introduce me to everyone. He was an excellent and thoughtful host, but religion wasn't for me so I think I unintentionally backed off from contact with him. I felt he was trying to foist it on me. He tried to draw me into a conversation about God and my beliefs and seemed very passionate, but having lost my mother to cancer I was in no mood to countenance a God that hadn't saved her. Justin found my anger and disillusionment hard to understand and I think this led to our relationship drifting apart,' Weaver says.

Gordon Holmes can confirm Justin's obsession with his faith around this time period. The boxing trainer says that when he spoke to Betty Jackson she revealed she was seriously concerned about Justin's state of mind. Sometimes the footballer called her and midway through the conversation started talking, erratically, in tongues. It scared the life out of her. The conversations got so bad that Betty eventually told him to stop calling unless he promised not to talk gibberish. Her testimony indicates the footballer was suffering from a fragile mental state and one that people were beginning to notice.

You can't write a chapter on Justin Fashanu's time in Brighton without mentioning the obvious: the city has long been known as the gay capital of Britain and that can't have been lost on the footballer. In the mid-Eighties, Brighton was a mecca for gays and lesbians who were attracted to a more bohemian and open-minded attitude. Unlike Nottingham it offered an array of gay bars and clubs, most of them located in Kemptown. If Nottingham had appeared like a metropolis compared to Norwich, Brighton was the centre of the universe next to Nottingham. Exactly how much Justin embraced the gay scene is uncertain, but he would have certainly appreciated the city's liberal vibe. Judging by what Weaver could tell, however, it didn't look as if Fashanu really embraced the local gay scene much, if at all. The main focus wasn't his social life but his Christian faith.

Down on his luck and with few friends, and unable to play the sport he loved, Brighton was anything but a bright chapter in Fashanu's life. Like Doney, Weaver also says that the flat the footballer rented was depressing. There weren't even any paintings on the wall. It was dark, empty and all the furnishings were owned by the landlord. One pleasant experience that did come out of this period of time was when the footballer was invited by the American televangelist Billy Graham to join him on stage and give a testimony. Terry Carpenter, Fashanu's friend who'd first introduced him to Christianity, drove the footballer to Sheffield where Fashanu gave a short speech in front of thousands of people. Graham packed the stadium and Fashanu said it was one of the best nights of his life. But as quickly as Fashanu's friendship with Weaver began, so it ended when the footballer's contract at Brighton was terminated at the end of the season. Chris Cattlin was sacked and his replacement Alan Mullery was not willing to risk keeping Fashanu on. With his knee still in bad shape, Justin found himself at yet another crossroads.

In Search of a Miracle

AFTER BEING told by specialists in England that he would likely never play competitive football again, Fashanu refused to accept this idea. He told friends: 'A life without football is no life at all.' Undeterred, Justin started looking overseas for an answer. He soon found the Kerlan-Jobe Clinic in Los Angeles, a private treatment centre that cared for America's top sports stars. Many of these athletes had managed to return to action despite facing crippling injuries. Fashanu booked an appointment to see a surgeon named Dr James Tibone who'd built a reputation as something of a miracle worker when it came to saving careers. Fashanu was hoping the specialist could resurrect his. He explained that the main problem with his knee was the weakness of the joint. While he could run in straight lines, the problem was when he made quick sharp turns. His knee felt totally unstable, clearly a huge problem when playing professional football. Tibone said that with arthroscopic surgery the footballer would be able to play the game he loved again but would likely experience a lengthy recovery. Fashanu didn't mind how long it took to get fit; at least the procedure gave him hope. The surgery wasn't cheap with some estimates putting it at more than $250,000. The high expense meant that Justin was once again forced to dip into his reserves and he also asked his brother John for money.

Before he embarked for America Fashanu called his old friend in LA, Neil Slawson. It had been a few years since the two men had last seen each other back in Nottingham and the American was delighted to hear from Justin. Since returning to his native country, Slawson had done a lot of growing and not just in height. He'd since swapped his football boots for a gun and was training to be a cop. Pleased that he had a chance to reciprocate the kindness Justin had shown him in England, he invited the footballer to stay with him in Upland, California, a 45-minute drive from LA. The footballer flew to LA towards the end of 1986. Slawson still lived with his parents so Fashanu was instructed to be on his best behaviour. When he arrived at the Slawson residence, one of the first things Fashanu did was walk up the stairs then slide head first down the banister on his belly. Mr and Mrs Slawson were left open mouthed. As someone their son had described as a mentor, the Englishman was not exactly what they'd been expecting. Within a week the cheeky player was calling them mom and dad.

Fashanu underwent the knee surgery in early 1987, and it was Slawson who shuttled him to and from the clinic for the intense rehabilitation sessions that followed. Although he didn't show it publicly, Fashanu was terrified at the prospect of not being able to play professional football again and prayed the surgery worked. He rarely showed his feelings or insecurities to anyone, but Slawson saw Fashanu's career fears first hand. The two men often discussed the subject late into the night. While Fashanu knew he was a minor personality in football, he wasn't sure if he was a big enough name to make it as a sports pundit or presenter. Slawson told him to keep the faith.

When the rookie cop graduated from the police academy later that summer Fashanu joined the celebrations with Slawson's family. The new cop hadn't forgotten what Fashanu had done for him in England and was proud the Englishman could see how far he'd come. If Slawson thought carrying a gun might stop Fashanu from reprimanding him, however, he was mistaken. When it came to giving a few lessons in life the footballer had not changed. When Justin introduced Slawson to tennis ace Tracy Austin in the clinic one morning the footballer was horrified when Slawson greeted her with: 'Nice to meet ya' Trace!' Pulling the rookie cop aside after Austin had left, Fashanu told him he'd been disrespectful and Slawson found himself in the bad books for the rest of the day. It was just like old times.

When it came to rehab, Fashanu had been placed under the expert supervision of one of LA's top physical therapists, Clive Brewster. Brewster also worked at the Kerlan-Jobe Clinic and placed Fashanu on an intense recovery programme.

'Justin was very optimistic when he came to me which was good. We tried to build up his mobility and in order to do that we had to try and decrease the swelling first. That's the only way we could get the range of motion back. When you look at the cut and pivot that is where he had his problems. Sometimes, the hardest part of my job is trying to prevent these high-powered athletes from getting discouraged, because they instinctively want to push themselves,' Brewster says.

Olympic gold medalist sprinter Sherri Howard knows just how gruelling those sessions were. She was being treated by Brewster herself for an inflamed Achilles tendon injury at the same time. Spying Fashanu from the other side of the treatment room, Howard could tell the footballer was putting all his effort into rehabilitation, but this was not the only attribute she observed.

'At first I thought he was just another track guy or football player until he opened his mouth then I realised he was from a different country. Clive informed me that he was a soccer player. He really was striking to look at and had a body to die for. He could definitely have been one of those underwear models. I thought he was just dreamy and would certainly make a nice date,' Howard says.

The two sports stars instantly hit it off and were soon pushing each other on during treatment. Coffees in the canteen quickly turned into lunches and then dinners. Howard felt a close connection to Fashanu even though he was guarded. Whenever she asked the footballer a personal question he always resorted to short answers. Like others before her, she wondered what he was hiding.

Within a few weeks, Fashanu opened up and told Howard about his past. The footballer mentioned being abandoned by his parents and how he'd strived to lead a happier life. With his career in jeopardy, Howard was surprised when he said he felt close to achieving what he'd always wanted to in life but was just falling short of glory. 'How can you understand glory when you've already won the gold?' he asked her. By that statement what Howard thought Fashanu meant was even when you get to the top of your game as a professional athlete it is never enough. If she's right, the comment is surprising given that Fashanu was only at the top of his game for a couple of years. He also told Howard that there were a couple of football clubs in England interested in signing him after he was fit but they weren't teams he wanted to play for.

In the spring of '87, Fashanu flew back to England to attend the annual PFA dinner and awards ceremony that was being staged at the Grosvenor House Hotel, London. Once again, the footballer was about to court controversy. Justin attended the event with his brothers John and Phillip, and the trouble started towards the end of the formal dinner when John stood up and shouted across the room at QPR player, Simon Stainrod: 'Hey Stainrod! Tell us what you've been saying about Justin behind his back!' he yelled. According to journalist and author Matt Allen, John had been told Stainrod had made disparaging remarks about Justin calling him a fag and poof. John was not happy about it. Rather than cause a scene, Stainrod ignored John but the younger Fashanu followed him into the toilet later that evening. Although nothing physical actually happened, there was clearly some kind of confrontation and Justin found himself the focus of an article about it in *The Sun* the following week. It was not the kind of attention he either wanted or needed. It's clear from this incident that John did not believe his brother was gay and was prepared to fight for his older sibling's honour. While it might actually have been a good opportunity for Justin to fess up the truth to John in private, it seems Justin believed things were too far gone for that. Sadly, hiding the truth would, ultimately, only cause him greater pain. Particularly with his brother.

Back in LA, Brewster delivered some exciting news later that year: Fashanu was ready to start kicking a ball. Not surprisingly, the striker was jubilant and wasted no time scouting for a local team to train with. He soon came across the Exiles: a club that was the creation of pop singer Rod Stewart who lived in LA. It was actually Stewart and the former head of Island Records in America, Lionel Conway, who founded the club for expatriates from Britain. Stewart was much better with a microphone than a ball, but created the team because of his passion for football, playing regularly himself. Most of the players worked in the entertainment industry and Justin was introduced to the squad before the start of a game. For whatever reason, Fash only played one game before he switched allegiances for a German based outfit called Autobahn FC that played in the Budweiser International League. The team's informal nature was a perfect set-up for

Fashanu because he could drop in and out whenever he liked, depending on how his knee fared.

In an interview with a local fanzine called *Soccer Match* Fashanu told a reporter that even though he'd been out of the English game for a while he hadn't been forgotten because several clubs were monitoring his progress: 'I spoke with my brother yesterday and he said it will be ten times better when I get back because it will be like I'm back from the dead!'[27] It's quite possible that his comment about clubs monitoring his progress was just a strong case of wishful thinking. He always did possess a healthy dose of bravado. With his knee strong enough to play football it meant Justin could also drive again and he was soon rolling around town in a sexy, black Mustang convertible. As someone who was at the cutting edge of fashion, the licence plate suited him perfectly: 1GQ RIDE. The car actually belonged to Slawson who was soon fighting his friend for the keys.

While Fashanu's relationship with the local media was still on good form the same could not always be said about how he handled other situations. The footballer presented Rod Stewart with a leather-encased Bible at the singer's birthday party and onlookers were not amused. Some of Stewart's entourage were offended at what they thought was the footballer's intimation that the singer needed saving. At the same party, Fashanu ran into the British pop star George Michael. Fashanu told him about the stories surrounding the footballer's sexuality which prompted the singer to reply: 'Relax. You're not a star until they've written about the gay rumour thing.' Michael knew this only too well as he was hiding the very same secret himself.

By early 1988, Fashanu's recovery appeared to be on track and he was now playing regular games for das Autobahn. Feeling it was time to switch things up a gear and play more competitive football, he contacted the general manager of California's biggest soccer club, the LA Heat. The team's Scottish coach John Britton subsequently took a call from the head office. 'The general manager calls and asks me if I'd heard of some guy called Justin Fashanu. When I told him: "Yes, of course" and asked him why, he said the footballer had just contacted him and was asking to play. My immediate reaction was: "You're bloody joking? Send him the heck down!" 'Britton says. Britton was delighted when Justin actually showed up. It hadn't been a wind-up after all. Fashanu explained that his knee was still on the mend so he had to take things at his own pace. For Britton that wasn't a problem. Having someone of Fashanu's experience in the squad was enough in itself.

As a less-experienced player, the coach was happy to let the footballer take the lead.

Fashanu's commitment to getting fitter proved unfailing. He worked hard in training and when each session was over went for a long run along the beach. Fashanu confided in Britton that the pace of his recovery was beginning to bother him. The coach explained that getting fit was not something he could rush and urged him to be patient. One bonus for Fashanu was the footballer managed to persuade the general manager Michael Hogue to pay him a small weekly salary. As someone who was well known for guarding his purse strings this was no mean feat. Britton noticed that Fashanu was very attracted to money and he tried to squeeze even more of it out of Hogue as the months passed. Fashanu also struck up a close friendship with the Heat's goalkeeper Bobby Ammann who rubbed his eyes in disbelief when he first spotted the striker at a training session. The American had stuck a poster of Fashanu on his bedroom wall as a teenager and now, ten years later, it appeared as if they were in the same team. It was surreal stuff.

Playing in a much lower league meant it didn't take long for Fashanu to re-discover his ability to score goals. After just a few games, the striker found himself the second highest scorer in the whole Western Soccer Alliance. The Heat had two minibuses at their disposal for transport and the team usually spent the night at a hotel if an away match was a long drive. Britton always roomed with Fashanu and while the coach read sports magazines in bed before the lights went out Fashanu digested the Bible. He carried it everywhere:

'I'm a huge Cliff Richard fan and I was impressed when Justin said he knew Cliff through various evangelical events they both attended. I was fascinated by what Justin thought about Cliff's relationship with women, God and the public. I liked Cliff for his music but Fash liked Cliff's beliefs instead. Fash and I had some heated debates about God and I used to wind him up because in his eyes God could do no wrong. Justin used to invoke the party line on religion. That gave me the impression that he was just regurgitating what had been fed him instead of thinking about the issues himself,' Britton says.

Britton and Fashanu also clashed on the tennis court. The first time the two men played a few sets was in Portland ahead of a game and Fashanu told Britton he was going to wipe the floor with him. While he may have been a competent player, what Justin didn't know was that his coach was a former Scottish junior tennis champion. The only thing that ended up getting wiped was the smug grin from Fashanu's face after he was trounced. Trash talk never pays. While Justin was in Portland that weekend he met writer and producer A.J. Ali who was visiting from Sacramento, California. Ali, at 24-years-old, was asked by the league to get his own soccer team up and running and he met Fashanu at a league soccer meeting. Ali will always remember the first time he saw Justin who was sitting at a board table surrounded by a bunch of boring old cronies in suits. The contrast with a smiling, energetic Justin Fashanu could not have been starker. As the sole black (and young) men in the room with a genuine passion for soccer, Ali and Fashanu found an instant connection. After the meeting was over, they headed to the nearest restaurant and a close friendship was sealed from that day on. Over the coming years, the two men would keep in regular contact. Ali, who would become something of a sounding board to the footballer in times of need, had no idea just how big a part he would actually play in the Justin Fashanu story.

According to Britton and Ammann, no one in the LA Heat team had any inkling that Justin might be gay. A friend of Britton's from Scotland once told him he'd heard the footballer might be and asked the coach whether he'd seen any 'signs'. Britton was shocked at the suggestion and told his friend he hadn't. In hindsight, Britton does remember a young male driver who sometimes chauffeured Fashanu around and wonders if he was more than just a driver.

Sherri Howard sometimes watched Fashanu play for the Heat but the athlete could not help being disappointed. It wasn't his performance on the pitch that bothered her, more that he didn't perform off it. She had always been slightly frustrated that their friendship had not developed into something more and she could never understand why. It wasn't as if Fashanu was married or had a girlfriend, so what was the problem? While Howard knew the footballer was determined to go back to England at some point, a kiss and cuddle would have been nice. 'He would always say to me: "God, you are such a great catch", and I'd be thinking: "Well, why don't you catch me?"' Sherri spoke about her frustrations to Slawson who could do little but offer a listening ear. He knew the rumours about Justin being gay but could hardly tell Howard. They were merely rumours, after all, and it was not his place to speak. As far as Slawson was concerned, he still didn't know whether Fashanu was straight or gay anyway. Despite what he'd heard, the footballer had dated women in the past, like Julie, and had chosen to live a celibate lifestyle in keeping with his Christian faith. The latter was just one plausible reason why he was not making a move on Howard. Of course, Slawson wasn't naive either. The two men once went on a double date with two girls he knew and at the end of the evening one of them asked Slawson if Justin was gay. The cop knew that women have good radar for such things so he remained open minded when it came to his friend's sexuality. Slawson didn't mind either way.

The LA cop got a much deeper insight into Fashanu when he took him out on patrol. The footballer could not believe how tough the streets were in LA compared to England. One evening Fashanu was riding in the patrol car when Slawson got called to a domestic dispute where a woman had been badly beaten by her husband. It wasn't the first time cops had been called to the residence. Justin was visibly shaken by what he saw and when they got back to the police station asked Slawson why the woman did not simply ask for a divorce. It was now Slawson who was the teacher, explaining why it's never easy for anyone to leave a violent relationship, period: shame, lack of money and fear just a few reasons. Another time, Slawson was called to a home where the conditions were filthy. Fashanu was upset that children were living there and couldn't understand why they had not been taken into protective custody. Justin's naivety reveals just how out of touch with the real world he was. While many people would be just as shocked to witness such sights themselves, most of us are experienced enough to realise that they exist on a huge scale. Fashanu's response was a lot more innocent and obviously stems back to his childhood. While he'd tasted the harsh realities of life in his very early years at the children's home, that experience had been short, and was in stark contrast to the years that followed. His privileged upbringing in Norfolk appears to have blinkered his perception of reality. What Fashanu considered the norm was anything but.

On a couple of occasions Fashanu was present when Slawson made an arrest. Back at the police department, the footballer got his first look at the county jail while the cop booked in his suspects. Slawson remembers how surprised Fashanu was at the size of the cells. He could not imagine being locked up in one himself and told Slawson he'd never be able to cope with it. They would prove to be ominous words. One amusing thing the cop did discover during those ride-alongs was how much the footballer hated driving fast. He was terrified. If Slawson ever found himself getting a lecture in the car from his famous mentor then he simply hit the police siren and accelerator. That soon shut Fashanu up.

One evening, Slawson was on patrol alone when he got a call from his mother. Justin had woken up in the dead of sleep and punched his hand through his bedroom window. The cut to his arm was so deep that it needed stitches. Fashanu had suffered similar nightmares when he was a child and the last documented incident was six years earlier when he'd smashed his fist through the door of his hotel room in Spain. He'd been playing for Nottingham Forest at the time. With these nightmares stemming back to his childhood, you can't help thinking those abandonment issues had something to do with them. Punching your fists through windows and doors is certainly indicative of sub-conscious rage and frustration. As an adult, Fashanu faced even more angst as a religious, closeted gay man. Given the circumstances and pressures he faced in life, it's surprising he didn't punch out more things.

In the summer of 1988, Fashanu gave an interview with the *Los Angeles Times*. He told reporter Stuart Matthews that he'd found himself at a crossroads. With his knee almost healed he felt that if he stayed in America the opportunities to work with a growing sport were endless, especially with the US about to host the upcoming World Cup. On the other hand a virtual fortune awaited him in England. Making money was clearly still a priority for Fashanu but his statement about a fortune awaiting him has to be taken with a huge pinch of salt. In reality, Fashanu was off the radar of most club managers in the UK and his days of commanding high fees were over. His comment to the reporter was either another case of wishful thinking or pure bravado and my money's on both. One person who can back this up is the LA Heat coach. Britton says that one of Justin's vulnerabilities was his vanity and he was forever calling reporters in England to keep them up to date with his success.

Ultimately, the decision to stay in America or fly home was out of Fashanu's hands. No English club recruited him meaning he was forced to play out the remainder of the American season. One person who was glad of that was Sherri Howard who had continued to see Fashanu socially. But their close friendship was about to come to an end. A Canadian team called the Edmonton Brickmen that played in western Canada was looking for an experienced player, and a friend recommended the general manager take a close look at Fashanu. Mel Kowalchuk was one of the top dogs in the Canadian Soccer League and flew to LA to watch him play. The Canadian was amazed to see three defenders marking Justin the entire game. The striker was obviously handy. After the game, Kowalchuk approached Fashanu and asked if he'd be interested in a move north. Fashanu's answer was blunt: 'Yes, if the price is right.' After he got back to Edmonton, Kowalchuk phoned the Heat's GM and a compensation deal was hammered out. By the end of the conversation, Fashanu was a free agent and free to join the Brickmen. Fashanu was more expensive than Kowalchuk had anticipated, but a contract was drawn up and the footballer ended up signing.

Howard was one of the first people Fashanu told he was leaving America. One or two nights before he left Los Angeles the two of them spent their last night together having fun: 'When we got close he said: "I'm gonna miss you, you are such a great girl but I can't do that." I thought: "Am I not attractive to this guy?"' Howard says. The athlete had finally developed a sneaking suspicion that Fashanu might be gay but it was only a guess. In the end, she put the footballer's lack of forwardness down to an unwillingness to start a relationship with someone in another country. She respected that.

John Britton and the rest of the Heat squad were also sad to hear of Fashanu's departure. Many of them had become good friends with him and would miss his bubbly personality. But one player who wasn't going to miss him was Ammann. That's because the keeper had also been signed by the Brickmen and would be travelling up to Canada himself. Justin had been so impressed at his goalkeeping skills that he'd persuaded Kowalchuk to sign him too. Assisting Ammann with his career was the third time Fashanu had helped a fellow player. While it certainly shows how considerate and kind Fashanu behaved you can't help wondering if there was also a desire to create some sort of family wherever he went. Again, it harks back to his abandonment issues. Whenever he made a solid connection with someone in a new city it must have been hard to walk away from. It's quite possible that he sometimes tried to create his own clan.

One thing is for sure, it was difficult for Fashanu to say goodbye to the Slawsons, who had shown him incredible hospitality while he was in LA. It had been a home away from home. Sadly, Justin would not pay them back in kind. While he'd stayed with Neil's parents the footballer had racked up a monstrous phone bill that exceeded $1,000. Despite promising to send a cheque the Slawson's never received a cent. When you consider the generosity he was shown then Fashanu's behaviour is very disappointing. Unfortunately, this kind of selfish conduct would only grow worse.

While Mel Kowalchuk was pleased at his new signing one thing he did have a nagging doubt about was Fashanu's knee. Although the footballer had lasted the soccer season in LA, Kowalchuk knew Justin's knee was sometimes a problem. Clive Brewster had told the footballer that these flare-ups required more rest or possibly more surgery. Neither of those options were what Fashanu wanted to hear.

Playing Tough

WHEN FASHANU arrived in Edmonton in August 1988, Mel Kowalchuk provided the footballer with two things: a swanky apartment on the grounds of Edmonton University and a car. The latter was not so swanky and when Fashanu complained he was told to lump it or leave it. Kowalchuk can't remember Fashanu's exact wages but they were the highest in the Canadian league at that time.

The Brickmen's coach was fellow Brit Len Vickery who'd moved to Edmonton a few years earlier. A few weeks after he arrived, Fashanu called an emergency meeting with Vickery and Kowalchuk in the team dressing room. When they exited ten minutes later, Vickery had relinquished control of the team and Fashanu was now in charge. According to one of the players, Gregor Young, Fashanu believed he was more suited for the job of coach than the less experienced Vickery. Fashanu told Kowalchuk that unless he was given the role then he'd walk. Kowalchuk had little choice but to accept his demands and Vickery was appointed assistant coach. In fairness to Vickery, he didn't try and fight the proposed change at all and willingly acquiesced.

As the new coach Fashanu set about making big changes. One of these was increasing the number of training sessions from once to twice a day. The move did not go down well with some players who resented the extra sessions when they were getting paid so little. When they complained to Fashanu they found the subject was not open for discussion. Kowalchuk wasn't complaining. He was happy that his new coach was milking the most out of a team that had, so far, failed to deliver results.

The soccer season in Canada was short, comprising 26 games stretched over the three month summer period, meaning teams played two games a week. Young, a centre back with the Brickmen, says it was a crazy schedule made even more extreme by Fashanu's training regime. The players usually enjoyed mornings off and were not impressed when the luxury of a sleep-in suddenly disappeared. Young says something else that didn't enamour the squad to Fashanu was the way their new coach sometimes treated them. Young saw him as nothing short of tyrannical, often resorting to humiliation as a motivational tool. While Vickery won't comment on that he does say a couple of the more senior players were not supportive of Fashanu and that this generated some tension. In Vickery's eyes, the new coach was simply bringing a new level of professionalism to the club that it badly needed if it was going to be a serious contender in the league. There's a fine line between discipline and tyranny and whether Fashanu crossed it depends on whom you speak to. There are always two sides to every story. What's worth noting is that Fashanu had always thrived under a positive manager and in a more family-centric kind of club himself, and here he was being accused of being a despot. Who knows what Brian Clough would have made of it?

Fashanu's tough approach to training was something the new player-coach also displayed in games. In one match against the Calgary Kickers the footballer jumped up for a header against three opposing players and the only one who landed back on his feet was Fashanu. One of the Calgary players was holding a broken nose and the other two were laid out on their backs. To this day, Kowalchuk still isn't sure what happened exactly but he has a good idea it involved Fashanu's elbows. As one of the injured players crawled past on his hands and knees Kowalchuk heard him mutter: 'Now I know what it takes to play First Division football.' In his first three games, Fashanu broke the noses of two opponents earning himself the same nickname as his brother: 'Fash the Bash.' Young witnessed both incidents in games against Winnipeg and Calgary. Young says:

'The Winnipeg Fury centre back was an old friend of Fash's and they spent most of the warm-up laughing and catching up as if the game had already been played. 15 minutes in, a long ball was played up to Fash and the centre back came to challenge in the air. An elbow was thrown with so much malice it serves as a great definition for juxtaposition given the pre-game friendliness between the two. I remember blood all over the white Fury jersey, a nose thoroughly broken, and a sub coming on who didn't look too keen on the task of covering Fash the rest of the game. It was a stunning, almost movie-like piece of violence. To top it off, two games later Fash did the exact same thing to Burke Kaiser of Calgary. Early doors elbow to the grill, Kaiser out with a broken nose.'

It's obvious that Fashanu wanted to stamp his authority on the CSL early on but Young's testimony suggests that he went way too far. With his injured knee still a concern, it's possible that Fashanu wanted to protect it by keeping opponents at bay. If that was the case then using his elbows certainly wasn't the way to do it. Fashanu's reputation for dirty play meant he soon had quite a few enemies in the league.

According to Young, Fashanu's sexuality was no secret amongst the rest of the squad. When he'd joined the team, players on other CSL teams who played in England announced to everyone: 'You do know he's homosexual don't you?' The fact these players stated it as fact reveals how much the rumour had circulated amongst the professional football fraternity in England. It also shows how quickly hearsay can turn into fact without any proof being provided. Justin had never mentioned he was gay to anyone in football circles and yet many people assumed he was. The *Sunday People* article from 1982 that first questioned his sexuality was certainly responsible for giving the matter wider attention. The only thing Fashanu, ultimately, wanted to do was play football and the rumours that followed him must have been frustrating.

The rest of the Brickmen team members lived in a separate apartment complex to Fashanu and rarely socialised with him. On the few occasions that Fashanu did go out with the team he would have one or two beers and then leave. He dictated the degree of interaction required and socialised only in situations where he knew he could slip away easily. Young realised that Fashanu only allowed people to get so close. Underneath his charisma and geniality was a solid wall that you hit if you delved too deeply. Justin had always been fiercely guarded, a natural response for someone who felt abandoned as a child. Of course, a wall of reserve has its own set of problems. While it was good at keeping his feelings hidden it also prevented others from getting close to him. One thing the Brickmen players noticed was

Fashanu's penchant for young men. During his time in Edmonton, the footballer usually had at least one male companion hanging around most times. Fashanu introduced one to the team after a training session. He said his companion was the son of a friend in California who he'd agreed to host over the summer holidays as a favour. The players might have believed their coach if his pasty, gaunt-looking companion didn't have 'rent boy' stamped on his forehead. Young says the guys didn't mind and were more amused by the footballer's cover story. Young claims that if Fashanu had come out while he was at Edmonton then none of the players would have cared. Like Young, half of the team was from Vancouver and very liberal. Young says they might have taken the proverbial out of Fashanu every now and again but it would only have been in jest. Although the Brickmen believed their coach was gay, Bobby Ammann didn't. The former LA Heat player hadn't seen any evidence in Canada, or back in LA, and was sure that if Fashanu was then he'd have confided in him.

As the season progressed the team's results improved under Fashanu's leadership, but one thing that didn't was his own fitness. It was fast becoming obvious that Fashanu's knee could not cope with the pace of playing so many games. When the swelling in his joint failed to subside, Kowalchuk booked an appointment for the footballer to see a specialist he knew. In a moment of serendipity, the doctor at Edmonton General Hospital was British surgeon Dr David Reid. Fashanu was stunned because Reid was the same surgeon he'd been trying to locate himself for the last five years. When he'd first injured his knee in Nottingham, Reid was the specialist everyone had recommended, but when the footballer tried to contact him the surgeon had vanished. Apparently, the good doctor had moved to Edmonton. Fashanu's delight was quickly replaced with a frown, however, when Reid informed him that his knee required more surgery. The good news was that the operation could be performed right away so he could be fit in plenty of time for the start of the next season. As before, the surgery would be expensive but Fash had no choice but to pay for it. The alternative of early retirement was still not an option.

While Fashanu recovered post-surgery in hospital Kowalchuk visited him every night. The GM knew the footballer didn't have any close friends in the city and could probably appreciate some moral support. Another person who visited was Bobby Ammann but his friendship with Justin had cooled. After they'd arrived in Edmonton, Ammann was disappointed that he and Fashanu no longer hung out together like they'd used to in LA. After Fashanu became coach he treated Ammann just as he treated the other players. Their social interaction was limited and it was obvious that Fashanu didn't want to mix his personal life with his professional one. The goalkeeper was disappointed but realised his coach was only being professional. During one visit to the hospital Kowalchuk decided it was a good time to quietly ask about a rumour he'd heard. The GM had been told by a few sources that his striker was gay and if it were true he wanted to warn Justin.

'I just thought I would come right out and say it. I told him: "Look Justin, there are a lot of rumours about you being gay. Try to understand that this is a bit of a redneck town and if you are gay then please don't bring it out in public or bring it near the team. What you do in your own home, I truly do not care,"' said Kowalchuk.

Kowalchuk said Fashanu didn't say a word and simply gazed into the distance. While the general manager liked Justin and was generally supportive it seems Kowalchuk was reluctant to stick his neck out and back a gay player. Even though he hadn't officially told anyone he was gay, I'm sure Fashanu would have appreciated the support.

At the end of the 1988 season, the Brickmen failed to win any silverware but they had won more matches than in previous seasons, thanks to Fashanu's presence and leadership. Though he didn't win any cups he had earned a reputation as the Canadian Soccer League's toughest player. The footballer had played 12 games and scored five goals. He'd also accrued the highest number of bookings. Overall, Kowalchuk was pleased with the results and invited him back the next season. In the meantime, Fashanu headed back to England.

All Over the Map

BACK IN the UK, Fashanu had something extremely important on his mind. While it wasn't related directly to football, to Justin it was equally big. The player called writer Malcolm Doney to discuss it. The last time the two men had spoken was back in Brighton when the striker had been injured and appeared down on his luck. Doney had been concerned for the footballer's welfare. Three years later and Fashanu now seemed in exuberant spirits.

'Justin called out of the blue and the first thing he said to me was: "This is fantastic! I have got hold of you! Just fantastic! I thought I'd lost your number. I was looking at an old address book for you and found it. I'm so glad that I did." He was very excited that he'd found me and told me it was through the guidance of God. He said he had something amazing to tell me about himself that was going to blow everyone's mind. Now was the time to tell it and he wanted me to write about it in a book,' Doney says.

The writer didn't have a clue what Fashanu wanted to reveal exactly, and if he had then he would, undoubtedly, have been just as enthusiastic. As it stood, Doney believed the footballer simply wanted him to pen his biography and the writer was not convinced that was something a publisher would go for. Fashanu hadn't been a big star for long when he'd played in England and had been out of the big league for quite some time. Rather than letting him down on the phone, Doney arranged to meet Fashanu the following week to at least discuss the idea, but the day before the meeting Doney was struck down with the flu. Unable to get out of bed he called Fashanu to cancel the meeting and asked him to call back the following week to re-schedule. When the next week arrived and Doney hadn't heard from Justin he tried to reach the footballer himself, but to no avail. Justin had disappeared. Of course, today Doney knows exactly what Fashanu was going to tell him and the writer is kicking himself. Because of a lousy bout of flu he lost the chance to reveal one of football's biggest stories. Doney put the whole episode down to fate. Perhaps his role in the Justin Fashanu story wasn't meant to be.

As it happens, the reason why Doney couldn't contact Fashanu was because the player was frantically moving between cities looking for a new club to sign him. This wasn't easy. He had been out of the English game for a few years, out of touch and, therefore, out of the minds of managers. Realising he needed help, the footballer hired the services of professional sports agent Ambrose Mendy. Mendy was better known in boxing circles and was currently managing the enigmatic Dark Destroyer, Nigel Benn. With the 1988/89 season already in full swing, one of the first calls Mendy made was to the Manchester City manager, Mel Machin. Mendy knew that Machin was looking for a striker and after a meeting in mid-December 1988 Fashanu was offered a trial run. Machin knew Fashanu from his Norwich City days where Machin had been one of his youth team coaches. Suddenly, the striker was back in the big league (or so it appeared). Mendy says that Fashanu dived headfirst into the Manchester social scene and revelled in it:

'Browns Bar was our favourite haunt and the media referred to the celebrities who went there as the "Black Pack" because there were so many of us. There were Paul Ince, David Rocastle and Michael Thomas to name but a few and, of course, Justin Fashanu, who just loved it. Every penny Justin made he spent on image and ran up bills on things I can't begin to tell you. All the other black players really looked up to him,' Mendy says.

But the fun in 'Madchester' would be short lived, at least for Justin. After just a few weeks, Machin terminated Fashanu's contract. The manager believed Fashanu's fitness was simply not up to par. Mendy's testimony about Justin again provides evidence of just how much Fashanu loved being in the centre of the action, away from the field. Even though he was short of money and should have been saving his funds, socialising appears to have been a bigger priority. Add to this the fact he was on a trial contract with

City and you get a good picture of the complex and, sometimes, irresponsible Justin Fashanu.

If the footballer was hoping another team would sign him he was disappointed. Not one club made an official approach. Fashanu's knee was obviously still a concern, so in the spring of 1989 he returned for pre-season training with the Brickmen back in Edmonton. This time around the New Year in Canada had brought a few changes in the line-up. Gregor Young had been loaned to Vancouver and Bobby Ammann was in England playing for Brighton and Hove Albion, a move that Fashanu had helped forge. Mel Kowalchuk was also preparing an exit after deciding to concentrate on his many business dealings instead of football. Fashanu's own departure from the Edmonton Brickmen came less than halfway into the new season. Although he managed to score 17 goals in 23 games, his contract was terminated. According to some sources, the footballer clashed with the new management and they sacked him fearing he was gaining too much control and influence over the club. It meant Justin was without a team to play for once again. Packing his suitcase, the footballer headed back to England.

In October 1989 he was back in Manchester. Bizarrely, Mel Machin had offered him yet another trial with City. But, just as before, things didn't work out. Fashanu came on as a substitute for one game against Aston Villa before his trial period was curtailed. Once again, the city manager believed the footballer's fitness was still not up to grade.

Next it was a trial at Ipswich Town, but Fashanu managed to sabotage that in sensational circumstances. After reportedly asking for an extravagant signing on fee (some say £300,000), Ipswich manager John Duncan was so outraged that he leaked the footballer's cheeky demand to the press. A headline in the *Daily Express* said it all: '£1m flop Fashanu puts amazing price on his soccer comeback deal!'[28] Needless to say, Fashanu was looking for another club to approach.

In early 1990, Mendy arranged for Fashanu to try out for Lou Macari at West Ham United. The striker was signed on a match-to-match basis and actually played a few first team games. However, according to Mendy, Justin's time at the club ended prematurely after an ugly incident involving a *News of the World* reporter. Mendy claims the journalist told Macari that Fashanu was gay and that the footballer was having a relationship with two of his new teammates. Mendy won't say which players but claims it was all an ugly lie that the reporter fabricated. Mendy said he was disgusted at it but there was nothing he could do. As a boxing promoter he knew full-well how dirty tabloid reporters played. This is Mendy's account of what happened, but Macari's is different. According to the West Ham manager it was Justin's fitness and attitude that were to blame for his exit. Macari says he was not impressed at the latter when he found out Fashanu had gone out drinking one evening before a game when he should have been resting. It was not the sort of behaviour or attitude he expected from a new player. Macari was spot on in his assessment. As in Manchester, Fashanu put socialising ahead of his career at a time when his career should have been the only thing that mattered. For someone who claims he was desperate to get back into the action of top-flight football he was doing a heck of a job of ruining it. There's no denying that, at times, Justin was his own worst enemy.

It's worth mentioning another incident that involved Fashanu at West Ham, albeit indirectly. Even though he had not officially come out, to me it seems very apparent that Justin's teammates believed the rumours about his sexuality were true. According to former West Ham player Mark Ward in his autobiography *From Right-Wing to B-Wing,* Justin was the target of blatant homophobia. Ward recounts an evening before an away game when he arrived at the team hotel late at night only to discover he was sharing a hotel room with Justin: 'I left the key on the reception desk and started to pace up and down looking for help. Being asleep in the bed next to Justin Fashanu? No f*****g way! I was panicking now and started to hunt for someone to talk to—where the f*** was Alvin? He would sort it out. Just at that moment I heard lots of sniggering. I turned the corner and there p*****g themselves laughing were Alvin, Galey and Dicksy (Alvin Martin, Tony Gale and Julian Dicks). It was a good set-up and I was so relieved to hear that Justin was rooming on his own that night,' Ward wrote.

What's disappointing for me is that Ward published this book in 2009 so obviously thinks the story is still amusing. Sadly, it just reinforces the stereotype that some professional footballers do not seem to care about the issue of homophobia.

Fortunately for Fashanu, after his brief career at West Ham ended the player was about to meet a couple of people in the game who did respect him. More than that, they genuinely cared for him. Mendy had convinced the manager of Leyton Orient, Frank Clark, that signing the more experienced Fashanu would be a good financial move. The striker was a big name for the Third Division club and could attract more fans. Realising he didn't have anything to lose, Clark agreed and signed Justin on a temporary contract. Clark had first met the footballer back in the late Seventies when Fashanu had been at Norwich City and playing for Nottingham Forest. The Geordie had not forgotten the fierce clash between Fashanu and Forest defender Larry Lloyd. He hoped the striker was still as physical. From the moment Fashanu joined the ranks of Leyton Orient, the footballer's commitment was unfailing. The club had a lot of young players in the squad who all looked up to him and Clark told them that they could learn a lot from Justin's hard work. Fashanu also struck up a close friendship with the club's resident physiotherapist, Bill Songhurst. The physio had a great deal of respect for him but sensed the footballer was hiding a lot of things. Songhurst thought he was a classic case of someone who looked confident on the outside but was, actually, desperately insecure.

Songhurst and Clark had both heard that Fashanu might be gay. Songhurst calls it football's worst kept secret. The physio says everyone at the club knew but that it didn't bother anyone. A big giveaway was a rotating cast of young male friends that were forever by the footballer's side. There was never a girl. Fashanu introduced his companions as his mates but he wasn't fooling Songhurst. It was obvious that they were rent boys but it didn't seem like the footballer really cared who knew. Songhurst believes that if Leyton Orient had been a First Division club then he might have acted differently. His so-called friends would have been picked up and plastered all over the news in a heartbeat. Playing in a lower league meant that his behaviour was, somewhat, below the radar and he was safe from prying eyes. At least that that's what Justin believed, anyway.

The only notable incident at Leyton Orient concerning Justin and his sexuality happened when the team was travelling home on the bus following an away game one Saturday. The captain at the time was John Sitton. According to Bill Songhurst, as he walked past Fashanu, Sitton asked: 'Come on then, are them rumours true or what?' Rather than retaliate like he had when Nottingham Forest's Kenny Burns had asked him the same question nine years earlier, Justin kept his cool. He turned to Sitton and replied: 'That's for me to know and you to find out.' Songhurst claims Sitton was lost for words and returned silently to his seat.

Songhurst was not only the club physio but also the resident joker. Since Fashanu also possessed a keen wit, they frequently engaged in amusing banter.

'One time Justin received a nasty cut to his lip and it was bleeding so badly that we called a doctor to give him some stitches. I grabbed the biggest forceps I could find and put on a pair of thick latex gloves. When the doctor asked me what I was doing I said: "Doctor, this guy is a homosexual who has been living in America. I'd advise you to put some thick gloves on too,"' Songhurst says.

Fashanu laughed and told the physiotherapist where he could stick the forceps. This particular incident shows that Justin's reactions to jokes about his sexuality depended on who was making them. Because he was comfortable with Songhurst the footballer accepted the teasing, but there weren't many other people who got away with the same, Pedro Richards to name but one. As it transpired, Fashanu secretly admitted to Songhurst that he was gay so that was probably another reason why he was okay with his jokes.

But behind the laughs Songhurst felt sorry for him. Fashanu appeared to be on a bit of a downer and a shadow of the man he'd once been. Not only was his knee injury holding him back in terms of pace, he often seemed melancholic. On top of that, Justin was also short of money. While he played for Orient, Fashanu rented a modest flat owned by a Greek businessman who also owned a well-known local Greek restaurant called The Apollo. The apartment was hardly luxurious and its bleak interior reflected the headspace Justin found himself in. It was depressing. The front window needed to be replaced one weekend after Fashanu returned home and smashed it in. According to Songhurst, it was not due to one of Justin's nightmares but the result of a pit of rage and shows just how unhappy the footballer was. Songhurst sensed that the footballer's relationship with his brother wasn't great and it was obvious there was no one in his family he could to talk to. Whenever he brought up the subject of John, Justin refused to talk about it. From what Songhurst could tell Justin had a much softer nature than his brother. He may have been a brute on the pitch sometimes, but he was a gentle giant off it. With all sorts of things going on in Justin's life it didn't come as any surprise to the physiotherapist when he found out that Fashanu looked to God for solace. As someone with a sports psychology diploma, Songurst recognised that people who feel despair often look for a higher power. Of course, Fashanu's own relationship with God was compromised by what he read in the Bible. The old conflict was still there.

In the spring of 1990, Fashanu spoke confidentially to Clark and Songhurst about his desire to come out publicly. The footballer said he'd been thinking about it for a long time but was, naturally, apprehensive. Just like Justin's friend Peter Tatchell had done years earlier, Clark and Songhurst laid out the pros and cons of coming out. Although Fashanu might find enormous personal relief in revealing the truth, Clark asked him whether he was prepared for the fall-out from the British tabloids that would attack like hungry sharks. Clark was concerned for the footballer's welfare but told Fashanu that if he chose to do it then the club would fully support him. After weighing up his options, Fashanu decided against it but told Clark he appreciated the support. Shortly after he made this decision the 1989/90 season ended, as did Fashanu's contract with Leyton Orient. Although he'd managed to play several games he'd lost a lot of his speed because of his injury and so Clark was forced to let him go. It was a big disappointment to the footballer who found himself searching for yet another club. Fashanu was probably also disappointed because he'd lost a close relationship with two people who supported him.

Unable to find another team in England willing to sign him, Fashanu looked overseas again. The footballer contacted the Hamilton Steelers, a team on the east coast of Canada based in a small city about an hour's drive from Toronto. Back in the Eighties, the Steelers were owned by Italian businessman Mario DiBartolomeo and the general manager/coach was a Scottish-born Canadian called John McGrane. While DiBartolomeo had never heard of Fashanu, McGrane certainly had. The Scottish-Canadian had spent most of his playing career in North America but was well acquainted with Fashanu's reputation and skill. He offered Fashanu a contract on the spot.

Once the deal had been hammered out, McGrane faxed a copy to Fashanu and mailed a one-way plane ticket from London to Toronto. The plan was for the footballer to arrive in Canada the following week, but when Fashanu received the plane ticket he was not happy about flying economy class. The GM told Fashanu that he wasn't dealing with an English First Division club and that the economy cabin was the best he could offer. Reluctantly, Fashanu acquiesced and the footballer ended up playing 16 games for the Steelers before agreeing to come back again the following season. If Fashanu was relieved that he was, at least, playing the sport he loved again, his happiness would be short-lived. Something he'd always feared was about to become a harsh reality and it would turn his whole life upside down.

The Truth is 'Out' There

FASHANU WAS staying at a hotel in Toronto in early October 1990 when he received a call that left the 6ft 2in striker quaking in his boots. A reporter with a British Sunday newspaper called to inform him that the paper was planning to run a front-page exposé. They knew he was gay and insisted they had the proof, though they refused to share the precise details of the supposed proof with Fashanu. Did he have any comments? Fashanu's heart hit the floor. All of a sudden, the opportunity to come out publicly in his own time had been snatched away. For years, Fashanu had contemplated revealing his secret and at one point had even approached Malcolm Doney. That obviously hadn't worked out and now it looked as if the whole thing was out of his hands. It was a cruel turn of events. Soon, the world would know he was gay and he had no control over it.

In a panic, Fashanu called the British sports agent Eric Hall for help. Nicknamed 'Monster', Hall was a brash and bullish agent who also worked in show business. He had a long list of clients and contacts in almost every field, particularly the media. Fashanu figured that if anyone knew what to do in his predicament then Hall would. He was right. After reprimanding the footballer for calling him in the early hours of the morning, Hall backed off when he heard how concerned the footballer sounded. Fashanu explained his dilemma and how the article could seriously affect his life. It was not only damaging but potentially embarrassing. Hall agreed. The agent told the footballer to remain calm while he made some calls. For someone who had previously been quite nonchalant about his open secret (some might say careless), Justin was beginning to realise the serious implications it could mean for his career. For many years now he'd felt like he'd been standing on a narrow precipice. While he'd often been tempted to take the plunge into the unknown below by revealing his secret he'd never actually done it, fearful of what might happen to him. Now he was being pushed and who knew how far he was going to fall.

Hall contacted Kelvin MacKenzie the hard-nosed editor of *The Sun* and a personal friend. After explaining the situation, MacKenzie made a suggestion. Why not run a front-page expose in *The Sun* instead? It would be more beneficial to Fashanu because the footballer would have control over what got published, plus MacKenzie would pay him. It was more than Fashanu would get at the rival newspaper. Hall relayed the offer to Fashanu who concurred. He didn't really have a choice. The story was going to get published regardless, so he might as well make some money out of it. While in later years Fashanu would earn a reputation for selling out to the tabloids, this particular instance was forced on him. Might this experience have set up his dirty habit for exploiting newspapers himself? It's certainly possible. The term agreed was £70,000 in return for an exclusive interview with the footballer about his secret life as a gay footballer. MacKenzie was a happy man. Justin Fashanu wasn't just any footballer. He was the first professional footballer in the whole world who was openly admitting he was gay. It was a massive story.

Knowing time was precious MacKenzie called one of his reporters in *The Sun's* New York office and told him to catch the next available flight to Toronto. The reporter was instructed to meet Fashanu at a hotel where they would stay the night and then fly over to London, together, first thing the next morning. *The Sun* reporter Allan Hall was a new recruit with the tabloid and the exclusive was his biggest assignment yet. Although he wasn't a huge sports fan he knew who Fashanu was and what a promising star he'd once been. The footballer's career had changed dramatically over the previous few years and Hall wondered whether Fashanu's secret might have had something to do with it. When Hall met Fashanu in the lobby of the hotel, he was struck by how calm the footballer appeared. For someone who was about to reveal his deepest and darkest secret to everyone he seemed amazingly relaxed.

Once the pleasantries between Hall and Fashanu were over they began the interview. MacKenzie had agreed to let the footballer dictate what he wanted in the upcoming articles but the editor was not a top dog in the British tabloid game for nothing. He wanted a few revelations in return. Fashanu was being paid a hefty bounty for the exclusive and Mackenzie was not going to settle for anything less than sensational. Fashanu would not disappoint. He began by telling Hall that the main point he wanted to get across in the article was that he was not interested in random, meaningless sex. What he really wanted was companionship, something previously unattainable because he'd kept his sexuality a secret. The footballer said that revealing the truth would be an enormous relief. One of the hardest aspects of life in the closet had been keeping his secret from teammates and that he'd often resorted to sneaking away after training sessions and matches to visit gay bars. Fashanu may well have sneaked off to gay bars but if he'd been trying to hide his secret from teammates he hadn't done a successful job. When he'd played for the Brickmen and Leyton Orient players from both teams suspected their teammate was gay because there was such a high turnover of pretty, young male companions by his side. It had been a classic case of 'don't ask, don't tell'. It's hard to believe that Fashanu was genuinely clueless. The footballer went on to tell Hall that he'd engaged in three-in-the bed romps with well-known MPs and pop stars. These claims seemed highly suspicious to Hall as the footballer wouldn't name the people he was referring to but *The Sun* news editor didn't mind. Following their flawed coverage of the Hillsborough tragedy, it was not as if the newspaper had a reputation to defend.

The next day Hall and Fashanu checked out of the hotel to catch their flight to London. Fashanu insisted *The Sun* fly him first class but MacKenzie refused. The footballer was told he'd have to settle for business class instead. At Toronto's Pearson Airport Hall says Fashanu wanted to make an international call and asked if he could borrow his corporate phone card. Reluctantly, the reporter handed it over. It would prove to be a costly mistake. A few hours later, the reporter and footballer were sitting on the plane and on their way to London. The countdown had begun to the revelation of Fashanu's sensational secret exposed for the whole world to see.

When they arrived in London the two men booked into the Waldorf Hotel in The Strand. It had been a long day and Hall told Fashanu he was retiring to his room and that he'd see him the next morning for breakfast. He told the footballer to get an early night himself since the next day was going to be a long one. Although the story was not due to be published for another two days there was more interviewing scheduled for the next morning. Fashanu, however, had no intention of getting an early night. It wasn't every day someone was paying to put him up in an expensive hotel in the centre of London and he was going to take full advantage of it.

The next morning Hall met up with a bleary-eyed Fashanu who'd obviously got to bed late. It seems incredible that despite facing one of the biggest days of his life Justin decided to hit the town instead of resting. While it might be true that he was only giving himself a much-needed distraction, it gives us a further insight into his complex personality. One moment he is panicking about the enormity of his situation only to blithely disregard it the next. I'd argue it shows that Fashanu was a man who loved to live in the moment and on the edge. While it appeared to Hall that Fashanu was being irresponsible, in Justin's mind there was nothing he could do to change his situation so he might as well enjoy it. Hall asked Fashanu more questions for the articles he was writing and a sports reporter from _The Sun_ turned up handing Fashanu a fistful of cash. Part of Fashanu's deal was to provide some stories for the sports pages of _The Sun_ and, apparently, he was being paid in advance. In Hall's opinion, this was not a wise move.

'Giving money was the worst thing you could have done with Justin because as soon as he got it he vanished into the night. The next morning I had written everything up and I am getting ten tonnes of shit from MacKenzie who wants to speak to Justin. When I called Justin's room no one answered, so I told MacKenzie who was not impressed. He was yelling: "What do you mean he's not fucking there? You're supposed to be minding him!" I went up and knocked on Justin's door and there was no answer, so I tried the door and it opened. As I walked inside, there was a big-mirrored wardrobe that looked back on the bed and in the reflection I could see two sets of feet poking out from under the covers. It turns out that Justin had only gone clubbing all night and brought back a rent boy. I told him: "For fuck's sake Justin, get that guy out of here. We've got a story to run!" Fifteen minutes later the kid was gone. I never said anything to the office and no one was any wiser,' Hall says.

We'll never know for sure whether Justin's companion was, actually, a rent boy but Hall says he seemed young. According to people like Ross Smith and Gregor Young, Fashanu always did have a penchant for younger looking boys and his taste had apparently not changed. After what he'd just witnessed, Hall wondered whether Fashanu really did want companionship or whether one-night stands were more his thing. With the story in place for the next morning's edition Hall waved Fashanu goodbye, wished him luck and headed to *The Sun* office.

After Hall's departure, Fashanu was left alone to face the daunting task of calling his brother and informing him about the next day's story. The younger Fashanu was still playing for Wimbledon and at the prime of his career. Justin didn't want him finding out he was gay directly from the newspaper but he knew it would be a difficult conversation. Not only was John about to find out that his brother was gay, but also that this fact would soon be common knowledge across the planet. As the first openly gay professional footballer anywhere, Justin was astute enough to realise the story would generate global headlines. While Justin knew that John would be unhappy he had no idea just how badly his younger brother would actually react. When he heard the news, John was shocked and angry. He begged his brother not to release the story and told him he would match whatever money *The Sun* was paying him. Justin told him it was too late for that leaving John furious. What the elder brother didn't say is that he had no choice in the matter as the story was being published regardless. While we don't know exactly why Justin didn't tell John the whole truth it seems likely that he wanted his younger brother to think that he had come out publicly on his own volition. Maybe it was because he wanted to show that he was in control of the situation. John told Justin he was making a big mistake and could not understand why his brother had chosen *The Sun* to reveal his story. Of all the tabloids in England, he felt it was one of the worst. Not only was it notoriously homophobic it was also considered racist. He believed that as a gay black man his brother could not have chosen a worse newspaper to trumpet his news.

After their conversation ended, John called Eric Hall and begged him to help quiet the story. He told the sports agent that Wimbledon was due to play Tottenham the following week in a local derby, and once news got out that Justin was gay John feared getting hammered by fans. No matter that his brother was about to put himself in the firing line.

Shocked at John's reaction, Hall said if anyone abused him then they could go to hell. Like Justin, Hall informed him that there was nothing anyone could do to prevent the story from coming out. It had already been written and would be hitting newsstands the next morning. Hall said the best thing John could do was brace himself. Later that day when a reporter from *The Sun* called John and asked him for a quote he reportedly said: 'Yeah, I have got something to say. When you write those billboards tomorrow that say: "Fashanu is Gay" make sure that you write: "Justin Fashanu is Gay."

One of the biggest stories in football finally broke on Monday October 22nd 1990, under a massive front page headline: '£1m SOCCER STAR: I AM GAY.'[30] Just under the headline were the words: 'Justin Fashanu confesses.' A photograph showed the footballer outside the Houses of Parliament in London with the phallic Big Ben in the background. The caption read: Commons romps with MP.' In typical tabloid style a smaller caption: 'Justin Fashan-ooh.' The story went:

'Soccer star Justin Fashanu confessed last night: "I'm gay - and I want everyone to know it." And Justin, who was Britain's first £1million black footballer, has revealed how he: Bedded a Tory MP and romped with him in the House of Commons.'

Inside the paper the story continued with the headlines: 'I Cheated on My Girl to Go Out with Men,' and: 'I Found God in a Garage.' *The Sun* had contacted Justin's ex-girlfriend Julie Arthurton for a quote. Surprisingly, given the way he'd treated her, Arthurton told the paper: 'I still love Justin. He's a nice person and we're still friends.' The article revealed how Justin had first discovered his sexuality at Nottingham's Part Two club and mentioned the homophobic incidents he claims he suffered at the hands of fellow footballers, Pedro Richards and Simon Stainrod. Justin also mentioned how he'd found God after a trip to get his car fixed at Terry Carpenter's garage in Nottingham.

The story wrapped up by promises of more sordid revelations the next day: 'Tomorrow: I slept with a married MP.' Over the course of the next week, *The Sun* squeezed as much mileage out of the story revealing how Justin had sex with a Conservative MP, a famous pop star and another footballer while he was living in Manchester. He revealed his torrid time and clashes with Brian Clough and how the Nottingham Forest manager had advised him to see a shrink.

As expected, the newspaper report caused an absolute sensation. Most people had no idea that Justin Fashanu was gay, despite the suspicions of many in the sport. So the story was indeed big news. While Justin fully expected John would distance himself from him after the revelations, he didn't seem to realise just how severe the younger Fashanu's reaction would actually be. In an interview with a weekly black newspaper called *The Voice* John publicly disowned Justin, calling him an outcast and a disgrace to the family: 'My gay brother has shamed the family name. If I saw him now I wouldn't be responsible for my actions.' He went on: 'I have no wish to contact Justin whatever. He is a stranger, an utter stranger.'[31]

The Voice editorial column blared: 'Soccer Star's Own Goal' and described Justin's revelations as tawdry: 'Telling the world you're gay is one thing, but claiming that your conscience and your faith in God led to the publication of such revelations is pathetic and unforgiveable.' A columnist with the same paper Tony Sewell joined in the condemnation calling Justin's actions an affront to the black community: damaging, pathetic and unforgivable.

'We heteros are sick and tired of tortured queens playing hide and seek around their closets. Homosexuals are the greatest queer-bashers around. No other group of people is so preoccupied with making their own sexuality look dirty,'[32] Sewell wrote.

To me, Sewell's comments are clearly homophobic. When I asked him to comment about his response to Fashanu's coming out he didn't respond. For someone who was once nominated as one of the 100 Greatest Black Britons Sewell should be ashamed. His comments were nothing short of outrageous and they cut Fashanu to the bone. But abuse from *The Voice* did not stop there. A Christian columnist called Marcia Dixon also put the boot in with studs raised. Her column was titled: 'Why Justin's Story Should Sadden Us All,' writing that the footballer had not completely accepted God and belonged to Satan. They were harsh, hurtful words from a woman of so-called faith. The fall-out between Justin and John continued when a television crew caught up with the younger brother at the Wimbledon training ground.

'He's come out publicly and said his sexual preferences. Every footballer doesn't come out and say they like women or they like men. That is nobody else's business, so now he will have to suffer the consequences. I wouldn't like to play or even get changed in the vicinity of him, that's just the way

I feel. So, if I'm like that I'm sure the other footballers are gonna be like that,'[33] John said.

If Justin was disappointed by Sewell's comments, he felt positively crushed by John's. While Justin had been hoping for a little verbal support from him, if that wasn't forthcoming then he might have at least expected silence. What's tragic is the Fashanus had been through so much together. Abandoned by their parents to fend for themselves at a Barnardo's home, they had only each other to rely on. It was them versus the rest of the world, a world they both, ultimately, conquered when they went on to forge careers in professional football. When they'd been kids Justin had always looked out for his brother and been his protector. Now that Justin needed John's support it was nowhere in sight. However, the elder Fashanu revealed later that his sister Dawn was supportive. His mother Pearl was okay with it and he hadn't spoken to Betty Jackson.

For those who knew Justin personally his admission provoked a mixture of shock, surprise and admiration. Some people who'd known his secret could not understand why the footballer had come out publicly in _The Sun_. Peter Tatchell was one of them. While he greatly admired the footballer's bold stance Tatchell was baffled by his choice of paper. In Tatchell's eyes, the right-winged _The Sun_ was one of most bigoted publications in England. When people asked him about it Fashanu said that if he'd come out in a serious newspaper then _The Sun_ would have been resentful and hounded him for the rest of his life. He also justified his decision with the argument that _The Sun_ was the newspaper most widely read by football fans. Of course Kelvin MacKenzie, Allan Hall and Eric Hall all knew different.

Former teammates of Fashanu's like Dave Bennett and Joe Royle were surprised by the news, but supportive of what they felt was a brave and noble decision. Several years earlier, Bennet had bet a hundred pounds with Forest's Viv Anderson that the rumours about Justin being gay were just that – baseless rumours. It looked as if he'd lost the wager after all. Other people from the football world claimed they were totally dumbfounded at the revelations. Justin's former manager at Norwich City, Ken Brown, said: 'Well, I still can't quite believe it. It just didn't make sense to me a fellow like that. Why does it happen? I couldn't tell you. It's a mystery to me.'[34] Football scout Ronnie Brooks took it one step further: 'There was certainly no indication, whatsoever, when he was a young man that there was any hint of any problem with his gender. None whatever.'[35]

Other football players like Mick Leonard, Peter Ward and Les Cleevely had heard about the rumours when they'd played with Fashanu in Nottingham, so they were less surprised. Over in America, Fashanu's former teammates in Los Angeles, John Britton and Bobby Ammann, were stunned. When they'd played together Ammann had always considered Fashanu one of his closest friends and was upset that the footballer had never said anything to him. After he heard the news Ammann called Justin right away. 'How come you didn't let me know? I feel like such an idiot. Here we are good friends and now I have all these people asking me questions and asking if I'm gay,' Bobby told him. Fashanu apologised and said he hadn't mentioned it because he thought it might have had a negative impact on their relationship. Ammann called Fashanu stupid for thinking that his admission would have changed anything. He didn't mind that Fashanu was gay, just upset he hadn't confided in him.

Fashanu told Ammann how confused he'd been about his sexuality his whole life. It had been a torment, especially since becoming a Christian. The footballer confirmed that he'd first begin to explore his homosexuality when he'd lived in Nottingham after he'd started hanging out at the nightclub, Part Two. The underground gay scene had been incredible in its freedom of expression and something he'd embraced wholeheartedly, at least in the beginning. The footballer disclosed that he'd attended some of the wildest parties with well-known celebrities where nothing was off limits. While that lifestyle was fun to begin with, Fashanu said it eventually began to take a mental toll and that's when he'd turned to Christianity. However, religion didn't change his feelings. Once he realised he was gay it was impossible to walk away from who he really was, even after God had entered his life. He said he'd tried but it was impossible.

To Ammann, it sounded as if Fashanu could have done with a listening ear, and the frustrating thing was the goalkeeper would gladly have provided both of his. He now realised why his friend had treated him so coldly when the pair had played together in Edmonton. Fashanu had obviously wanted his privacy. As well as Ammann's support, John Britton also called Justin and told him he was proud of him. In Baltimore, A.J. Ali felt the same way as Ammann. He admired Justin's bravery but was disappointed the footballer had not confided in him. Ali told him he was there if he needed anything. In LA, Neil Slawson was surprised but not shocked. Apparently, those rumours he'd heard had been true after all. He hoped his friend would now find more peace in his life.

After *The Sun* article was published Fashanu immediately contacted his spiritual mentor, J. John. Justin's news was a complete surprise to the Nottingham based preacher. J. John was sympathetic but as a Christian could not condone homosexuality. Fashanu was caught in an impossible position.

While many people generally applauded Justin's decision to come out publicly, some believed his claims of having sex with politicians and pop stars seriously undermined it. It made the whole thing seem slightly seedy. If Fashanu had chosen to come out in a more serious publication like *The Guardian* or *The Independent* then he might not have resorted to such sensational claims, but because he'd made a deal with *The Sun* it was like making a pact with the devil. Its readers demanded sensation and that is exactly what Fashanu gave them. Unfortunately, that also meant losing credibility. While there was some initial speculation about which politicians Justin claimed he'd slept with, people would learn later that the claims were false. Throughout the week after the news first broke *The Sun* squeezed as much juice as it could out of the story and ran a series of other articles on Justin's revelations. One headline that would not have improved his relationship with his brother was: "'I'll have to quit Britain!' That's what our kid John said when I told him I was gay.'[36]

A week after *The Voice* first assassinated Justin in its pages, there was such uproar against its sentiments from the gay and lesbian community that the publication was forced to do a spectacular U-turn. Threatened with boycotts from readers and advertisers, the paper posted the following on its front page:

'*The Voice* has received a number of complaints from the gay community who have suggested that our coverage of the recent Justin Fashanu story was irresponsible and gave the impression that *The Voice* is anti-gay. It goes without saying that *The Voice* is opposed to all forms of prejudice against any group in society because of their race, sex, religion or sexual orientation. We have examined our treatment of the story in question and we accept that in some respects it could be interpreted as homophobic. This was not our intention and we therefore regret any offence that may have been caused.'[37]

It was commendable the publication had, at least, acknowledged its errors. Three months later the editor was replaced and homophobic editorials duly banished. Sadly, there was no retraction or apology from Tony Sewell.

In the midst of the media circus surrounding the footballer's fantastic revelations, there was still the little matter of his career. Fashanu was due back in Canada the following season with the Hamilton Steelers and now that his secret was out the striker wondered whether the club still wanted him. Team coach John McGrane first heard about the revelations when Mario DiBartolomeo had stormed into his office a few days earlier. The club owner's face was ghost white. Clutching a copy of The Sun in his hands he shouted: 'Look at this!' before slamming the paper onto McGrane's desk. McGrane only had to read the headline to realise why his boss was so fired up: Justin Fashanu gay? McGrane couldn't believe it either. It was certainly a first in soccer. According to McGrane, DiBartolomeo was concerned the news could bring unwelcome attention to the club, but the Steeler's coach was not so convinced. Secretly, McGrane could not help admiring Fashanu. The footballer was only being honest about his life and McGrane knew plenty of other people in the sport who had much worse secrets. What was important was how the footballer performed for his new team. He told the team owner that as long as Fashanu promised not to bring any unwelcome attention to the club, the move could still be good for all parties. When McGrane spoke to Fashanu, he reprimanded the footballer for not giving the club a heads up. Fashanu giggled and apologised. He told McGrane it was something that he'd wanted to get off his chest for a long time plus he'd been paid well. McGrane explained that while the club was still willing to hire him Fashanu had to promise to keep his private life out of the spotlight. The Steelers coach said that he greatly admired the footballer's decision to come out but the owner of the club did not want him being a poster child for gay athletes, at least not while he was with the Steelers. Fashanu stopped giggling and agreed.

A fortnight after Fashanu's big news was broadcast around the world, the person who reported it, Allan Hall, got a call from his office. It was a lady from the accounts department who wanted to know why he'd spent thousands of pounds on calls through his corporate phone card. She was not happy. It was news to the journalist as he hadn't made one single call since arriving in London. When he explained as much the accountant told him: 'Well someone's been using it and you'd better figure out fast before MacKenzie finds out.' Hall was perplexed and tried to think who he'd lent it to. It didn't take him long to figure out the culprit: Justin Fashanu. The reporter had given him the card at Toronto Airport to make a call and the footballer must have written down the details. Incensed, Hall tried to get hold of Fashanu to give him a piece of his mind but, fortunately for Justin, could not get hold of him. The calling card was cancelled and, to this day, the journalist will never forget how brazen Fashanu had been to pull such a stunt. It reinforced Hall's view that there was a selfish and devious side to the player that wasn't cool at all.

Hall wasn't the only person after Fashanu. There were some angry folk at _The People_ who desired a word too. Back in 1982, the footballer had successfully sued the _Sunday People_ for thousands of pounds after it ran a story about him being gay which he claimed was false. It was quite obvious now that he'd been lying and _The People_ was demanding its money back. Reporter John Smith wrote:

'I don't doubt that Joystick Justin received a substantial fee for finally coming out of the closet. But before this two-faced tittle-tattler starts congratulating himself on a healthy bank balance I should warn him that we plan to take steps to ensure he returns every penny of the cash he screwed out of _The People_. [38]

Fortunately for Fashanu, no action was taken, but he'd certainly made some enemies in the world of newspaper publishing. _The People_ would eventually get its own back in spectacular and devastating fashion.

Breaking Free

ACCORDING TO those who knew him personally, Fashanu loved his newfound freedom. Not forced to hide his sexuality any more made him feel like his life had been unshackled. One of his friends is the former advertising director of *Gay Times* magazine, Terry Deal, who he met in early 1991. Deal says the early Nineties was an exciting time to be on the gay scene in London as there was a lot happening. A multitude of new gay bars and clubs were opening up everywhere, and you'd often see pop stars like Jimmy Sommerville or the Pet Shop Boys at the many events. Compton Street in Soho was also just starting to establish itself as the capital's gay centre. If you were on the A or B list like Deal, there was always a party to go to every night of the week if you wanted. It seemed that Justin Fashanu had picked the perfect time to come out and the perfect man with whom to share those good times.

Deal and Fashanu's paths first crossed in the Village West One bar in Soho. The advertising director had dropped in to see to the owner of the bar on business and found him talking to the famous footballer. As a football fan himself, Deal recognised Fashanu instantly. Ironically, Deal was a

Wimbledon supporter and had met John Fashanu too. After introductions and pleasantries were exchanged, Deal elbowed Fashanu in the ribs jokingly and told him he should give an exclusive interview with *Gay Times*. He was surprised when Fashanu asked for his number and promised he'd phone the next day at 2pm. Not thinking for a moment he'd ever hear from him, Deal was shocked when Fashanu actually called the following afternoon. When Deal looked at his watch it was dead on 2pm. He was impressed. Fashanu instructed him to jump into a taxi and meet him outside Earls Court an hour later. Sensing that an exclusive might just happen, Deal wasted no time. Grabbing his coat and wallet, he bolted out the door and flagged down the nearest cab. When the taxi reached the front of Earl's Court, Fashanu appeared from nowhere and jumped into the cab. Deal hadn't been dreaming after all and instructed the driver to head straight to the *Gay Times* office before Fash changed his mind. As a trained advertising director, not a reporter, this would be Deal's first interview and he hoped Fashanu would not hold back. Since *The Sun* article was first published eight months earlier, the footballer had said very little publicly about his decision to come out so the interview was a big coup for the magazine.

When the Dictaphone was switched on Fashanu did not disappoint. In fact, Deal could not believe how candid the footballer was. Fashanu told him that there were two reasons why he came out. The first was because the timing had seemed right. Fashanu said that over the years there had been many backdoor approaches made to him regarding his sexuality, and it had finally been time to stand up and be counted. When Justin talks about these 'backdoor approaches' one assumes he's alluding to the few times the media had tried to 'out' him, but rather than telling Deal he'd actually been blackmailed by a tabloid newspaper he gave another reason why he'd revealed all. He said that a young friend in Canada who was gay had committed suicide after his family could not come to terms with his sexuality. Fashanu said the boy's death made him realise that everybody should accept the responsibility of being truthful, and being open was better than hiding things. Of course, we know the real reason why Fashanu came out. It was an impressive story but not exactly true.

Deal asked the footballer why he'd chosen *The Sun* to publicise his homosexuality. Fashanu explained the tabloid was the newspaper football fans read the most therefore it seemed the sensible choice. He stated that if he hadn't chosen to run his story with *The Sun* then the paper would have picked it up and hounded him for the rest of his life. Fashanu would stick with this story in later years. He admitted that the stories *The Sun* published about him romping around with unnamed MPs, pop stars and other football players were untrue. While Justin made it seem as if *The Sun* had made up those stories however, it was actually the footballer himself who had mentioned them to Allan Hall when they'd met. He forgot to mention that part.

Another discrepancy in the interview concerns the footballer's career. Fashanu said the backlash that followed his very public coming out had greatly affected his earning capacity and that no club had offered him a full-time contract since. The truth was different. It was Fashanu's injured knee that was the problem, not his sexuality. No club was willing to risk signing him because he'd undergone several surgeries and had not played in England for three years. No one had been willing to take a chance on him. He'd recently tried out for a couple of English clubs but they hadn't rejected him because he was gay. It was his form that had been questionable and doubts about his knee. Despite the way he'd been treated, Fashanu said that he was confident that he would eventually be able to break back into the English football league. He also said something else that was interesting: 'I've made a lot of money in my career and I understand the shallowness of it. But money equals power and I want to use that power. I want to use it in a way that is helpful to other people. Keeping it to yourself is the most unsuccessful thing you can imagine.'[39] What's interesting about it is that Fashanu didn't have any money. He'd spent most of it on expensive surgeries in the United States and Canada and had even borrowed from his brother. Moreover, Fashanu was about to embark on a dark period in his life where he would rip people off rather than helping them. He'd already started this bad habit by fleecing Allan Hall and the Slawsons. Deal would see it first hand for himself the following year.

Fashanu said that out of his family only his sister was still talking to him and that his brothers Phillip and John were, noticeably, absent. He said John still believed he had let the family down. Justin said his brother obviously needed space but hoped he would get in touch soon: 'If you keep pushing people, sometimes you can drive them further away. The key is love and understanding. Sometimes, love can mean leaving people alone,' he told Deal.

Fashanu did not hold back about the vitriolic article that was written about him in *The Voice* newspaper. He was bitterly disappointed by the bigoted, prejudiced views and said it was time that black people realised homosexuality was not a white man's disease and something that also hit black families and lives too. The footballer also talked about being a Christian. He said that the most important aspect about Christianity is how much people care and love. It doesn't matter whether you have anal or vaginal sex, what matters is awareness of the thoughts behind what you do. 'Homosexuality is not a sin,' he told Deal, and if it were then millions of people were going to hell.

Gay Times editor John Marshall also joined the interview and asked Fashanu questions. Both Marshall and Deal were surprised when Fashanu agreed to have his photograph taken for the front cover. Being splashed on the front of any magazine means it will be staring at people from newsstands all over the country for months after. Here was someone who was definitely not afraid of letting the world know he was gay, Deal thought. Fashanu's interview would be published in July 1991 under the headline: 'Justin Fashanu: Soccer's Enigmatic Gay Star.' Chillingly, Marshall included the following words: 'He's as rare in the football world as wasps are in winter, but it's not clear if his story will end in triumph or tragedy.'[40] Those 25 words would come back to haunt everyone.

A week after they first met, Deal was at home one Friday night when Fashanu surprised him with another call. 'He told me he was going to the Fridge, a nightclub in Brixton, and asked if I wanted to go. I wasn't doing anything so I told him to meet me outside my house in Tooting. I was 32 at the time and living with a 23-year-old boyfriend. When Justin arrived and saw him, his mouth dropped open and he said: "Oh Terry, your boyfriend is so lovely. You are so lucky. You are on the gay 'A' list and I have to say I'm a little jealous." I've met a lot of famous gay people in my line of work and it didn't surprise me to hear he was envious. Some celebrities are paranoid under the surface and feel they can't lead the normal life that they would like to,' says Deal.

Over the next few months the two men forged a friendship that would last a couple of years, but Deal was under no illusion why Fashanu liked hanging around with him. As someone who was connected to the social scene, Deal was a ticket to some of London's hottest parties. It was VIP central all the way and Fashanu lapped it up. Whereas in the past Fashanu attended gay bars and clubs covertly, now there was no need for such secrecy. Deal described Fashanu as the ultimate gay ligger and someone who attended the opening night of absolutely everything. Deal didn't mind that he was being used as he had a great deal of respect for Fashanu. The footballer was good fun and gracious. He always had a smile on his face and had an incredible knack for remembering people's names. A year after the *Gay Times* article was published he sometimes dropped into the magazine's office and was still able to reel off everyone's names.

When it came to men Deal says that Fashanu was mainly interested in younger guys between the ages of 18-23: skinny, white, preppy looking men. Two of the footballer's conquests eventually included an ex-boyfriend of Deal's and a young man who worked in the office of *Gay Times*. When Deal spoke to one of the men who'd dated Fashanu he described the footballer as caring and affectionate but like a wet lettuce under the sheets. For someone who was so tough on the football field Deal was surprised at that revelation. Sometimes, Fashanu called Deal at his office to ask him for the telephone number of a model who was being featured in the latest *Gay Times* edition. He also wrote to the editor of a pornographic magazine for the same reason.

While the footballer was happy to tell anyone he was gay it gradually became apparent to Deal that, under the surface, Justin still had his problems. He wasn't convinced that the footballer was as free and happy as he sometimes made out.

Ultimately, Deal believes that Justin was lonely. He didn't seem to have a best friend and craved attention. He loved nothing more than hanging out at VIP bars along with other famous people and was obsessed with getting his face in as many newspapers and magazines as he could. If a photographer was present at an event Fashanu positively flaunted himself. Deal sensed his master plan was publicity and wondered if he might have been jealous of his brother's success in front of the TV camera. Deal noticed that Fashanu had a habit of dominating conversations and rarely spoke about himself. It was a good trick at keeping people at a distance and not revealing too much. It was the 'façade' in full effect and similar to what the Canadian footballer Gregor Young had said about Fashanu when they'd met in Edmonton. Deal rarely managed to breach the surface himself, but Fashanu did admit how badly he felt his brother was treating him. John was still refusing to speak to him but had 'allowed' him to continue contact with John's young niece, Amal. Justin absolutely adored her.

In relaxed mood at the City Ground, but the smiles masked a deep turmoil
and rift with manager Brian Clough that would become a chasm.

Fash in the danger zone and goalmouth action at the City Ground.

Exasperation: this picture sums up Justin's whole time with Forest. With his manager on his back, as well as some Forest fans, Fashanu was glad to make his escape to local rivals, Notts County in 1982.
Credit: John Lawson

Above: '*That Bloody Poofs Club*' is how Brian Clough famously described
Nottingham's Part Two nightclub. Justin spent many happy hours
inside its doors during the early 80s.
Below: A poster advertising Part Two shortly after it opened in 1981.
Credit: David Edgley

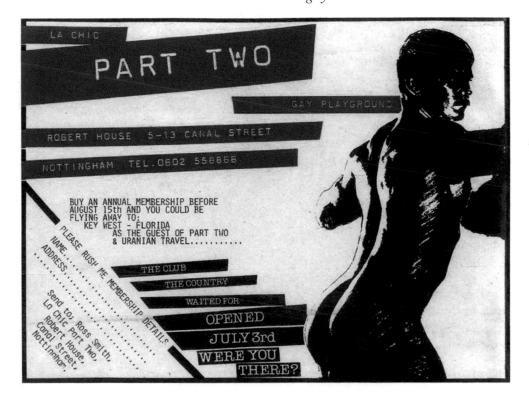

Justin with goalkeeper and
friend Les Cleevely.
Credit: Les Cleevely

Back to back with personal fitness coach, Osman Raif. This photo was taken inside
the footballer's home in The Park, Nottingham 1981. *Credit: Les Cleevely*

Despite his fame, Justin still found time to connect with family. Here the footballer shares some laughs with the Jackson clan (Edward, his wife Rachel, and their children plus friend). *Credit: Jackson family*

Dark days: Brighton, 1986. Despite suffering a career threatening knee injury, Justin still manages to crack open a smile in the home of his friend Kevin Wheeler. *Credit: Kevin Weaver*

Seeing the light: With his career in pieces, Justin turned even more to religion for guidance and solace. He attended church most days in Brighton. The footballer would soon leave the city for L.A. where he hoped cutting edge surgery might save his career. *Credit: Kevin Weaver*

Fashanu's American mate, Neil Slawson, hosted the footballer at his home in L.A. in 1987. Slawson became something of a confidante to Fash who was terrified his career might be finished. *Credit: Neil Slawson*

Above: When Slawson graduated from the L.A. Police Academy in 1988, he was proud Justin could attend the ceremony.
Below: Fash the Flash: When Slawson lent Justin his prized Mustang convertible it was only supposed to be for the night. He never saw it again. Fash always did like living life in the fast lane but it would come back to haunt him. *Credit: Neil Slawson*

Post surgery and Justin is back playing the sport he loves. Looking slightly gaunter, and sporting a slick haircut, the striker is determined to rekindle his ailing career.
Credit: Soccer Match

Fashanu reignites his career with L.A. based soccer team Autobahn FC. He's soon their top-scorer and looking to play at a higher level.
Credit: Soccer Match

Never mind the elbows! Fashanu shows he can still jump with the best of them despite his weak knee. Here he is playing for Canada's Edmonton Brickmen in the autumn of 1988. *Credit: Neil Slawson*

The Jackson clan visit Justin in Atlanta, Georgia. The footballer is working at a local YMCA after a spectacular fall from grace in Scotland. His smile hides a fragile psyche.
Credit: Jackson family

Happier times, Baltimore, USA, 1998. Justin shares a laugh with friend and Maryland Mania FC president, A.J. Ali and Ali's wife. A few months later Fashanu's life would be blighted by unimaginable controversy.
Credit: A.J. Ali

Ashton Woods Apartment Complex at 8465 Oakton Lane, Ellicott City, Maryland.
No one will ever know exactly what happened in apartment 2C on March 25th,
1998 but it would lead to tragic circumstances.
Credit: Stevey Long

The Justin Campaign: The organisation wants to see football and wider society value the contributions made by all people, regardless of their gender and sexuality. It's an ongoing battle.
Credit: Jason Hall

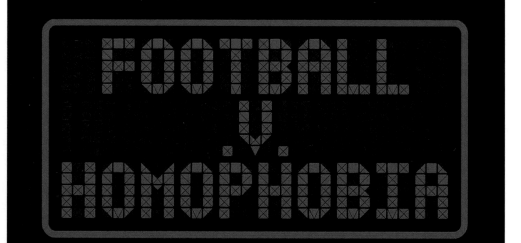

Football vs Homophobia: An international initiative opposing homophobia in football at all levels - from grassroots to professional clubs. Spread the word.
Credit: Jason Hall

Fighting the Cause: Jason Hall (pictured) and Juliet Jacques
both started *The Justin Campaign* in 2008.
Credit: Jason Hall

Political campaigner Peter Tatchell (centre) supporting the cause with Hall and the Justin Fashanu All-Stars team. Tatchell was one of Fashanu's close friends and confidantes. *Credit: Alan Quick*

Alan Quick (right) met Justin in Torquay in 1992. They became instant friends. Quick is an active member of *The Justin Campaign* and exhibits a huge collection of Fashanu related memorabilia across the country. *Credit: Alan Quick*

For a short time after his big announcement, Fashanu dated a London based actor and singer called Mark Anthony who he met in London nightclub, Kinky Gerlinky. One of Anthony's flat mates was Brett Gordon who got to know Fashanu quite well. Gordon, who's straight, says whenever they went out Justin was incredibly generous and always insisted on paying for everything. The footballer said that although he'd found it tough when he'd first come out, overall, he was happy with his decision to tell the world he was gay. He told Gordon it felt like a huge weight had been lifted off his shoulders. Fashanu's boyfriend was a lot younger than Justin and, along with his friends, worshipped the ground he walked on. Gordon says Fashanu revelled in the adulation. As far as Fashanu's career was concerned, he spent a quick spell with Southall FC in west London before heading back to the one place where his talents really were appreciated: Canada.

Happiness vs Heartache

IN JUNE 1991, Fashanu jumped on a plane and headed to the east coast of Canada. A brand new season with the Hamilton Steelers loomed. Fashanu didn't know it but right after news of his sexuality broke, the Steeler's general manager and coach, John McGrane, had met with his players and asked if any of them had objections to a gay footballer joining the team. No one raised their hand. McGrane was impressed. To the players, performance was the only thing that mattered. When Fashanu arrived in Hamilton the Steelers arranged a press conference to give local reporters a brief opportunity to ask their new star some questions. Naturally, the footballer's recent revelations were a hot topic. Justin told them that his decision to share he was gay had been long overdue and now his secret was out he was free to concentrate on winning games for the Steelers.

True to his word, Fashanu worked hard in training and in matches. McGrane was instantly pleased with what he saw and even happier when Fashanu started calling him 'boss.' Not even Larry Lloyd had been afforded that honour. McGrane described his new recruit as friendly, respectful and approachable. McGrane never hesitated to ask Fashanu for tactical advice and within a few weeks he promoted the footballer to captain. One bit of good fortune for Fashanu was his knee wasn't causing any serious problems. On the odd occasion when the joint did flare up rest and ice were the only remedies required. A lot of the football matches were played on grass, not artificial turf, and that helped as there was less impact on the footballer's body.

The Steelers coach had decided that the best way to deal with Fashanu's sexuality was to be completely open about it and inject a bit of humour into proceedings. With that in mind, when Fashanu first turned up for training McGrane presented all the team with their own personal soap-on-a-rope. The players were informed that if anyone happened to drop their bar of soap in the shower then they would be taking their lives into their own hands. It was clearly insulting. It's impressive Fashanu managed to keep his composure. McGrane says Justin was actually relieved that his sexuality was not going to be an issue with anyone and didn't seem to mind a little banter.

McGrane also introduced something called the 'yellow bib award.' At the end of each week, the player deemed to have performed the poorest in training was awarded a yellow bib that he would have to wear on the Friday night before game day. If it happened to be an away game with the team on the road for the night, then the recipient of the bib would have to room with Fashanu. While it may sound like an insult to Justin, McGrane insists this joke was a great way of releasing the tension and was well received by everyone, Fashanu included. Justin might well have laughed along on the surface, but I doubt he was smiling inside.

Fashanu might have got on with McGrane, but the same could not be said about the footballer's relationship with Mario DiBartolomeo. According to McGrane, his boss and the team's newest recruit had a classic personality clash and sometimes the fall out incurred wasn't pretty to watch. Case in point was shortly after Fashanu had first turned up. According to McGrane, when Fashanu first arrived in Hamilton DiBartolomeo lent him his Mercedes to drive. In the early Nineties, there were less than half a million people living in Hamilton and not many of them drove a brand new Merc. There weren't many gay bars in town either: just one, in fact, located right in the centre of town. The bar wasn't well publicised and if you didn't know it was there you'd probably have driven right past it. But it didn't take Justin long to locate it and his boss' Mercedes was soon parked regularly outside the front entrance. When he'd lived in England, Fashanu had never shown much interest in respecting parking regulations and it seems he didn't care for them much in Canada either. Parking his car on the sidewalk was no big deal in his reasoning. Of course parking attendants beg to differ, even in Canada, and Fashanu's indifference soon resulted in a stack of tickets. As the unpaid fines began to pile up, an officer from the local police force felt it necessary to contact DiBartolomeo and ask him when he was planning to pay up. The Steelers owner demanded to know what tickets and the officer calmly explained: the one's accrued outside 'the bar.' What the businessman did in his private life was no one's concern, but the cop recommended he pay the tickets before tongues wagged. According to McGrane, DiBartolomeo was none too happy and Fashanu was given the dressing down of his life when the club owner eventually caught up with him.

Generally speaking, Fashanu was good at keeping his private life under wraps while he was living in Hamilton and there were only a couple of instances when McGrane felt it necessary to have a word with his captain. The first was during a training session when a muscular bald guy wearing a pink tank top and spandex shorts showed up at the touchline. The players were involved in a scrimmage and whenever Fashanu touched the ball the man shouted: 'Go, Justin, go!' It was a little disconcerting for the rest of the team, especially McGrane.

'When I first spotted the man I thought to myself: "No, that's not possible. He's far too big and strong to be a gay." However, when he started jumping up and down on the sideline like a big girl and cheering Justin on I realised that he was obviously a friend of his. All the guys were looking at each other wondering what the hell was going on. I took Justin aside and said: "Don't tell me he's with you?" When Justin nodded I said: "Well get him the fuck out of here because it's a distraction and I don't want that shit around here." What made matters worse was that there was a local reporter watching the training session who'd noticed the man himself and was trying to interview him,' McGrane says.

You can't help wondering if McGrane would have done the same if his captain was David Beckham and it was Posh who was cheering from the sidelines. I doubt whether she would have been given her marching orders. It seems that the Steeler's players and coach dealt with Justin's sexuality at arm's length. While they were fine talking and joking about it they really didn't want to see or deal with it first hand and couldn't handle the gritty details. What seems to confirm this is another occasion when McGrane felt impelled to reprimand Fashanu. It was when the team was on the road for an away match. The captain had a room of his own at the hotel and the next morning a few of the players complained that they'd heard strange noises coming from Fashanu's room the whole night. McGrane pulled the footballer aside and told him to be more discreet. If it had been another player who'd had sex with a woman then he might have got a slap on the back instead for his efforts. Fashanu's sexuality was clearly met with double standards when it came to his teammates.

Other than these two instances McGrane can't recall any disciplinary problems with Fashanu and really liked him. He found the footballer genuine and someone who always stuck up for his players. The Steelers coach also found Fashanu intriguing. It was obvious the footballer had some demons inside him that only someone in the same circumstance would truly understand. After his very public outing, it seemed he was happier but it was difficult to tell because Fashanu was good at hiding things: 'When you hide things from people like Justin did then it's difficult to have close friendships. You can't be real with them when you are withholding things. That's probably why Justin felt so alone and why he didn't develop many real friends here,' McGrane says. Although he only knew Fashanu for a short period, McGrane has one of the most perceptive analyses of Justin's personality. As the world's first coach of an openly gay professional football player, the Scot says he learned a lot of things about himself too. Before they'd met, McGrane admits he was slightly homophobic, but after he worked with the footballer that quickly changed. In time, if anyone made a homophobic comment about Justin then the coach was the first to admonish them.

Ultimately, Fashanu's time with the Steelers eventually ended prematurely when McGrane announced the following year that he was leaving the club. After a string of poor results DiBartolomeo informed the coach that he wanted to be part of the team selection process. The owner may have been a successful businessman but he knew nothing about the intricacies of football and McGrane told him as much. His resignation followed. After announcing his departure to the team at the end of a training session Fashanu immediately stood up and said that he was leaving too: 'You're the gaffer and you should be picking the team, not the owner,' the striker proclaimed. It was a bold stance and, to McGrane, just showed the measure of the man. No one else displayed such loyalty. Fashanu's move might have been commendable, but he must have realised that his time with the Steelers could potentially be over too. DiBartolomeo wasn't exactly Fashanu's number one fan so you can't help thinking there was a little bit of pragmatism involved in Justin's decision. McGrane was secretly pleased that Fashanu was publicly supporting him but concerned the footballer might not find another club. He needn't have worried. A few weeks later, Fashanu signed for the Toronto Blizzard where he played out the remainder of the season. For McGrane it would be the last time he worked for a professional soccer club. After his stint with the Hamilton Steelers ended he went on to open his own soccer academy.

In a bitter twist of destiny the paths of Fashanu, McGrane and DiBartolomeo all crossed again a few weeks later, but not in good circumstances. According to McGrane, Fashanu was playing for the Blizzard against The Steelers at Hamilton and a friend of McGrane's invited the former coach to watch the action. Sitting in the stands McGrane was pleased to see the striker was on good form and still giving defenders a hard time. McGrane says that DiBartolomeo was also watching from the press box and, incredibly, began heckling Fashanu during the second half. Whenever the striker touched the ball he unleashed a torrent of abuse. The comments were loud enough for McGrane to hear them from where he sat several metres away. According to McGrane, it soon became obvious that Fashanu had heard them too, because as the game progressed, he began to get noticeably flustered. No sooner had the final whistle sounded the footballer sprinted across the pitch, jumped over the billboards and into the stands. As he ran up the steps towards the press box where DiBartolomeo was standing it was obvious what was on his mind. McGrane says the look on Fashanu's face indicated he wanted to rip DiBartolomeo's head off. Realising his safety was in serious danger, McGrane says that DiBartolomeo dived into the press box and locked all the windows and doors. It was just in the nick of time too. When Fashanu got there seconds later, he tried to hammer the door down and it took several people to restrain him. McGrane says that if the footballer had managed to break down the door there is no doubt he would have done serious damage to DiBartolomeo. After a minute or two, Fashanu managed to regain his composure and walked away towards the dressing room. It was an ugly scene sparked by a series of ugly comments. When McGrane caught up with Justin later the striker was understandably upset, hurt and embarrassed. With tears in his eyes, he told McGrane that no one deserved that kind of treatment. This incident was also confirmed by some Steelers fans on a Canadian soccer website. McGrane eventually said goodbye to Fashanu and it would be the last time the two of them would meet. It was the tenth and final game Fashanu played for the Blizzard before he headed back to England where yet another uncertain chapter awaited him.

The Toast of Torquay

WHEN FASHANU returned to the UK in the autumn of 1991, the 30-year-old had bounced between three countries and played for a multitude of clubs, all within the space of a few years. But if he hoped for some normality in his life his nomadic existence would only continue. In October, Fashanu was signed on a match-to match basis with Newcastle United but only got the chance to play twice before his services were terminated by manager, Ossie Ardiles. The footballer's second and final match was against Peterborough United and his friend from Christians in Sport Graham Daniels watched from the stands. Daniels had been hoping to catch up with Fashanu after the match was over, but it was impossible to get near him. A throng of reporters was eagerly trying to get a quote from him about his decision to come out. A year on and it seemed the player's sexuality was still big news.

When it became obvious that no other First Division teams were going to sign him, Fashanu approached lower level clubs and soon found himself at Leatherhead FC in Surrey. After several games the striker was on the move again, this time to the picturesque south west of England. The chairman of Torquay United, Mike Bateson, was looking for a marquee player and Fashanu fitted the bill perfectly. After a day of negotiations at one of Torquay's top hotels the footballer was offered a one-year contract at the beginning of December. The pressure was now on. It had been 18 months since he'd last played regularly in England and it was impossible to predict how his knee would hold up. As if that wasn't enough, there was also the little matter of his sexuality. The world's first openly gay professional footballer was still making headlines and there was no telling how the fans would react. History was in the making.

One person who didn't mind whether Fashanu was straight, gay, bisexual or anything else was Bateson. It was he and club secretary Dave Turner who had signed the footballer and both were convinced they'd made the right choice. Bateson respected Fashanu, not only as a player, but someone who had taken a huge career risk by admitting he was gay. It was an admirable decision. As a successful businessman, the Gulls' Chairman knew a thing or two about risks and was wise enough to realise that you never got anywhere without taking a few. Of course, he was also shrewd enough to know that risks could sometimes backfire and he hoped Fashanu didn't turn out to be one that did.

Being a businessman, Bateson hadn't signed Justin Fashanu from the goodness of his heart and expected something in return. In Fashanu's case he was hoping the footballer would boost ticket sales. The striker's wages were £1500 per week, three times higher than the club's previous record for player pay, meaning the only way to keep him was to sell more tickets. When Bateson hammered out the contract he learned that the footballer was no pushover when it came to negotiating. By the end of the meeting, Justin had not only convinced Bateson to shell out a bumper wage packet but pay him 50 per cent on any future transfer fee. As a sweetener, Fashanu also persuaded the chairman to throw in a black XJS convertible. When the meeting was over Bateson had a strange feeling like he'd just been fleeced. The footballer had been adamant about his demands and refused to budge: 'I have to look after Justin Fashanu,' he'd said.

Before the contact had been finalised, the Torquay United chairman had spoken to the players to find out whether any of them objected to Justin joining the ranks. Bateson knew that there was a big difference between thinking a person might be gay and someone who had openly come out. This was extremely new territory as far as professional football was concerned and who knew how a player might react? There was a chance someone might feel uncomfortable changing in the same dressing room as Justin or sharing a room with him on the road. To the chairman's relief there was not a single objection from anyone in the team. On the contrary, the players announced they were delighted at the prospect of playing alongside Justin. As a young team the players realised that it was a great opportunity to learn from a more experienced player. It was just like the reception Fashanu had experienced in Hamilton, and impressive that the Torquay players were more focused on playing better and getting results than on the sexuality of their newest recruit. As professionals, they acted accordingly. Bateson was pleased that his striker's sexuality was not going to be an issue, at least not with the players. As far as the fans were concerned, that was a different matter.

With everything seemingly in place, Bateson was eager to squeeze as much publicity as he could out of his new acquisition. Getting his money's worth was his number one priority and so the chairman arranged for Justin to sign his contract in front of the home fans when Torquay played Bournemouth. The deal was sealed at half time and as Justin ran on to the pitch, pen in hand, there was a mixture of cheers and howls from the crowd. Aside from a few catcalls, the reception from fans was respectful. Like the Torquay players, the real fans were only concerned about how Fashanu played. They paid to see good football and nothing else.

It's fair to say that Torquay United had been going through something of a rollercoaster ride since Bateson had become chairman 18 months earlier. Three managers had come and gone and there were also allegations in the local press that some of the club's players were partying too much. Incredibly, despite the turmoil, Torquay had managed to win promotion. This meant that when Justin Fashanu touched down at Plainmoor the dizzy heights of Division Three football beckoned. Albeit faintly.

Since Fashanu didn't know a soul in Torquay when he first arrived, Bateson paid for him to stay at a four-star hotel until he found his own place. When the bill arrived a few weeks later, Bateson was shocked to find that Fashanu had been charging him for absolutely everything. There was even a bill from a local taxi firm that had fetched him newspapers. It really shouldn't have come as too much of a shock considering what had happened a week earlier. The footballer had made the headlines after walking into the local River Island store and dropping thousands of pounds on clothes. Bateson would come to learn that money ran through the footballer's fingers fast. It had been more than a decade since Fashanu had first turned professional and he had yet to master the art of saving money. Fortunately for the chairman's wallet, Fashanu only remained at the hotel for a few weeks before moving into an apartment overlooking the ocean along the town's fashionable Marine Drive. Bateson was glad that Fashanu had found his own place, less because of the expense and more because it meant the footballer was putting down some roots and appeared serious about staying.

After Fashanu had sorted out his digs it was time to do what he was getting paid for: play some football. The striker made his home debut at Plainmoor against Preston in December. Not surprisingly, the world's first openly gay football star attracted a big crowd. It wasn't just the number of fans that had increased, so too had the number of journalists eager to see what kind of reception he received. Despite some cat calls the reaction from both sets of fans was warm and courteous. There were no homophobic chants or any visible hostility towards Fashanu. The game wasn't a classic by any stretch, but the striker put on a solid performance that helped the Gulls clinch a 1-0 win over their northern opponents. Although he didn't score, Justin worked hard enough to quiet the small section of Torquay United fans who believed he was no longer fit enough to play competitive English football and that he was going to be an expensive failure. When Justin walked back into the dressing room at the end of his first game for Torquay he must have felt incredibly relieved. He'd managed to get through his first game unscathed. He was still upset at how his big news had been received generally, and it would have been too much if his home fans had been abusive too.

According to Bateson, Fashanu's fellow teammates had decided that the best way to deal with Justin's sexuality was the direct approach. When their new striker walked into the dressing room his teammates grabbed their backsides with both hands. It was exactly the same thing that had happened back in Hamilton. While Fashanu laughed along and appeared unfazed by the comments you have to wonder how much they hurt him. Being singled out because you had a bad game or scored an own goal is one thing, but receiving comments about your sexuality is another. Of course, Justin knew there was no use fighting it.

One hint that Fashanu was not entirely comfortable with the comments was that he often dressed in the referee's room, preferring to get ready for a game alone. It had nothing to do with being a prima donna so the only conclusion is that there was some unspoken tension about his sexuality, at least as far as he was concerned. Banter aside, the Torquay players and management actually all looked up to Fashanu and when he wasn't in the team due to injury then he was sorely missed. He was a key player with many of the set moves centered round him. Fashanu always slathered himself with baby oil before a match and the ritual amazed Bateson. When he asked him about it the footballer replied: 'Packaging Mr Chairman, packaging.' There's no obvious reason why Fashanu felt the need to apply so much oil. It would have certainly made it more difficult for defenders to grab on to him but it was most likely down to good old-fashioned vanity. As well as the oil, Fashanu made a point of tucking his socks into his shin pads to give himself a gladiatorial look. Unlike a real gladiator, Justin didn't need a sword as his elbows were just as lethal.

Unfortunately, when it came to the footballer's sexuality with away supporters it was a different matter. To them, Fashanu's recent revelations were too good a target to ignore and one they exploited with vicious intensity. While Fashanu obviously expected some remarks nothing could have prepared him for the abuse he faced in Torquay's game against Fulham. It was only his second match for the Gulls and from the moment he ran on to the pitch the hostility was unrelenting. Insults rained down on the poor footballer: 'You fucking poof!' 'Faggot!' The horrific name-calling was coupled with homophobic chants: 'He's bent, he's queer he takes it up the rear, Fash-anu, Fash-anu.' It was particularly nasty when the footballer was near the sidelines as some fans stood up and openly spat insults at him. You'd like to think that if a fan sitting next to you shouted similar obscenities at a gay professional footballer today then you or a fellow supporter would tell them to shut up. Back in the early Nineties that wasn't the case. Justin Fashanu was considered fair game. Football fans targeted Justin's sexuality in the same way that fans abused Britain's first black players a decade earlier. The sole object was to target what they perceived to be a player's weakness and attempt to distract him accordingly. In Fashanu's case they hoped to make him lose his cool. Local Torquay sports reporter Dave Thomas was at the Torquay/Fulham game and says it was sickening to hear. He felt very bad for the footballer. Here was someone who'd been treated as a hero at Norwich City, and now he was being treated like a leper. To add insult to injury, Torquay went on to lose 2-1. Unfortunately, if Justin thought that experience was bad he hadn't seen the worst yet.

In light of the disgraceful reception he'd received, it's a testament to Fashanu's character how he responded. Rather than let his detractors affect him he was more determined than ever to play well. Not long after the Fulham game, Torquay took on local rivals Exeter City, and it was Fashanu who scored the only goal of the match: a wonderful strike from ten yards out. It marked his first goal in the English league for six years.

Sadly, Fashanu's next home game against West Bromwich Albion would be marred by more sickening homophobic behaviour from away fans. In the Nineties, a section of West Brom fans were notoriously racist, so when it came to gay, black Justin Fashanu they were literally rubbing their hands. No sooner had the Torquay striker run on the than field he came under fire. A barrage of insults reigned down on him, along with bananas. Following footballer John Barnes' lead a few years earlier, Justin picked up one of the bananas, peeled it and took a huge bite. It was a smart response. Despite a few hard challenges on opponents early on in the game, Fashanu resisted the temptation to get sent off. Some West Brom fans might have been giving him hell but he wasn't about to make their day by being shown the red card. Rather than losing his head, Fashanu channelled all the aggression he felt building up inside into his football. Using the hateful comments to spur him on, Fashanu found the ultimate way to silence his detractors: a stunning header that won the match. The glorious goal came towards the end of the game, and as the ball flew past the helpless West Brom keeper he wasn't the only one left open-mouthed: so too were the away fans. Savouring the moment Justin ran up to away stand, turned his back to them and wiggled his butt under their noses. It was a truly wonderful moment. Thomas was pleased that Justin had managed to keep his head and made his point the best way he knew: with his head.

Unfortunately, when the Gulls played West Brom away the following month, Fashanu could not contain his anger. Once again, homophobic and racist comments were the order of the day from a section of home fans. As the level of abuse towards the player intensified, so did the footballer's rage. Fashanu couldn't directly fire his anger back at the crowd so he aimed his frustrations on the nearest thing: his opponents. Elbows and studs were soon flying. After one dirty foul too many Fashanu was eventually shown a red card and ordered off the pitch. As the footballer made his way back to the dressing room for an early shower, his pain was plain to see. For the most part, Fashanu had always enjoyed a good relationship with fans therefore this kind of reception was completely alien to him. As a sensitive soul the abuse cut deep. Torquay lost the match 1-0.

While away supporters occasionally gave Fashanu abuse, one thing that wasn't giving him strife was his knee. Despite training and playing every week it was still holding up and that in itself was a relief.

While Fashanu was an enigma to most people at Torquay United he was an enigma that especially intrigued Thomas. The reporter suspected that the public persona he put on show was just that: purely a façade that concealed a more sensitive soul. Thomas always travelled with the Torquay team on away games and often sat next to Fashanu. Despite getting to know him, Thomas says he only managed to penetrate so far before the footballer clammed up or changed the subject. Getting through was a near impossible task but he respected Justin's boundaries and didn't try to push him. Another person who couldn't peel away Justin's layers was the Torquay youth team coach, Paul Compton. While Compton considered himself a good friend, he too says he could only get so deep with the footballer. Fashanu always tried to portray that everything in his life was okay. He'd often tell Compton: 'Always make sure people see that life is good for you, always.' It's a good indication of how Fashanu's internal defence operated. Some of the Torquay players joked that Justin would have made a good poker player.

Two people who often sensed Fashanu's insecurities were Bateson and his wife, Sue. They knew he didn't have many friends in town and so regularly invited him to their home for dinner. Although the couple never managed to delve that deeply into his psyche, there were some animated discussions about life and the universe. Fashanu's faith was always one hot topic.

'Religion was always a subject we argued a lot about. He was always going on about Jesus and God and I used to tell him that he was talking bollocks. I didn't believe he was serious about it. He only talked about religion because it sounded like the right thing to be talking about,' Bateson says. John Britton would, undoubtedly, agree.

On the odd occasion, Fashanu lowered his guard and opened up about some of the things that were bothering him in life. His main concern was his relationship with his younger brother that was still in tatters and causing him pain. Justin could not understand why John still refused to speak to him and he longed for them to reconcile. Justin seemed so low around Christmas 1991 that it prompted Sue to contact John herself. When she got hold of the Wimbledon footballer she begged him to call. She told him: 'Look, you chaps are brothers and blood is thicker than water. You both need to speak.' John's reply was short and to the point: 'Yes, but you can't choose your brother can you?' Despite his ambivalence something obviously resonated because around midnight on Christmas Eve the Bateson's phone rang. On the line was an ecstatic Justin who announced that his brother had called and they'd had a long chat. In tears, he said that it was the best Christmas present he could have wished for.

Torquay United's performance on the field, however, was enough to bring Bateson to tears. In a surprise move he asked Fashanu if he would consider taking on the role of assistant to manager, Ivan Golac. Since Fashanu had never managed a team before it was risky. It was a surprise to Justin, too, but he happily accepted. He knew his career as a player would not last forever and team management seemed the obvious succession. But the move was not enough to stop the club from being relegated. It was a disappointing blow for Bateson who had obviously hoped for a much better finish. As the team went down Ivan Golac left and the chairman promoted Compton as Fashanu's equal as joint assistant managers. In his new role, Fashanu would continue playing but also assist with training and team selection. From Bateson's perspective, he was giving him a chance to prove himself and if it worked out then maybe there was a long-term future for him at the club in management. In Fashanu's eyes, Bateson was giving him more responsibility and that in turn deserved a pay rise. When the striker knocked on his office door asking for a hefty salary increase, therefore, the chairman could not help being disappointed. Yet again, it seemed that the only thing that really mattered to the footballer was money. While a modest rise was one thing the increase Fashanu wanted was something else. From Bateson's point of view, Fashanu didn't seem to appreciate that opportunity is sometimes more valuable than anything else.

Off Target

WHEN THE new football season started in August 1992, there was a fresh sense of optimism at Torquay United. Even though the club was now playing in a lower division, the fans and players believed that the new management team of Fashanu and Compton would help the club vie for promotion. Fashanu was enthusiastic too, but as the months progressed it quickly became evident that his heart was no longer in things. His main interest in playing football was, seemingly, replaced with a desire to party. Whenever there was a celebrity event happening in the capital he made a point of attending, especially if his friend Terry Deal had arranged it. Deal was still Fashanu's main meal ticket as far as glitzy parties were concerned. As assistant manager and a player, Justin should have been working even harder than the previous season but this wasn't the case. Thomas says that the striker's football became second rate and he only seemed to try if he thought a scout from another club was watching. Bateson also noticed a diminished sense of fervour from his striker. He always believed that if Justin put as much energy into his football as he did with his appearance before each game then he'd look more like the million-pound player again of old.

On the occasions when Fashanu did make an effort the fans were treated to rare glimpses of brilliance. Torquay United's away game at Doncaster

Rovers was a good example. The ball appeared glued to his feet and defenders could get nowhere near him. The magic had momentarily been re-ignited and he scored two amazing goals, helping the Gulls win the game 3-2. At the final whistle Fashanu was the hero of the day. Thomas watched the game and when it was over he waited for Fashanu outside the dressing rooms. Doncaster's stadium Belle Vue didn't really reflect its name back in the Nineties with a depressing feel to the place that matched the Doncaster sky. The dressing rooms were in dire need of attention with paint peeling from the walls and musky odour in the air. When Fashanu walked out the doors the contrast could not have been starker. Walking tall after his killer performance and wearing a designer suit, he looked and smelled like a million dollars. As he walked towards Thomas a group of children ran up to him and clambered for his autograph. Fashanu seemed surprised but happily obliged. When he'd played for Norwich City he'd signed a lot of autograph books but times had changed. Sitting down next to Thomas on the team bus Fashanu was positively glowing: 'Wasn't it great all those kids waiting for me? Just fantastic!' he chirped. It was definitely one of Fashanu's better days at Torquay United and confirmation to Thomas that what the footballer really wanted in life was to be loved. If that's true then the irony is that most of his other performances for Torquay didn't reflect that desire. The Torquay fans would dearly have loved Justin more if he'd only tried harder. Sadly, yet again, Fashanu seemed intent on sabotaging another promising future.

Terry Deal watched a few Torquay United games and says exactly the same as Thomas. When Fashanu made an effort he was head and shoulders above the opposition and a force to be reckoned with. But these occasions were getting rarer. One thing Deal was impressed with, generally, was the reaction Fashanu got from supporters. Apart from a few catcalls and homophobic comments directed at the striker at the start of games, Deal says the abuse was minimal. As a gay football supporter standing in the middle of the terraces Deal didn't feel intimidated or threatened by the name calling at all. He knew what some football fans could be like and was surprised there wasn't more heckling. When Deal met up with Fashanu after one home game the footballer introduced him to his new personal assistant. The assistant was a camp 19-year-old boy who was clearly more than just a PA (certainly in Deal's view.) Deal was astonished at how brazen Fashanu was. He and the boy appeared glued at the hips, and the footballer didn't seem to care what people thought. The PA in question was, actually, a live-in assistant who Fashanu had found after advertising for one in *Gay Times*. Of course, Justin didn't tell Deal that.

If there was one place Fashanu was always guaranteed a great reception, at least on Tuesdays, it was at a nightclub in Exeter called Boxes. On every other night of the week Boxes was just an average club that attracted an average crowd, but Tuesdays was gay night. The DJ and promoter Alan Quick says that when Justin first turned up at the club the footballer was practically mobbed:

'Justin showed up out of nowhere in his Jaguar and caused quite a stir. He parked his car right outside the club on double yellow lines and just walked in. It was a bit cheeky really but we didn't mind because it was Justin Fashanu. When he walked inside the whole blooming club went mad. Well, you can imagine can't you? Complete bedlam!' says Quick.

Since his early clubbing days at gay haunts in Nottingham, Fashanu had, apparently, not lost his flair for an entrance or his disregard for parking regulations. While there were a few gay bars in Torquay and a gay club called Rocky's, Fashanu never ventured inside because they were a little too close to home. He'd once been reprimanded by Bateson after being spotted hanging around a street in Plymouth that was well known for cruising. The Torquay chairman didn't mind what the footballer did in his spare time so long as it didn't produce bad publicity. After a quiet chat in Justin's ear there was never any similar problem again. Twenty miles north in Exeter and Fashanu was off the grid and free to do what he liked. Boxes was his favourite club and the fact cameras were banned inside made it even more attractive. Quick says the footballer often brought friends to the venue and always sat in a corner booth listening to the music and chatting. Justin sometimes hit the dance floor himself and when he did always requested his favourite song, Clivilles and Cole's *A Deeper Love*. If the footballer really was searching for true love as a marginalised gay man then it was the perfect song title. Quick says Justin felt right at home in the club and also turned up alone. It seemed at Boxes he could relax and just be himself. Whenever the enigmatic footballer showed up a horde of groupies floundered after him, but he never minded and often bought his fans drinks.

Conversely, while Fashanu was making friends at Boxes his popularity with Torquay fans was waning. The 1992 season had not started well for the Gulls with the club losing a string of matches. Fans were growing frustrated. By Christmas, the club was languishing near the bottom of the division and supporters were beginning to get the impression that the player-coach was more interested in being a celebrity than how his team fared. They may have been right. Throughout 1992, Fashanu was in the spotlight just as much as he was on the football field. Media appearances included being a judge in the final of *Mr Gay UK* and as a guest on *Tonight with Jonathan Ross*. His appearance with 'Wossy' is memorable and not only because Justin decided to wear a tracksuit for the interview. As someone who prided himself on wearing the finest designer suits Ross must have been horrified. Once again Fashanu proved himself to be a natural in front of the camera with his relaxed demeanour and witty insights proving a hit with the studio audience. When Ross asked him whether professional footballers really did have sex all the time Fashanu replied: 'It's not a totally sex-orientated thing but it's there, and we've got to be careful now because we're not dealing with gonorrhoea and syphilis we're talking about Aids which can kill.'[41] It was an important message at the time. You can tell Ross admired Justin for coming out publicly and having the courage to speak about it on national TV.

When John Fashanu appeared on the same show a few weeks later, Ross put the younger Fashanu on the spot by asking him when he'd last spoken to Justin.

'It's been eighteen months now since I last spoke to him and for Justin and myself that's a long time. As you know, we were fostered together and we were very, very close. It's disappointing. I'd like to think that some day we will get together but I don't know what he is. This week he's a born again Christian, next week he's gay or he might be a Jehovah's witness the next week, we just don't know,' John replied.

As the studio audience sniggered Ross wasn't smiling and said: 'Just pick up the phone, give him a call and you'll find out. That's the way to do it.'[42]

Aside from his candid interview with *Gay Times*, it's worth mentioning two other interviews Fashanu gave in the early Nineties as they are also insightful. The first was an appearance on BBC's *Open to Question*. The half hour show gave the studio audience a chance to directly ask Fashanu any question they wanted. It was incredibly brave of Fashanu to put himself in the hot seat and, consequently, he suffered a few burns. As usual, the footballer's bravado was on full display. When someone suggested that he was using his sexuality to hide the fact that his career was over the footballer replied: 'I'm proving it's not. I'm playing and scoring goals. I've done well enough in football to sit on a beach in Malibu and enjoy life. Coming back and subjecting myself to aggro is not something I would do unless you are masochistic.'[43] If Bateson had been watching he'd have wondered what goals Fashanu was talking about. The Torquay striker was not on top form and neither was his eagerness to play for the club. As for having enough money to be able to relax on a beach, we know that wasn't true unless someone else was paying for the trip. The truth was Fashanu didn't have any money to speak of and what he earned he certainly wasn't saving.

Asked about his treatment at the hands of Brian Clough the footballer did not hold back: 'If you buy a player for a million pounds then there is no guarantee you are going to produce. It's like a racehorse, you take your chance. It's up to the manager to bring out the potential. He made a mistake of not nurturing me.' Not content with Justin's answer another member of the audience suggested that maybe it was the footballer's attitude that hadn't helped matters. To this Fashanu replied: 'I could have been a little conceited. Clough should have done some background on Justin Fashanu. Football is not just about scoring goals but can I work with him?' From his comments its obvious that Fashanu was still angry at the way things had gone down at Forest but there's a touch of arrogance too. He knew in advance that Clough was not the nurturing type but took the risk of playing under him all the same. Not all risks work out. One thing Justin did come clean about was his social life while in Nottingham: 'I enjoyed myself too much,' he said. At least now he was being more honest.

Fashanu went on to say that while he was happy to be a role model to other people, martyrdom was not for him: 'I have the responsibility to be true to Justin Fashanu. I have to look after Justin Fashanu.' He'd uttered the very same prose to Mike Bateson when he'd hammered out his contract with Torquay United. Talking in the third person suggests the footballer regarded himself as something of a business package and the bottom line was looking out for number one (himself.) It also shows that he really wasn't that interested in being a spokesperson for minorities.

It was only a matter of time before someone asked about the state of his relationship with his brother and Justin replied: 'It's hurt me and disappointed me because I thought he had more depth about him than that because we've been through so much together. I thought he was better than that. We will meet and I hope when we do he throws his arms around me, gives me a big kiss and tells me he loves me.' They were warm, loving words for a younger brother who had, effectively, abandoned Justin. Even though John continued to treat him with contempt it's obvious that Justin was willing to forgive the past and move on. It shows a strong, compassionate spirit.

As well as TV appearances, the footballer also penned an essay for the gay rights organisation *Stonewall*. Entitled *Strong Enough to Survive* Justin wrote that he had been wrong to come out in the tabloid press, mostly because the tabloids didn't like black people being successful. He said that his brother's prejudice was fuelled by ignorance and that he'd felt abandoned by the church. The lack of support from fellow Christians had made him look long and hard at his faith. Justin was also critical of the gay and lesbian community in general that he felt had not supported him.

'When I came out I thought I would meet my true family. Sometimes I would listen to transsexuals and they would talk about how they were trapped in a body that wasn't theirs. I knew exactly what they meant: I felt I was living my life as a lie. I thought that when I came out all my problems would be over; all I would have to do was stand firm and I would be welcomed into the gay community. But it didn't happen like that. I felt isolated and alone and none of the people who could have helped me did. I felt used and abused by the gay machine, which seemed to say that I was just another celebrity to be exploited for the cause.'[44]

Fashanu was wrong about one thing: not everyone in the gay community had effectively abandoned him, his friend Peter Tatchell for one. The activist had been a huge support to Fashanu in earlier years and would have gladly supported him now, but the footballer no longer kept in touch with him. Terry Deal was another friend and supporter. To many people in the gay community it seemed as if it was Fashanu himself who was doing the isolating. Considering Justin was in his thirties when he wrote the Stonewall essay you can't help wondering about the naivety of some of his prose. For instance, did he honestly believe that coming out publicly would solve life's problems?

What's evident from the essay is that Justin was most probably bisexual because he stated a frustration that many people in the 'gay world' feel threatened by bisexuality: 'There is so much fear and ignorance about what makes up a lesbian, gay man or bisexual. But the gay world wants us to have an identity that is just as fixed. Lesbians and gays feel very threatened by bisexuality. They seem to think that you can only be gay or straight,'[39] he wrote. Just as Fashanu's own personality was made up of different shades, so it seems, was his sexuality. Judging by his comments it was not black and white and involved the love of men and women.

After making appearances on television and in newspapers it was, perhaps, not surprising that Justin also tried his hand at radio. He presented a pilot for a BBC series called *Loud and Proud*. Ultimately, the job went to another presenter, much to Mike Bateson's relief. The Torquay chairman was beginning to tire of Fashanu's celebrity moonlighting.

In December 1992, Fashanu caused tongues to wag even more after declaring he'd started dating actress Julie Goodyear who played Bet Lynch on the TV series *Coronation Street*. The 'relationship' generated a lot of headlines in the British tabloids, especially *The Sun* who ran the headline: 'My Bet on the Side: Gay soccer star tells of affair with Julie.'[45] For those who knew Fashanu well, like Deal, the relationship was nothing more than a publicity stunt and some Torquay players saw it as an unnecessary distraction. In the team's eyes, as assistant manager, Fashanu's sole focus should have been on helping the club getting out of the relegation zone. What didn't help his cause is when people found out he'd failed to turn up for an important game against Colchester United electing to attend the *Coronation Street* Christmas party instead. Admittedly, he was injured at the time but as a coach his presence would have been appreciated. Torquay lost the game 2-0 which didn't help matters.

Bateson wasn't a Julie Goodyear fan by any stretch, and it wasn't just because of the *Coronation Street* Christmas party debacle. After Justin and Julie started dating the chairman had spotted the chance of some good publicity, but it almost backfired and Bateson blamed Goodyear. The plan had been for the actress to pull the last ever pint at Plainmoor's old wreck of a social club before it was pulled down. The event was set to take place after a home game against Millwall, and Bateson had invited a reporter from *The Sun* and photographer to get exclusive pictures of Julie and Justin in the dressing room at the end of the match. Goodyear always loved a bit of exposure and *The Sun* had promised to run the story in the next day's edition. But midway through the second half of the game, Goodyear's assistant sidled up to Bateson and informed him that the actress had decided not to go ahead with the pint-pulling stunt after all. She said Goodyear had spent most of her career pulling pints on television and she'd finally had her fill. Literally! Talk about short notice. Bateson was fuming, but rather than make a big scene he thought of how to get his own back. It didn't take him long to figure a way. At the end of the game, while Goodyear was being escorted down to the dressing room for the photo shoot, he gathered all the local reporters and photographers together and told them to meet him outside the dressing rooms. As Goodyear was led in to meet Justin, Bateson kicked open the doors and shouted for the whole press pack to pile in. It was an absolute circus as several photographers, including *The Sun's*, clambered to get snaps of the stars. With his exclusive ruined, *The Sun* reporter was furious and Goodyear was none too happy with the mêleé either. It was a wonderful moment of revenge for Bateson who whispered to Goodyear's assistant: 'Two can play at that game!'

As many people suspected, Justin and Julie's relationship turned out to be nothing more than a sham designed to make money. Given Fashanu's love of the green stuff Bateson wasn't surprised in the least. The actress herself also confirmed that she and Fashanu were never more than good friends. Not long after the dressing room incident *The People* reported that the couple had broken up because the footballer believed the actress was too old for him. Justin told the paper: 'I love Julie more than I've ever loved anyone. And all the ingredients were right except her age. If she'd been ten years younger, I'd probably have married her.'[46]

Once again, Fashanu was publicly humiliating someone in the press and not just anyone but a person he'd counted a friend. He'd done the same thing to his ex-girlfriend Julie Arthurton in *The Sun*. It wasn't nice behaviour. Understandably, Goodyear was livid and never spoke to him again. Ultimately, Justin's comments would not come without a price. In a big dose of irony, the footballer would soon find himself being ridiculed in the national papers himself.

Fashanu's romance with Torquay United was also on its last legs. It was now obvious to everyone involved with the club that Torquay was not a priority. Justin's recent performances on the pitch had been average at best and he clearly wasn't serious about being an assistant manager. While Compton, the team's assistant manager, had tried his hardest to make things work he lacked the experience needed for the club to succeed. The end came when Bateson asked the former Notts County manager Neil Warnock to manage the team instead. While Compton accepted the decision with grace Justin wasn't happy. Surprisingly, given the circumstances, he believed that that the job should have been his.

Warnock's appointment ensured Fashanu's position at the club was now untenable and in March 1993 the striker told Bateson that he was leaving. While the chairman understood the decision he couldn't help being disappointed. From the moment he'd arrived at Torquay, Bateson had tried to support Justin in every way he could. He'd even given Fashanu a shot at management. If the footballer had been serious about the job then he certainly hadn't shown it. Thomas agrees and says that the opportunity to manage the club was never matched by Justin's own commitment. As his spell at Torquay ended it was time for the footballer to pack his bags and head for pastures new. Moving cities was becoming a common trait. Before he left Torquay Justin asked Bateson for one last favour.

'He told me a story that he needed £11,000 and then, boom, he was off. I never saw him again. Money was always an issue with Justin and he had a problem understanding that if you earn a thousand pounds a week, then you don't spend eleven hundred. On one side, you had this very personable bloke who could charm the birds off the trees but the other Justin Fashanu was this money grabbing bastard,' says Bateson.

By the time the chairman realised he wouldn't be seeing his cash again Fashanu had already left the country. The next stop for the transient footballer was Scotland where a team near Glasgow was vying for his services. Fashanu didn't know it but the final whistle had been blown on his career in England. He'd never play football there again.

Star of Scotland

FASHANU HAD not travelled to Scotland in the vain hope that a club might sign him. The footballer may have been an opportunist but he wasn't that much of a chancer. While he was still at Torquay, Fashanu had contacted the chairman and manager of Airdrieonians FC, George Peat and Alex MacDonald, who'd both agreed to hire him on a match-to-match basis. Airdrie was a smaller club located just outside Glasgow, and towards the end of the 1992/93 season it was struggling to keep afloat. MacDonald was hoping Fashanu's experience would help prevent the team from sinking completely from the Premier Division.

When Fashanu's plane touched down at Glasgow Airport, Airdrie's assistant manager John McVeigh was waiting in arrivals. McVeigh had been instructed to meet and greet the star then drive the footballer to his digs. The club had arranged for its newly signed member to stay at the city's Crown Plaza Hotel and on the way there McVeigh made a point of passing the legendary Ibrox and Celtic Park stadiums, homes of the Old Firm. Fashanu was impressed, but if he hoped Airdrie's own ground was just as striking he was in for a big disappointment. At the time, the club played at a little ground called Broomfield Park, but a broom cupboard was a more accurate description. With a couple of rickety sheds for stands and a tight field the ground was no Ibrox. Opposing teams hated playing there because the fans were so close to the pitch that it was intimidating. As McVeigh drove past Broomfield he told Fashanu it was where Airdrie trained. McVeigh might have been the assistant manager, but there was no way he was going to be the one to tell Fash it was where the team actually played.

Fashanu's arrival at Airdrie was a shocker for most fans but no one was more surprised than local reporter, Alex Dowdalls. The sports editor of the *Airdrie and Coatbridge Advertiser* says his appointment was a very big deal. The player was the club's biggest and most flamboyant signing in its 100 plus year history. The first time Dowdalls met Justin for an interview the footballer suggested they meet in the dressing room after a training session, and Dowdalls brought along a female photographer to take some snaps. It was a good job that she'd remembered her wide-angle lens because as they entered the changing rooms a near-naked Fashanu was just exiting the shower. Dowdall's jaw hit the floor and the photographer almost dropped her camera. Dowdalls didn't know who was more embarrassed: him or his colleague. It certainly wasn't Fashanu. The Scottish reporter got the bare essentials from Airdrie's latest signing and was impressed at how cordial the cheeky striker came across.

It didn't take long for Fashanu to settle in at his new club and everyone warmed to him. He was particularly popular with the young apprentices whom he paid fifty pounds if they scrubbed his boots and ironed his kit. Fifty pounds wasn't much money to Fashanu, but it was more than the youngsters earned in a whole week. If the apprentices thought he was extravagant with his cash the rest of the team soon learned that he was flamboyant, period, after the footballer hosted a 'Meet Justin Fashanu' evening. Ever the self-promoter, Justin moved into a beautiful penthouse right in the middle of Glasgow and invited everyone around for a house party. McVeigh tagged along with Airdrie defender, Sandy Stewart.

'Everyone who was anybody in Glasgow was invited to this party and it was a posh black-tie affair. Justin's apartment was right at the top of the building and it had its own private elevator that opened into the living room. Sandy had brought a dozen McEwan Export beers with him but when the lift doors opened he realised he needn't have bothered. Two beautiful girls greeted us and one of 'em handed us a drink while the other played a harp. Everyone was looking at us as we entered and there was Sandy, rather embarrassed, clutching his tinnies! The champagne flowed the whole night and it was one of the best parties I have ever been to,' says McVeigh.

Fashanu's extravagance with the apprentices and party are further indications that he really did fancy himself as a bit of a superstar, even when times were a little rough. In Scotland, he found he was a big fish in a little pond and he certainly made the most of it. Once again, he was the centre of attention and truly relishing it.

Fashanu's arrival in Glasgow was like a breath of fresh air. 'Big Fash', as McVeigh called him, was unlike anyone he'd ever met. The assistant manager remembers the day he took the footballer to collect his sponsored car. The owner of the local dealership threw him a set of keys for a Ford Orion and Fashanu was not impressed: 'That's not quite me,' he said. Throwing the keys back he asked the man what else was on offer, before disappearing towards the back of the shop. A few minutes later, McVeigh heard the sound of screeching tyres and the next thing he knew Fashanu came screaming around the corner in a brand new Ford XR3i Cabriolet. Pulling up next to McVeigh he wound down the window and proclaimed: 'Now this is me!'

Like Norwich City years earlier, Airdrie was a good fit for the footballer. Not only was he welcomed by the players and fans but the team's style of play matched his own. Dubbed the 'Beastie Boys' by the Scottish media, the Airdrieonians were a notoriously physical side that took no prisoners. The midfield unit hunted in packs and the team had one of the worst disciplinary records in the league. Fashanu felt right at home. In one memorable game against Aberdeen, the striker was left in a heap, dazed and confused, after Aberdeen's Alex McLeish and Brian Irvine sandwiched him mid-air. Running on with a stretcher McVeigh asked him if he needed to come off. Shaking his head, Fashanu announced he'd be alright and just needed a moment to regain his composure. Fifteen minutes later and it was McLeish and Irvine who both needed stretchers after finding themselves on the receiving end of Fashanu's elbows. As they were both being attended to the striker looked over at McVeigh, winked and shouted: 'I'm alright now!'

In the same game, Fashanu scored the second most spectacular goal of his professional career. It was almost identical to the one he'd scored for Norwich against Liverpool 13 years earlier at Carrow Road. Dowdalls was there to witness it himself: 'It was a blinding right foot volley from 30 yards out on the left-hand side of the pitch, near the touchline. Seeing the keeper was off his line, Fashanu flicked the ball up, turned, and smacked it into the top corner of the net. It was, by far, the best goal at Broomfield that I ever saw,' says Dowdalls.

The Airdrie fans really took to their new signing and soon designed their own special chant for him: 'He's black – he's gay – he plays for Air-der-ray – Fash-anu – Fash-anu!' As football chants go it cut close to the bone but to supporters and players it came from the right place. From the fans perspective it was a fun, honest cheer celebrating Justin as one of their clan. Being black and gay was true, but not things the footballer defined himself by. Fashanu was a physical player who never took grief from anyone, and if he'd had a choice in the matter then he would, undoubtedly, have opted for something that reflected that characteristic instead (think former Forest player Stuart Pierce, aka 'Psycho'). If any opposing fans gave Fashanu grief about his homosexuality then he wiggled his well-trimmed backside at them and smiled. It was the same way that Fashanu often dealt with racism. The footballer knew he would never win by showing his disapproval so the best policy was to just accept it as part of the game and make it appear as if it didn't bother him. In a way it was like so many other aspects of his life where he also felt conflicted inside but had to put a public face on. He was gay and comfortable with that inside yet felt intense guilt because it conflicted with his faith. He also lived and acted like a superstar while, in reality, he was way past his prime and fading fast. He pretended like nothing bothered him but the truth was he was only mortal and, as such, hurt like anyone else. It's tragic that Justin's outer life in all its stoicism could never quite mirror his inner-one. What seemed like reasonable and mature coping strategies masked how he really felt.

As far as his Christianity was concerned, Justin was still upset at the way his friends in the church had treated him after he came out. Many of them had publicly denounced him. Despite this, the footballer started attending the Whitburn Pentecostal Church just outside Glasgow. He didn't make a big song and dance about it and kept a low profile whenever he went. His faith had been tested to the hilt but it's obvious that he still wanted God in his life.

The fierce Airdrie midfielder Kenny Black was a huge fan of Big Fash's and says the striker's presence in the team was good for morale. Black says no one had a bad word to say about him. Justin always mucked in on the pitch and was always the first to turn up at training. He even had his own set of designer warm-up exercises that the rest of the team assumed he'd learned from America. When it came to Fashanu's sexuality the players were very open about it with some even calling him a 'big poof' to his face. According to the Airdrie players, Justin didn't mind at all and often retorted: 'Don't knock it til' you've tried it.' The footballer would later reveal to his friend A.J. Ali that such comments hurt but that he elected not to show it. The Airdrie players were only acting the same way the Hamilton Steelers and Torquay United players had treated Justin themselves, but you have to wonder why they felt a need to joke about the footballer's sexuality so directly. Being upfront and joking about it was a great way of diffusing any awkwardness but it certainly wasn't beneficial to Fashanu. After all, he was the one on the receiving end. Some might argue that because Justin never told anyone that such homophobic comments hurt him then the players didn't realise it. Given how much Fashanu's teammates respected him they would probably have stopped if he'd just asked.

Sadly for Airdrie, not even Fashanu could stop the rot as far as results were concerned. A string of defeats towards the end of the season made the prospect of relegation a painful reality by the time the 1992/93 season wrapped. The club may have been going down but Fashanu was not planning on joining them. Given his itinerant history no one was totally shocked when the footballer announced he was leaving Scotland altogether. His next destination was Sweden where he'd been signed by Trelleborgs FF. Fashanu's chapter at Airdrie had been short but, for the most part, sweet. He'd played 16 games for the club and scored five goals. His knee had managed to withstand a demanding schedule plus, when he left, he didn't owe the chairman any money. That itself was an achievement.

Caught in a Lie

AFTER MOVING to Sweden, everyone was surprised when Fashanu showed up back in Scotland just six weeks later. Heart of Midlothian FC (Hearts) had signed him. Playing in Sweden might have been an attractive proposition for the summer, but Hearts offered him more money: £2,000 per week. It was also a far more serious club. The footballer was officially unveiled at a press conference where he told reporters that since Hearts was one of the biggest clubs in the country, joining them was a 'no-brainer.' The Airdrie players were astonished to see him playing in Edinburgh, but it's a testament to how much they liked him that no one wished him ill at the rival club. The manager at Hearts, Sandy Clark, was a former Airdrieonian himself and, like Fashanu, the big Scot had played as a centre forward. He'd always admired Justin and liked what the footballer had done for Airdrie. Concerned that his knee might pose a problem, however, Clark only offered him a short contract. He wanted to see how things worked out before he committed to anything longer. It would prove to be a wise move.

One of Fashanu's first duties for Hearts was joining the team for a pre-season tour of Germany. Local sports reporter David McCarthy accompanied them and says it was the first opportunity the players got to meet the footballer. According to McCarthy, Justin fitted right in with the rest of the squad. The striker was on the receiving end of some of the team's banter when the team arrived in Germany and, once again, it was contentious stuff. Incredibly, the players openly discussed who should room with the 'gay footballer'. With no volunteers it was put to the vote and the player who was chosen reportedly said: 'I'm gonna make sure you are asleep and snoring before I even shut my eyes.' As always, Fashanu laughed along but the comments obviously stung. 'You have to understand that footballers are very narrow-minded people. It's the nature of the business. When you put yourself in the firing line, you are open to attack. I know I'm there to be shot down in flames,' Fashanu said.

Again, some might say that Fashanu's teammates were simply dealing with and attempting to diffuse a unique situation the best way they knew how, through humour. While this may be true it's easy to say that when you're not the one on the receiving end. While it may have made the other players feel better about the situation, what they didn't consider is how Fashanu felt as the sole recipient and it only encouraged the footballer to reinforce the emotional wall around him. The footballer faced a lonely and challenging predicament. Occasionally, there was even joking about Fashanu publicly in the local media. One notable example was when a reporter commentating on a game for a local radio station informed listeners that Fashanu had been pulled off the field. This prompted a fellow broadcaster to retort: 'Pulled off? The best thing we used to get at half-time was an orange.' It was predictable stuff that got a cheap laugh.

When he first arrived in Edinburgh, Fashanu rented a quaint Georgian townhouse in the centre of town and found his nearest florist. Since he'd last been in Scotland the footballer had developed a penchant for white lilies and was soon ordering a hundred pounds worth of the flowers every week. When the rest of the Hearts team found out then Fashanu was again the centre of their jokes, but this time the footballer saw the funny side. Florists weren't the only places in town he visited. Chapps and The Laughing Duck were two gay bars also frequented.

Fashanu's career, however, was no laughing matter and this chapter in Scotland would end up resembling something of a Greek tragedy. Things at the club certainly started well. Like at Airdrie, both the Hearts players and fans really took to Justin. The fans, in particular, loved the striker and were soon calling him their 'Queen of Hearts.' In reality, a knight might have been a more accurate description because Justin's elbows sometimes did just as much damage to opponents as a lance. Unfortunately, Fashanu's physical style of play resulted in more bookings than goals earning a rebuke from Clark. Unable to execute what he was hired to do, score goals, Fashanu was soon dropped and began spending more time on the bench. When Clark signed another striker, Mo Johnston, Fashanu's fate was sealed. Rather than fight for his place he seemed to simply give up and started to miss training sessions. When Clark heard the footballer was spending time in London when he should have been in Edinburgh he fined him and banished Justin to the reserve team. This only seemed to make the footballer even more reluctant to try.

Fashanu wasn't making himself any friends away from the club either. He made the local newspaper headlines one week after the owner of a local furniture store complained that he owed her two thousand pounds. The woman claimed she had decked out his flat and he hadn't paid her a penny. When the article was published, Fashanu wrote out a cheque but the damage was already done. The footballer was earning a reputation around town as someone who stitched people up. His erratic and self-centered behaviour was not only confined to Scotland and others who helped him out were also treated badly. One of those people was Graham Morgan. Justin's former youth coach was now working for Adidas and when Fashanu discovered he could get new football boots at a knock down price he called Morgan and asked for a few pairs. It had been several years since they'd last spoken and Morgan was delighted to hear from him. Two pairs of boots were immediately dispatched. Fashanu promised to pay on delivery but the ex-coach never heard from him again. It was disappointing behaviour from someone who Morgan had always admired.

Someone else who got burned by Fashanu was local Edinburgh reporter, Gillian Glover. The footballer asked her to pen his autobiography, but the day the contract was due to be signed he pulled out. Justin told her that after praying to God he'd had a change of heart. Glover had spent a great deal of time making all sorts of arrangements and was none too happy: 'He was a fantasist. He had very grandiose ideas and was brilliant at getting other people to pay for them. He had incredible charm. But none of his stories added up. He was always on the verge of making it big globally, always on the verge of breaking through. People were drawn into the fantasy and how fabulous it was all going to be,' [47] she said. Reporter Conal Urquhart was even more damning. 'When he lived in Scotland he built up an image of a charming and suave gentleman. But the reality was a cynical manipulator who bled dry anyone with whom he became involved.'[48]

Sadly, it was the same story with a friend whom Terry Deal had introduced Fashanu to. The friend in question owned a gay travel company and over the years he'd treated Fashanu to a couple of free holidays abroad. When the footballer asked him to fix up a vacation in Lanzarote the owner was happy to oblige, but told him he would have to pay for some of the services himself. Fashanu agreed but when he returned from his vacation forwarded a personal cheque that bounced. When Deal asked Justin about it the next time they met the footballer said it was none of his business and their friendship was never quite the same again. It's hard to fathom exactly why Justin began treating people this way. It certainly wasn't down to his upbringing. Alf and Betty Jackson had instilled the very best of values into both Fashanus as children and would have been horrified to find out some of the things Justin stood accused of. Exploiting people, especially so-called friends, was Justin's dark side at its worst.

Halfway through the 1993/94 season and the player's career at Hearts looked in pieces. One weekend he met up with his old friend from America, John Britton. The LA Heat coach was visiting Edinburgh with his wife and taking a much-needed vacation. When they got together Fashanu told Britton how unhappy he was with the way things were turning out with Hearts. He was not at all pleased to train with the reserve team. 'It's funny because as Fash and I were talking in a McDonald's restaurant on Princes Street who should walk in but Sandy Clark and his family! I was introduced to Sandy and pleasantries were exchanged. There didn't seem to be any obvious tension between him and Justin but Fash told me that the reserve team issue had caused a problem between them,' Britton says.

In February 1994, Fashanu received a surprise call from George Peat. The Airdrie chairman had heard the footballer was out of favour at Hearts and wondered if he was interested in playing for his former club again. 'Justin's exact words were: "I will come back to Airdrie on the condition that I tell you how much my wages are gonna be." I am convinced that Fashanu used to sit down every night and work out how he was going to make a couple of hundred quid the next day. That's how his mind worked. He was always scheming,' Peat says. Despite his precious demands Peat was still keen to lure him and the Airdrie players and management wanted him back, too. But his return to Airdrie would only be waylaid by scandal. Fashanu

thought he could earn some easy money from the tabloids but, instead, learned a painful lesson that when you try to get one over on the devil you get can sometimes get burned. In Fashanu's case, it was a scorcher.

The debacle started in early February when Fashanu skipped yet another Hearts reserve team training session to travel to London. The footballer, along with his agent, had arranged to meet a reporter from *The People* who believed that he had an amazing story to sell. That's what Fashanu claimed anyway. It was salacious stuff: secret trysts with well-known Tory MPs from the British Cabinet. It might well have been sensational had any of it been true. Unfortunately, it wasn't. Just as scandalous was the sum Fashanu demanded for his lurid tales: more than a quarter of a million pounds. When it became apparent that the footballer's narrative resembled more of a fairy tale than a real-life story the reporter at *The People* was understandably upset. He called his news editor and, together, they decided to get their revenge. The story about Fashanu and gay MPs would still go ahead, but with a slightly different slant and without any money being handed over at all. The next day's headline said it all: 'Gay Soccer Star Top Tory Sex Scandal!'[49] The report read:

'Gay soccer star Justin Fashanu says he had three-in-a-bed sex romps with two Tory ministers. Now he's trying to sell the story of his sensational affairs for £300,000…and says: This will topple the Government. The hypocrisy of these men makes me sick.'

The report called Fashanu a money grabber who demanded £1000 expenses in cash and complained the hotel room the newspaper had put him up in was like a broom cupboard: 'I live in a £250,000 house and I don't expect treatment like this!' he was quoted. Once again, Fashanu's name was publicly soiled, but this time it was all over the country. The article was not only an embarrassment to the footballer but also to Hearts. Clark was furious. As reporters converged outside Tynecastle looking for any kind of sound bite it brought unwelcome attention to a club that was tiring of Fashanu's antics. To make matters worse, when Clark asked him if the article was true Fashanu denied it. He said he'd never spoken to the newspaper and planned to contact the Press Complaints Commission to lodge a complaint.

Rather than cutting his losses and lying low, incredibly, Justin only dug himself deeper into the mire. Things got plain bizarre when the footballer contacted detectives in London who were investigating the recent death of

prominent Tory MP, Stephen Milligan. Fashanu said he had information about the death that could help and invited officers up to Scotland to meet him. (Back story: Milligan had been found dead in his London home wearing lady's suspenders with an orange stuffed in his mouth, causing quite a sensation. Although a coroner would later conclude it was a case of autoerotic asphyxiation gone wrong, Scotland Yard was initially called in to investigate the possibility of foul play.) When detectives flew up to Edinburgh to speak to Fashanu the meeting was short. It didn't take the police long to conclude the footballer knew absolutely nothing about the case and had wasted their time. Fashanu must have believed that he could earn some cash if he sold it to the tabloids, but the only thing it actually generated was more bad publicity and wrath from his club.

The *Daily Mirror* soon got hold of the story and it ran the headline: 'Fash the Trash: "He wasted our time," say angry cops.'[50] When news of his latest escapade became public it was the last straw for Hearts and the club chairman instructed Clark to sack the footballer forthwith for unprofessional behaviour. Fashanu was interviewed by reporters later that day and he finally came clean: 'Maybe I should have come out earlier and just denied everything, but I was in a situation where I thought that this was easy money because people were convinced I was involved. I have never had any sexual contact with any MP. We just made it up,' he said. At least this time he was being truthful.

With his reputation and career both in tatters, Fashanu considered his next move. Playing football in Scotland was no longer an option. Not even Peat could risk hiring the footballer now and he told Justin as much. Fashanu was a tainted man and there was no one he could blame but himself. He'd not only let himself down but others too and all because of money. Fashanu's love of the green stuff was starting to look like a major addiction. The irony is that his desire for more money is exactly what left him jobless and without an income. Sadly, the latter was clearly lost on Fashanu who, once again, found himself in a hole.

One option the footballer considered was investing what little money he had left in a bar in the centre of town. It was a stereo-typical thing for a footballer to do, trading on his name and notoriety to make some cash, but at least it was a plan. Right now, he didn't have many others. The City Café was a busy pub on Blair Street, just off the Royal Mile. While it's uncertain how much money the footballer was actually planning to invest

in the bar, one of the main backers was a friend of Fashanu's who owned an upscale restaurant called The Witchery. According to Britton, Fashanu was extremely excited about the project and had big ideas about refurbishing the place and opening it as a nightclub. He clearly wanted to stay in Edinburgh and was telling Britton about the bar one evening when a man standing nearby interjected. In the thickest of Scottish accents he said: 'Ya dinnay wanna buy that bar man. Its fil' o' frickin' queers.' Fashanu and Britton both fell about in stitches. But for whatever reason, Fashanu wasn't able to get the City Café project off the ground and was soon packing his bags. It was time to move on to pastures new. Again. Although he hadn't exactly been run out of town, even Fashanu realised he'd burned too many bridges to remain in Scotland, never mind Edinburgh. It was time for another chapter.

Nomad

FASHANU'S FIRST destination was Los Angeles, but he didn't stay long. When no opportunities presented themselves he flew to Canada and then back to England. At one point he even risked a return to Scotland staying briefly with a friend in a little village just outside of Edinburgh. The one time hot shot had turned into a nomad desperate for another chance at glory. Unfortunately, with his reputation still in shreds, no one dared touch him. As far as football and broadcasting were concerned he was too much of a liability. It was a sad situation but the footballer only had himself to blame. In the spring of 1995, Fashanu flew to Atlanta, Georgia where he was hired as Director of Youth Sports at the YMCA in Buckhead. It was a new direction for Fash who was, finally, relieved to be away from Britain following his scandal. His main remit was to organise soccer schools. Fashanu didn't tell any of his new recruits who he was, likely because he was still embarrassed at what had happened to him in Scotland.

As it happens, he wasn't the only Brit in Atlanta that summer. Graham Daniels was now director of Christians in Sport in the UK and had travelled there himself with a group of young English footballers. Daniels was coaching one afternoon when someone asked if he knew a guy called Justin Fashanu who was working down the street. Daniels called the YMCA right away and was delighted when Fashanu picked up the phone in person. After a quick conversation they arranged to meet at a local diner later that evening. The last time they had seen each other was when Daniels had watched Fashanu play one of his few games for Newcastle United a few years earlier. It was after Justin had come out and had been a complete circus as reporters scrambled to get a soundbite from the player.

When they met up Daniels could not help noticing Fashanu seemed in low spirits and Daniels let Justin do most of the talking. The conversation was very candid with the footballer revealing some of the tougher challenges that he'd faced in his life. It's no real surprise that his biggest test had been the struggle to come to terms with being homosexual and discovering who he was as an individual. After becoming a Christian, it had been difficult hiding his sexuality from people in his church and he told Daniels he'd felt like he'd been living a lie by not being honest. While he'd enjoyed a strong network of support from people in his church in Nottingham, he said that he'd struggled a lot when he'd moved down to Brighton. Fashanu described that chapter of his life as a dark period and he missed the support of his friends and fans from the Midlands. He also talked about the pressure he'd faced in his younger days by being thrust into the public arena at seventeen years of age. He'd found it hard to adapt.

By the end of the two-hour conversation, Daniels had hardly said a word but was pleased to see that Fashanu had, noticeably, lightened up. Just talking about his problems had clearly been therapeutic for the footballer who had obviously been keen to get things off his chest.

'When I reflect on that conversation it is not Justin's homosexuality I reflect on. It is a guy who was a very young man from a fragile background who became a poster boy and wasn't able to work the implications of his Christian faith outside the public glare. Here was a guy who had to do all his thinking in public. Becoming a public representative of Christianity at such a young age and having such a vulnerable profession, that is what exacerbated his inner conflict,' Daniels says.

At the end of the meeting, the two men said their goodbyes and parted company. It would be the last time they ever met. While he was staying in Atlanta, Fashanu paid for his birth mother to travel out from London to see him. Justin kept in touch with Pearl even though their relationship was often strained. The visit was marked by intense conversations that Pearl would recount to a BBC reporter two years later. In short, her son wanted to know why she had abandoned him. Pearl told Justin that she'd had no other choice as bringing up five children alone would have been an impossible task, but Justin seemed unable to accept this and he kept repeating: 'Why did you abandon us? Why? Why?' It was obviously still a huge issue with the footballer and one that he'd been unable to deal with after all these years. Pearl felt extremely guilty about what had happened but there was nothing she could say apart from 'sorry.' If Justin had hoped his mother would provide some other answer it wasn't forthcoming and he was unable to forgive her. He still viewed it as abandonment. Alf and Betty Jackson's son Edward also met up with the footballer in Atlanta. Jackson was visiting with his family and, like Daniels, also got the sense that Justin seemed down.

Fashanu didn't stay in Atlanta long, but while there he got involved with a local professional soccer team called Atlanta Ruckus. The Ruckus played in the North American A-League and Fashanu played several games for the club. But not long after he joined he was suspended by president, Robert Heller. No one knows for sure why he was sidelined but it's believed he fell out with the German coach, Lothar Osiander, about playing time. Fashanu felt that he should have been playing more.

In 1996, Justin flew back to England. He was now 34-years-old and, sadly, the footballing landscape appeared just as desolate as when he'd left it. His age didn't help. By contrast, John Fashanu had hung up his own boots and was forging a new career in television. The 32-year-old was presenting the hit ITV show *Gladiator* alongside Ulrika Jonsson. Justin could not have missed the irony. For most of their lives it had been him who'd always led the way and been a knockout success in everything he'd turned his hand to. It was him people had raved about. A decade on and the brothers' fortunes had been reversed. Now it was John who was in the public spotlight with Justin standing in his shadow. It was a bitter pill to swallow. To make things worse, the two siblings who had once been so close were still not on speaking terms.

With no offers in the world of football, television or any other field in England the elder Fashanu spoke to a sports agent in New Zealand. Nick Mills owned a sports management company in Wellington with his wife, Gina. Mills had lots of contacts including one with a local football team called Mirimar Rangers AFC. Mills approached the club and asked them if they would consider taking on Fashanu as the club's celebrity striker. Mirimar jumped at the chance and once the deal was in place Fashanu was on his way to the other side of the world. When Fashanu's plane touched down at Auckland Airport it was the first time the footballer had set foot in New Zealand and he was instantly smitten. According to Mills, the footballer was bowled over by the country's beauty and when they met at the airport Fashanu was jumping around like a little school kid. Mills was impressed when the footballer gave him a big smile and a warm embrace. He could tell the two of them were going to get on just fine. Mills dropped the player off at the Museum Hotel in the centre of Wellington and told him they would hook up the following day. He knew Fashanu had endured a long flight and was most likely exhausted (at least that's what Mills thought). The next day he called Fashanu and arranged to see him in the hotel restaurant later that night. Mills had a business associate he wanted the footballer to meet. When Mills and his friend entered the hotel reception the agent's jaw dropped to the ground.

'There is Justin sitting in the foyer looking absolutely immaculate, and sitting next to him is this scraggly looking guy who looked as if Justin had just met at a brothel. He looked dirty and unwashed. The guy I was with was a well-to-do businessman who had a high reputation around town and he certainly didn't want to be seen with this rent boy. I went over to Justin and I said: "Listen, let's get one thing straight. When we have arranged to have a meeting then it is just you I want to meet." Justin replied: "Oh, this is just my assistant who will be helping me out while I'm in Wellington." I said: "Justin, you've only just arrived in the friggin' country. You don't know who this clown is or what is going on. Just get him the hell out of here." Justin apologised and said he didn't mean to offend and I said: "You're not offending me, but I'm just telling you the way it is," Mills says.

The way Mills describes the scene it's easy to picture the contrast between Fashanu and his young companion. Considering how fastidious Fashanu was with his appearance, you have to wonder why he was less bothered about having someone exactly opposite in appearance by his side. It was the same situation back in Edmonton when he'd hung around with similar characters there. We'll never know whether he was oblivious to the dissimilarity or simply didn't care. One thing is for sure: Mills was totally justified in his reaction because the agent was genuinely trying to help him out. Once Fashanu's companion had been sent on his merry way the meeting went ahead as planned.

Despite this small incident, Mills and Fashanu rarely clashed other than the time they had a slight difference in opinion over a sponsored car. Mills had arranged for Fashanu to drive a Ford Escort from a local dealership but Justin, as usual, wanted something a little flashier. He was told his options were either the Escort or public transport. The two men would actually go on to become good friends. The footballer appreciated Mills had his back and Mills, in turn, found the feeling was reciprocated. He once introduced Fashanu to a business associate and friend of his in New Zealand whom Fashanu took an instant dislike to. There was something about the man that made him suspicious and he told Mills to watch his back. A year later, the footballer's instincts were proven right when the supposed friend ripped Mills off for thousands of dollars. It proved that Justin really had been looking out for his New Zealand mate after all.

In the mid-Nineties football was still a growing sport in New Zealand, therefore Justin Fashanu was a big name. Any football loving-Kiwi worth half his salt had heard of him. The excitement surrounding his signing was evident in an article written by local Wellington journalist, Grant Stantiall. Penning a piece for a Rangers match programme, Stantiall still didn't know whether the deal to secure Fashanu had actually gone through:

'Will Miramar pull off the major signing of the Smokefree Summer National League? That has been the question that has been asked most frequently over the past few days in soccer circles throughout the country. The possibility of Justin Fashanu playing in our top league is just the sort of attraction that could give the club a high profile and boost attendances. At the time of writing, the deal has yet to be signed... If the signing has fallen through, well, Miramar you gave us plenty to talk about!' Stantiall wrote.

Secretly, the deal had gone through it just hadn't been officially announced. Ultimately, Fashanu would, indeed, provide plenty to talk about in the 1996 season. The striker played his first match wearing Miramar colours in November against Melville United and would go on to make 18 appearances, scoring 11 times. *Waikato Times* journalist Bruce Holloway interviewed Fashanu several times and was struck by the contrast between the way Justin looked and how he talked. Here was this large, physical footballer who was known for leaving no prisoners in his path with a very posh, high-pitched English accent and impeccable manners. Holloway says he has two overriding memories of Fashanu's stint at Miramar. The first is that Rangers misspelt the striker's name in the match programme of his opening game, calling him 'Justin Fashan', and the second is when Manchester United legend George Best stopped off in Wellington on a speaking tour. A reporter asked Best how he rated Fashanu, to which he replied: 'Well, I think he will certainly stiffen up the back four.' It was a cheap shot that made local headlines. Fashanu also participated in a revealing little question and answer session that was included in a Rangers match programme in March 1997. It's worth including here because it gives a glimpse into the footballer's mind.

What is your personal philosophy?
To achieve my personal potential each and every day. To lead a varied and interesting existence that will help to overcome the twin barriers of success and failure. I feel that even success has its own set of difficulties. Always to be aware of my own identity and self worth and grow old disgracefully.

Ten years from now where do you want to be?
I have regarded my life up to now as being one long learning curve. I feel I have acquired personal skills which I would like to impart and teach others within the context of the game and the game of life. The prospect of full-time coaching does not appeal to me. I feel it can be one of the most unrewarding and unsatisfying jobs in soccer.

What has life taught you?
Whatever choices you are faced with in life, make a decision and accept the consequences because the act of making a decision makes you stronger in yourself. Be prepared to laugh at yourself and don't believe your own press releases. Getting older is fine as long as you get wiser. Finally, a personal relationship is the most important thing in your life, for to be successful in your career and to have someone to share your life with is the ultimate achievement.

For someone who'd spent the best part of his life shielding his true feelings and emotions it's a fascinating insight. The answers he gives are classic Justin. While there are elements that seem genuine, Justin's words are tinged with desperation and bravado. The footballer's personal philosophy is a point in fact. He talks about being aware of his own identity and self worth but, in reality, Justin really didn't know who he was. For years he kept a big part of himself, his sexuality, a secret and rather than being open about it he felt forced to hide it. There were two main reasons for this: the macho world of sport and religion. When God entered his life then his sense of self worth took another hit when he was told that homosexuality was wrong.

The wisdom Justin says that he gained was something he actually had trouble putting into practice. Being able to share his own life with someone special was, regrettably, also something he was never able to achieve. His brother had long since abandoned him and he never had a serious, loving relationship with another man. Justin had enormous love to give and it's tragic that he wasn't able to share that with another person in a long-term relationship. What's evident from his prose is that the footballer had not lost his cheeky sense of humour. 'Growing old disgracefully' was something he was doing for real.

It's clear that Mills and his wife were the two people who got closest to Fashanu while he was in New Zealand. Fashanu rarely talked directly about his sexuality, but admitted to Mills that there had been a time in his life when he had been more open and honest about who he really was. Just before he'd found God, he confirmed that he'd begun to explore his homosexuality, but that God had told him it was wrong forcing him to close up again. For Mills, it was frustrating to hear his friend and colleague had suffered so much angst. Justin was a warm, loving guy who always insisted on a hug rather than a handshake yet seemed down on his luck. He was lost and Mills was sympathetic. Beyond his fading career and conflict with his sexuality, Fashanu was also affected by the rift in his relationship with John. This really tore at him.

While he stayed in New Zealand, John Fashanu was actually going through a crisis of his own. In May 1997, the footballer stood accused of fixing football matches along with two other players, Bruce Grobbelaar and Hans Segers, as well as a Malaysian businessman. It was alleged that the three players provided match forecasts for betting syndicates in the Far East. After months of testimony at Winchester Crown Court the footballers would eventually be acquitted. Reporter David Thomas spent every day at the trial and went on to write a book on the case called *Foul Play*. Over the months he was in court Thomas got to see John Fashanu up close. Thomas says:

'The John Fashanu I observed over several months was an absolutely classic alpha-male: for good and ill. He never said a word in court, other than 'not guilty' when asked his plea. Yet he was very clearly the dominant one of the four defendants and had more sheer presence than anyone else in the courtroom, lawyers and (two) judges included. I always found him very pleasant in the very minor encounters I had with him. But equally, I absolutely would not want to cross him. Without ever making the slightest threat, he still exuded a very powerful air of sheer physical strength and the will to use it.'[51]

Towards the end of 1997, both Fashanus were devastated when they learned that their foster mum Betty Jackson had died. As soon as he found out the news, Justin flew back to England to attend her funeral. John was unable to do the same because of other commitments. This was unfortunate because if he had returned then maybe it would have forced him to speak to his brother and something positive come of it. At Betty's funeral, Justin acknowledged everything his foster mum had done for both siblings: 'We know it was Mama Jackson who gave us the strength of character and foundation we needed in life to make our assault on football. She was faithful, loyal and loving,' he said.

When the 1997 summer soccer season finally wrapped up, Fashanu waved goodbye to his friends in New Zealand and returned to his second home, America. Georgia's Atlanta Ruckus was under new ownership and the president wanted Fashanu to rejoin the troops. Unfortunately, Fashanu discovered the club had changed a lot in the last two years and not in a good way. The new management didn't have a clue on how to run things. He called his friend in Baltimore, A.J. Ali, to ask his help in reviewing and negotiating his contract. Ali obliged and flew to Atlanta to meet him. Ali discovered the footballer was right to be concerned. The club's operations were a disaster and it wasn't just the club in disarray but the whole soccer league set-up. As a gifted businessman and entrepreneur, Ali offered his help and within a few months things with the Ruckus and the league looked in a lot better shape. The organisers were so impressed with Ali that they offered him the chance to take over a team in North Carolina. While he was reviewing the opportunity, however, the owner of the team decided he couldn't part with the club. Undeterred, the league offered Ali the opportunity to start up his own franchise in Maryland. Ali took them up on the offer and returned to Baltimore to start Maryland Mania FC.

Once the operation was up and running, Ali contacted Fashanu and invited him to join the club. While management in Atlanta had improved, things were still not working out as he'd hoped so Fashanu accepted. The prospect of starting a professional soccer team from scratch was, at the very least, a fresh challenge. Justin didn't know it but Maryland would be his last ever stop in America. The footballer's life was about to take a dark and chilling turn.

Madness in Maryland

UNTIL NOW, AJ. Ali has never spoken publicly about his friendship with Justin Fashanu or what he believes happened to the footballer in Maryland. The Baltimore native has always been fearful that what he says might get twisted. Ali only agreed to speak to me after a great deal of persistence and only face-to-face. Justin considered the businessman one of his closest confidantes so I was eager to speak to him. As such, I hopped on a plane and met him in Maryland. As we talked it soon became clear how much Justin's friendship had meant to Ali. During our conversation he paused several times to regain his composure. The former Mania president (turned author and TV host) was a little guarded at first but gradually opened up.

When Fashanu first arrived in Maryland in the fall of 1997, he stayed with Ali and Ali's wife at his former home in Columbia. The two men shared a connection not only professionally, but also spiritually. Like Fashanu, Ali was a practising Christian whose faith was an integral part of his life. Fashanu quickly learned that his new president was also a straight talker. The first serious conversation Ali had with him concerned the footballer's career. Ali told him he was only interested in employing him as a coach not as a player. The Mania president felt bad because he knew how much Fashanu liked being in the centre of the action, but he needed someone to put together a team and Fashanu was the man he wanted for that job. When Ali explained that his role would also entail developing soccer camps for the local community, Justin perked up. He'd enjoyed his time running soccer camps in Atlanta and felt he could put the skills he'd learned to good use in Maryland.

Founding Maryland Mania FC was a dream-come-true for Ali. He'd always wanted to run another sports franchise and the opportunities seemed limitless. By the time Justin arrived in Maryland in September '97, Ali had brought in several investors from the local business community to help the club get started. It was understood that Ali would focus on the business side of things while his colleague focused on his own strengths, recruiting new players and coaching. At first, this arrangement worked out great. Fashanu developed various soccer curriculums and was soon coaching his first camps. He looked happy. He had a natural ability for communicating with people and seemed to thrive in a teaching role. He shared the president's optimistic visions for the franchise. There was even talk of building a big indoor and outdoor soccer centre just outside Baltimore, complete with a 10,000-seat stadium modelled on one Ali had fallen in love with in Italy.

A couple of months after he arrived in Maryland, Fashanu bought himself a sleek black Volvo and rented a plush apartment in Ellicott City, about five miles outside Baltimore.

Fashanu fell in love with Ellicott, a historic mill town built in the late 18th century. With a mix of quaint brick houses, museums and old-fashioned stores Ellicott is also renowned for having a record number of ghosts haunting various buildings. The footballer felt right at home here because it reminded him of England.

Given the footballer's limited finances (Ali was not able to pay Justin much in the beginning), the Mania president tried to persuade Fashanu to buy a cheaper car and rent a less luxurious home. The advice went unheeded. Ali was amazed at how bad Fashanu was at managing his finances. He didn't seem able to grasp the main concept of a budget that what you spend should never exceed what you earn. Even if he were a billionaire Ali is convinced the footballer would still have managed to blow his budget. Ali felt his poor money management skills were the result of a problem that plagued many players who became stars early in their careers: he'd been paid too much, too young, with no sound advice about managing his newfound wealth. As an 18-year-old player at Norwich City, Fashanu's monthly salary had been way above what most people earned. Once he'd tasted the finer things that money could get him, Fashanu had become hooked. While some people were addicted to drugs, Justin got his high from spending money. As such, Ali quickly learned not to lend him cash. If he did, he knew he'd never see it again. Ali believes the footballer didn't borrow with malicious intent it just didn't register with him that he needed to pay a loan back. Sometimes, Ali would give Fashanu ten dollars only for the footballer to give it to a homeless person a few minutes later. Ali says that was just part of Fashanu's quirky personality. Whether the chairman of Torquay United, Mike Bateson, would agree with those sentiments is another matter. Fashanu still owed him eleven thousand pounds and it was unlikely the footballer had put any of that cash towards a charitable cause. Despite Fashanu's flaws, Ali admired him. Justin was the kind of guy who people were instantly drawn to when he walked into a room. He had an aura about him and when he talked you felt like he cared.

Since they were both Christians, no one got more of an insight into Fashanu's own faith than Ali. The two men talked about God for hours. On many occasions the discussions became heated, especially when it came to interpreting verses from the Bible. Fashanu said that he could never quite get the religious side of his life together because of the other side of his life, his homosexuality. Apart from Graham Daniels, of everyone I interviewed for this book Ali was the only religious friend of Justin's to whom the footballer admitted he was gay. Justin revealed he loved God more than anything in the universe, but that being gay was impossible to suppress and something he had no control over. Ali says one of the reasons he and Justin were so close, and why the footballer opened up to him, is because he never judged or condemned Justin. He says:

'I never told him he was a bad person because he did whatever. It was not my role to do that. We had a lot of deep conversations about religion and we would both look at the scripture together and talk about the parts where the Bible deals with the issues of homosexuality. At the core, Justin felt a certain way and he knew that acting on those feelings would take him away from God. It was frustrating for Justin and he was sad that the Christian church seemed so focused on singling out homosexuality. He said there were a lot worse sins.'

One morning in late 1997, the two men attended a prayer session at a friend of Ali's. According to the Mania president, there were about 15 people present and no one apart from himself knew Justin was gay. The man leading the meeting designated random verses from the Bible for people to read. When it came for Justin's turn to read, his assigned passage was Romans 1:26 27:

> *Because of this, God gave them over to shameful lusts. Even their women exchanged natural relations for unnatural ones. In the same way, the men also abandoned natural relations with women and were inflamed with lust for one another. Men committed indecent acts with other men, and received in themselves the due penalty for their perversion.'*

Ali says it was pure coincidence that the passage Fashanu had been asked to read focused on the 'sins' of homosexuality: 'Justin looked at me, I looked at him and it was like: "You see?" He and I talked about it after and he felt like God had just told him that he needed to make a decision. He really, really wanted to commit to Christianity and to his faith, but he had this other thing going for him as well. It was a struggle,' Ali says.

Despite the 'sign' the footballer remained caught between a rock and a hard place. Although he wanted to be a devoted Christian, he still could not abide by the Christian stance on homosexuality. 'Why is it that way?' he always asked. Ali says that Justin's favourite question was always: 'Why?' The footballer often repeated it on a basic level, almost like a child. When it came to his faith it was: 'Why?' With his family relationships he continually asked: 'Why?' The question also extended to Justin's abandonment as a child: 'Why?' To the Mania president Justin was a manboy, an adult who acted like a child because he could not understand what was happening around him. A big part of Justin's perplexity, undoubtedly, stemmed back to his childhood. It was probably also why he could never seem to settle down in any one place for long.

'Justin was a wandering soul who never could quite find his place. This was probably from his upbringing. He could not trust stability and could not have real stability. When things got comfortable he would run and go off to the next town. He couldn't believe that he could be comfortable and that is probably the most profound thing that I remember about him. He was an enigma. When he had an opportunity to have some kind of peace in his life then he would go and vanish and go to the next country with no warning and start over. We vibed on a deeper level because my own father was not good in the home so I have always had issues with trust myself. I know where it comes from and Justin and I talked about that,' Ali says.

That might be true but it's also fair to say that Justin sometimes left town when things got heated. Rather than face the consequences of his actions he fled. Torquay and Edinburgh are just two examples. There's no doubt that Ali was a very close and dear friend who supported the footballer as much as he could, but not even he could change Justin's inability to reconcile his homosexuality with the rest of his life.

Things first started to go wrong for Fashanu in Maryland when a few businessmen who'd invested money with the Mania approached Ali with a concern. They'd heard a rumour that Fashanu was gay and were worried that he was working so closely with children. In short, they wanted him gone. Ali was shocked and disgusted at their demand. He told the investors in no uncertain terms that as long as he was the president of the club Justin wasn't going anywhere: 'Some of these people were close friends, but I refused. They made it very hard and it really brought out the worst in people. On one hand there was Justin trying to do the best he can and then you have these people judging him on things that they shouldn't have been judging him on,' Ali says. But shortly after Ali's colleagues broached their concerns, a serious complaint was filed against Fashanu with the police.

No one will ever know for sure exactly what happened on the morning of Wednesday, 25th March 1998. Much has been written about it and interpretations differ. Only two people were actually there and so only they can tell us. Unfortunately, one of them is dead and the other no longer talking. When I contacted the police department involved in the subsequent investigation its representatives weren't saying much either. What the Howard County Police Department did provide, however, was something much more valuable: the official police report. The 25-page dossier has never been released and sheds some remarkable light on what may actually have taken place inside Justin Fashanu's rented apartment on the night in question. It also contradicts what many British newspapers reported as fact after Fashanu fled Maryland. The names of everyone who the police interviewed, except Fashanu, were deleted in the police file that I received. British reporter Brian Deer wrote the most detailed article on the incident for the *Mail on Sunday* a few months after the complaint against Fashanu was first reported. Deer flew to Maryland to interview the police and the alleged victim himself. Unlike other reporters and writers who have since repeated what Deer wrote as fact, the following information is based on the official police report alone along with A.J. Ali's personal testimony.

The evening before the incident in question, Tuesday 24th March, started off as just a regular night. According to the police report, Fashanu was having trouble wiring some speakers to his home stereo system so he called a girl he knew through his association with the Maryland Mania for assistance. The girl spoke to her boyfriend who was good with electronics and, together, they drove over to the footballer's apartment to help out. While she was at Fashanu's place, the girl called her ex-boyfriend. The 17-year-old's name was not mentioned anywhere in the police report but he was known as DJ (short for D-Junior). According to the report, DJ asked if he could join the group and he arrived at Fashanu's place a short time later. A.J. Ali was acquainted with DJ through soccer circles. Although DJ never played soccer he hung around with friends who did.

According to the police report, DJ says that when he arrived at Fashanu's apartment a few other teenagers were already there, drinking beer and smoking marijuana. DJ says he drank a few beers himself and then smoked a joint that was doing the rounds. Everyone was relaxed and having fun. At around 9.30pm, DJ asked Fashanu if he could call his girlfriend. Fashanu directed the young man to his bedroom where his phone was located next to the bed. DJ claims that as he sat on the bed talking, Fashanu entered the bedroom, sat down next to him and started rubbing the youngster's crotch. Embarrassed, DJ told his girlfriend that he'd call her back. When he hung up, DJ says he turned to Fashanu and told him he preferred women and wasn't gay. DJ claims that Fashanu apologised and said: 'Thanks for telling me. It will not happen again.' Rather than leave, DJ told Fashanu that everything was cool and that he would not tell anyone about what had just happened. Fashanu left the bedroom and DJ called his girlfriend back. He told her what had just happened. After finishing his conversation, DJ re-joined the others in the living room and carried on drinking. He also smoked another joint.

At approximately 11pm, the beer had run dry and Fashanu offered to drive to a nearby liquor store to buy some more supplies. DJ asked if he could go with him and jumped into the footballer's car. When they got to the liquor store it was closed so DJ directed the footballer to another one nearby. Fashanu purchased a case of 22-ounce beers then he and DJ headed back to the footballer's apartment. When they returned, DJ says everybody had left except one person who departed a short time later. Despite what he claimed had happened earlier in the footballer's bedroom, DJ decided to hang around. He says he drank two more beers and smoked another joint.

According to the police report, around midnight DJ says he suddenly felt very tired and asked the footballer if he could stay the night. Fashanu told him it was no problem and DJ called his mum to let her know he would not be coming home. DJ says he took off his shirt, laid down on Fashanu's couch, pulled a blanket over himself and fell asleep. According to DJ, the next thing he recollects is waking up around 8am in Fashanu's bed with his jeans off and his underwear pulled down around his knees. He says he was alarmed to see his penis erect and the footballer performing oral sex on him. In shock, DJ told the footballer to stop and immediately jumped out of bed. As he tried to regain his composure he claims the footballer said: 'You're a sound sleeper.' DJ claims he collected his belongings, ran out of the apartment and walked home. When he arrived back home around 9.30am he immediately broke down and told his mother what had happened. The report says that DJ's mother tried to contact her husband at work but couldn't get in touch with him. She decided to wait until she'd spoken to him before she alerted police. At around 10.30am the report states that DJ felt the urge to go to the bathroom. DJ said that when he defecated it was painful and he noticed blood in his stool. Police were then called.

This is the account that DJ gave a police officer from the Howard County Police Department, PFC King, who first responded to the call and travelled to the young man's home to speak with him. After recounting what he claims had happened at Fashanu's apartment, DJ said that as he'd rushed out the door he'd left his wallet behind. Once the interview was over, Officer King collected DJ's underwear and shirt, placed them in an evidence bag and drove the youngster to Howard County General Hospital for a medical examination. The case was then handed over to Howard County Police Detective Glenn Case who worked in the Violent Crimes Unit.

The doctor who examined DJ found some tearing around DJ's rectum but no sperm. DJ's clothing, along with swabs, were packaged up and sent to the Maryland Police Crime Laboratory for further analysis. In his article, Brian Deer claims the laboratory confirmed the presence of semen in the samples that had been collected at the hospital. This is not mentioned in the police report. This could be because the results of the lab report were not added to the police report when they came through a few days later. According to the report, once the examination was over detective Case drove DJ and his mother home where they then conducted another interview. In his report Case noted that DJ described a hazy memory from the previous evening.

'He vaguely recalls something during the night when he was passed out. He felt that he was just having a bad dream. (DJ) advised that he woke up for a few seconds and remembers being in Fashanu's bed lying face down with Fashanu behind him. (DJ) admitted to drinking heavily the night before but described a terrible hangover feeling when he woke up. He advised that he has never had a hangover from drinking beer and did not drink anymore than in the past,' read Case's notes.

From DJ's testimony it's clear that he believes he was possibly raped by the footballer and that Fashanu might have drugged him. Case asked DJ to give some information about his family and the young man said that his parents were having financial difficulties. He explained that his mother was currently out of work after being injured in a car accident and that his father didn't have a stable job. He told Case that he'd dropped out of high school and had recently lost a part-time job he'd held at Pizza Hut. While he'd been working, he'd helped pay some of the household bills and expressed frustration about never having his own money to buy the things he wanted. He told Case that in a previous meeting with Fashanu at the footballer's apartment, he'd told the footballer about his financial woes and Fashanu had offered to give him money for clothes and to help him out. After concluding the interview, Case spoke to DJ's girlfriend. She confirmed that DJ had called her from Fashanu's apartment the previous night and had to cut the conversation short because Fashanu had 'made passes at him.'

The following afternoon, Case and his partner drove over to Fashanu's apartment at Ashton Woods: #2C, 8465 Oakton Lane. They hoped to talk to the alleged perpetrator himself. The footballer's car was parked outside the apartment but there was no answer at his door. As Case and his colleague waited outside in his car, they saw a young woman who appeared to be looking for someone. She was actually a friend of Fashanu's and trying to locate the footballer herself. Case approached her and she told the detective she was DJ's ex-girlfriend and had been at Fashanu's apartment the previous night. Case asked her some questions. She denied there'd been any alcohol present at the footballer's apartment but said she had seen Fashanu and DJ drive away in the footballer's car around 11pm. She told Case she didn't know where they were going and had left the apartment herself shortly thereafter. The girl told Case that she'd heard the allegations DJ was making and said she believed DJ was lying. She stated that the youngster had told her that he intended to sue the footballer for what he claimed had taken place: sexual assault. It seems incredibly early for the gossip mill to have started working, but judging by what the girl says it appears that DJ had already contacted her and told her what had happened.

After he finished speaking to the girl, Case and his partner returned to their car and decided to wait for Fashanu to return home. Their patience paid off when the footballer arrived at his apartment a short time later. Fashanu appeared surprised when the detectives introduced themselves but said he didn't mind answering any questions. He invited them in for a chat. The player told the detectives right away that he knew about the allegation being made against him. The police report doesn't state how he knew this but it's possible that DJ's ex-girlfriend had told him. Fashanu denied that he'd given DJ a blowjob or had any sexual contact with the youngster at all. Case asked Fashanu if he was a homosexual and the footballer said he wasn't. Fashanu said it wasn't uncommon for people of all ages to hang out at his apartment and that he had not met DJ before. This contradicts DJ's own account that he'd met the footballer on previous occasions. Fashanu said he didn't observe any alcohol being consumed on his premises the previous night. When Case asked him whether he'd driven anywhere with DJ in his car the footballer denied it. The detective told the footballer that a girl he'd just spoken to outside the footballer's apartment contradicted that statement and that she had seen Fashanu and DJ leave together in his Volvo around 11pm. Advised of this, Fashanu did recall going to the liquor store, after all, to buy someone cigarettes, but said he did not take DJ with him. Fashanu had been caught in a lie.

As they were talking, the detective noticed a leather Bible on the floor of the apartment. It seemed as if the footballer was religious. Fashanu confirmed that DJ had asked if he could sleep on the couch. The footballer told Case that when they'd got back home from the liquor store he went to bed alone. The next thing Fashanu says he remembered is hearing DJ leaving the apartment around 6am the next morning. Fashanu concluded the interview by telling Case that he wanted to clear his name and was willing to take a polygraph test if necessary. The detective told the footballer he'd be in touch with him again soon and left.

On the Run

IN REALITY, Case would never see Fashanu again. The very next day, March 27th, the footballer packed a small bag and left town. The first time A.J. Ali heard anything about what was happening was when Fashanu called him from England after the footballer's plane touched down at Heathrow Airport. Fashanu told the Mania president that he'd had to leave Maryland in a hurry, and needed Ali to pick up his Volvo that was parked at the airport. At first, Ali was annoyed but his irritation quickly turned to shock when Fashanu informed him why he'd fled.

'Justin told me that he was in trouble and that the kid DJ was trying to frame him. Justin said he didn't stand a chance and that he had to sort it out. I tried to convince him to come back. I really wanted him to come back and fight it. I thought running was a big mistake, you know? He shouldn't have gone,' Ali says.

Not surprisingly, Fashanu appeared concerned on the telephone, but despite Ali's pleas for him to fly back and face the allegations head on the footballer flatly refused. He said he'd never get a fair trial. The Mania president wasn't the only person trying to convince him to return. So was a friend from the footballer's local church in Maryland. Lonnie Wortham, his minister, says Fashanu also told him that DJ was blackmailing him. Fashanu said that he and DJ did have sex but that it had been totally consensual. Fashanu claimed that he had woken up the next morning and that DJ had demanded money. If he didn't pay, then DJ said he was going to tell everyone that the footballer had raped him. Fashanu says he told DJ that he didn't have any money to give and claimed the youngster left saying: 'You'll see.' Wortham tried to persuade Fashanu to come back and face his accuser but the footballer said he was too scared. Given Fashanu's life experience and the general attitude towards gay men, you can understand why he felt he wouldn't get treated fairly but there's no getting away from the fact that he lied to police. He'd told detectives that he and DJ did not have sex. If consensual sex did take place then his motivations for lying were obviously because he felt he would not get a fair trial.

One person who didn't know Fashanu had left the country was Case. The detective was still conducting his investigation into the alleged assault, and was arranging for a sample of DJ's urine to be sent to a specialist laboratory in Mississippi to test it for the presence of Rohypnol (also known as the date rape drug). Case wanted to know if the youngster's drinks had indeed been spiked. If that were true then it would account for how confused and impaired DJ claimed he felt the day after the alleged assault. Clearly, Case didn't believe Fashanu's claims that the footballer hadn't observed any drinking at his apartment. Three days later on March 31st, Case received information from an unnamed source that the footballer had not been in contact with any friends or associates since the detective had interviewed him. The source also revealed that Fashanu's career in England had been damaged after the footballer had 'come out of the closet as a homosexual.' The detective wondered why Fashanu had not been truthful to him about being gay. It was another lie.

Case visited the liquor store that Fashanu said he'd visited the night before the alleged assault. An employee told Case he recalled seeing a black male with a British accent who matched Fashanu's description visit the store accompanied by a younger white male who matched DJ's description. Yet another lie. The employee said he'd carded Fashanu because he looked young. Although the police report does not state whether Fashanu actually purchased beer from the liquor store, it seems from the employee's statement that he did.

As Case continued his investigation in America, back in England Fashanu travelled to Norwich to see his friend, Ronnie Brooks. The football scout had now retired from the game and was working in boxing. According to Brook's wife Stephanie, Fashanu was in a real state. He looked worried and concerned. It had been a number of years since the Brooks had last seen Justin and they were shocked at what he had to tell them. As a former magistrate, Ronnie was hugely concerned about the legal implications of his situation. Fashanu had essentially fled a criminal investigation after offering to undergo a lie detector test and to give a blood sample. He told Justin that hampering an investigation was a serious crime and that by fleeing he had not done himself any favours. Regardless, Brooks offered his help and support. The footballer thanked him but said there was nothing anyone could do. Next, Fashanu dropped in to see Mel Richards. The hair stylist says Fashanu explained what had happened to him and that his biggest fear was being jailed in America. Richards got the impression that Fashanu was telling him the truth about the boy and that he was being blackmailed. One thing Richards was certain of: Fashanu was scared.

Meanwhile, Detective Case was employing the Internet to help in his investigation. He researched Justin Fashanu's name and was surprised to learn just how successful the footballer had been in England. He also found Justin's name listed on several gay and lesbian websites. On 2nd April, the detective decided it was time to speak to Fashanu again in person, but when he turned up at his apartment complex Fashanu's black Volvo was nowhere to be seen and neither was the footballer. Case obtained a search warrant and together with three other detectives entered the apartment to look around. It was immediately obvious that Fashanu had made a speedy escape. There were piles of mouldy dishes in the sink and Fashanu's answering machine indicated the footballer had not answered his telephone for a few days. The detective noticed that the Bible he'd spotted lying on the floor of the apartment a week earlier was also no longer there. Oddly, inside the closet Case found several letters from an unidentified person in the UK who accused the footballer of preferring young men for sexual gratification. Given the investigation he'd found himself in, it seems strange that Fashanu would have left such letters behind for police to find. It points to a hasty departure. Case collected several items from Fashanu's apartment including a comforter, two bed sheets and two blankets.

Wondering where exactly Fashanu had gone, Case called A.J Ali to see if he could help. Ali told the detective that he was well aware that Fashanu

was the subject of a police investigation and had spoken with Justin a few days earlier. Fashanu wouldn't reveal his exact whereabouts but had said he was in England. He'd needed to go away for a while and think some things through. To Case, fleeing the country did not seem like the actions of someone with nothing to hide.

In England, Fashanu travelled from Norwich to a religious retreat in Leicestershire where he'd once visited with his Christian mentor, J. John. Fashanu had gone to Mount St Bernard Abbey in the mid-Eighties to pray for help with his injured knee. A decade on and the footballer had a lot more at stake. The Abbott Father Rufus says that when Fashanu first arrived he called himself Justin Lawrence. Fashanu eventually admitted his real name and told Rufus his version of events in America. Fashanu proclaimed his innocence and repeated his story that he and the DJ had engaged in consensual sex and that the youngster had blackmailed him.

It was clear to the father that Fashanu had hit rock bottom. Fashanu said that he'd always felt like a contradiction and had been pulled in different directions between his faith and being gay. He'd continually struggled with this conflict and had been unable to resolve the issue in a healthy way and move on. He said the conflict had been a very destructive force in his life. Father Rufus said he could sense Fashanu regretted a lot of things. The footballer told him he knew he'd been given a lot of opportunities but hadn't always done things the best way. It's clear from this comment that Fashanu was admitting that he had squandered some of the chances he'd been given in life. Justin also said he realised that his brother had only been trying to help him and that he regretted the road he'd gone down. Fashanu told the abbot that if he had his life to live all over again then he would do things differently. The footballer remained at the abbey for a few days and then left.

Fashanu might have been out of sight, but he was not out of Detective Case's mind. Despite his departure from America, the detective now believed he had enough evidence to charge the footballer with assault. Case prepared a statement of charges against Fashanu for a second-degree sexual assault offence and first and second-degree assaults. An arrest warrant was issued on 3rd April 1998. The following day, Case contacted an associate of Fashanu's in England whose name has been removed from the police report. The person said he didn't know where Fashanu was but if the detective checked the footballer's phone records they might lead to his whereabouts. Later that same day, Case dropped off two subpoenas at the state attorney's

office. One was for access to the footballer's bank account and the other for access to the phone number of the anonymous person who the detective had just spoken to in England. Case contacted Interpol, Atlanta Police, DeKalb County Sheriff's office in Georgia, Strathmore RCMP in Alberta and New Scotland Yard in London to find out if any of them had a criminal record for Fashanu. There was nothing on file.

Meantime, Fashanu was renting a room in a house in North London for the month of April. The footballer was obviously trying to put what happened in America behind him. People who met him during this time say Fashanu seemed positive and he told some he was even thinking about trying to forge a new career as a television presenter. On 30th April, Fashanu had lunch with his brother's ex-girlfriend Maria Acuna who he'd remained friends with even after she and John had split up. Acuna would later testify that Fashanu seemed in good spirits and looking forward to spending time in England. Two things seem clear: only a handful of people in England knew what had happened to Justin in America, and the footballer didn't realise that a warrant for his arrest had been issued.

If Justin believed that the investigation in Maryland would fizzle out now he'd left the US, however, he was wrong. He was certainly concerned because he called his old friend Neil Slawson in America. Slawson was now a police sergeant in the Los Angeles Police Department. Fashanu inquired about the extradition protocol between the two countries and was told that Great Britain had no problem sending its citizens across the pond if an arrest warrant in the US had been activated. It wasn't exactly what the footballer wanted to hear. Fashanu asked Slawson if he could check into his case concerning DJ, but the sergeant told him he couldn't. Doing that could cost him his job, plus he wouldn't be able to get the information over the phone anyway. When he explained that to the footballer, Fashanu thanked him and said goodbye. According to Slawson, Justin didn't sound particularly alarmed. But that was about to change.

Game Over

THE SAME day that Fashanu was meeting Maria Acuna in London, Thursday, April 30th, 1998, Detective Case was meeting the public information officer with the Harrison County Police Department. Together, they compiled a press release on the case concerning the footballer. The American detective wanted to find out exactly where Fashanu was residing and hoping the British media might be able to help. The press release was faxed across the Atlantic and quickly picked up by news agencies the next morning. As word of 'Fugitive Fashanu' began to be broadcast it kick-started a series of events that would lead to tragic consequences. Over the years, Justin Fashanu had never exactly enjoyed a love affair with the English press. While he'd earned thousands of pounds by selling illicit and, sometimes, false stories to reporters he'd also, just as frequently, been burned by them. All his life the footballer had played a dangerous game, especially with the tabloids, and the last time he'd messed with them in Scotland he'd been left licking his wounds. This time around there was far more than just his reputation on the line.

It was the UK's Press Association (PA News) that picked up the story first reporting: 'Police Hunt Soccer Star Over Gay Assault Claim.'[52] When newspapers and other media learned the footballer was wanted for sexual assault against a boy, naturally, it made for a sensational story. It spread like wildfire. In an instant, the footballer's hopes for a fresh start back in England had just evaporated. When a reporter caught up with John Fashanu he told them that he hadn't spoken to his brother for more than seven years: 'I have not a clue where he is. It doesn't interest me one iota what he does,'[53] he said. John would later claim that the same day he made that comment he received a call on his mobile phone from an unlisted number. When he answered, all he could hear was heavy breathing. Thinking it was his brother he immediately hung up. When he heard the news himself, a frantic sounding Justin called A.J. Ali in America. Ali says:

'He feared what was going to happen to him. I was very concerned for him at that point. He wanted to make sure that I knew he didn't rape this guy and he wanted to make sure that I knew that they did have sexual relations, but that it was consensual and he hadn't seen this coming. He said he felt betrayed and persecuted. When talk began about him possibly being arrested and having to do whatever time, I thought that was going to be extremely rough but that he was going to be able to do it.'

Judging by Ali's comments, if Fashanu had returned to America to face his accuser then the Mania president believed the footballer would likely have gone to prison. Ali always believed in Fashanu's innocence, but realised that the odds would be stacked against his friend in a court of law. Justin had certainly not done himself any favours running back to England.

As news of his alleged deeds in America were being broadcast on TV, radio and by newspapers across Britain, Justin Fashanu made the biggest decision of his life. Unlike others he'd made in the past there could be no going back with this one. Unwilling to face his accuser back in America, and unable to bear the shame in England, Justin chose the one option that enabled him to escape it all. It was a dark and chilling choice but, apparently, the only way the terrified footballer could see out of his predicament.

In the late afternoon of Friday May 1st 1998, Justin visited a gay sauna called Chariots Roman Spa in Shoreditch, east London. The footballer spent a few hours at the spa and, according to staff, seemed happy. He chatted to other customers and didn't seem anxious at all. John Pickford was working the reception that day and would later testify that Justin seemed totally relaxed. Of course, today we know better. In reality, Justin was an emotional wreck. For most of his adult life he'd always been able to mask his true feelings, and it seems this was a skill he'd maintained to the bitter end.

When he left Chariots Justin walked a short distance down the road and turned into a dark, cobbled side street. Fairchild Place was a small, innocuous dead end road of warehouses and industrial buildings. Walking slowly, Fashanu eventually stopped next to what appeared to be an empty brick building at the end. The warehouse was actually a car park where commuters left their vehicles during the day, but at night it was mostly empty. No one knows exactly how long he stood there but at some point Justin decided the building was suitable for what he had in mind. Throwing a bag he was carrying over his back, Justin grabbed the top of two crude corrugated iron sheets that served as doors and hauled himself up. Despite his six foot-two-inch frame, Fashanu had no problem climbing the front of the building and after squeezing through a small gap above the entrance he dropped down the other side.

Inside the building, Justin spotted a mirror on a wall next to a corner office and removed it. The owner of the building, Norman Keen, used the mirror to keep a watch out for anyone entering the space when his back was turned, but Justin had other plans for it. Placing it on top of the sink in the bathroom one can only guess he wanted to look at himself one last time. Picking up a sharp instrument, Justin slashed his right wrist three times. The pain from the symbolic act was nothing compared to the torment he felt inside. Pulling a handful of paper towels from a nearby dispenser, Justin wrapped them tightly around his wrists. Norman Keen would stumble across the bloody towels a few days later. Grabbing his Filofax and a pen from his bag, Justin wrote a short note to his family and friends. The dark rhetoric said it all.

'Well, if anyone finds this note hopefully I won't be around to see it. But let's begin at the beginning. What a start, everything going so well then I felt that I was abandoned, left alone without anybody to turn to. Being gay and a personality is so hard, but everybody has it hard at the moment, so I can't complain about that.

I want to say that I didn't sexually assault the young boy. He willingly had sex with me and then the next day asked for money. When I said no he said you wait and see. If that is the case, I hear you say, why did I run? Well, justice isn't always fair. I felt I wouldn't get a fair trial because of my homosexuality. (Silly thing really but you know what happens when you panic.)

> *The blood is from my wrists cut because I want to die rather than put my friends and family through any more unhappiness.*
>
> *I wish that I was more of a good son, brother, uncle and friend but I tried my best. This seems to be a really hard world. I hope the Jesus I love welcomes me home. I will at last find peace!*
>
> *Please let Maria Sol and Amal know that I love them with all my heart and to know that I was the person they knew me to be. Please send my love to John, Phillip, Dawn, (Aatu), Remi, Delli, mum and Daniel. Special thanks to Edward, Rachel, Jemima, Simeon and the boys. Love to my friends in the US and say that I had the best time of my life there. Love!!'*

Justin placed the Filofax on top of the sink. The book contained the names and numbers of hundreds of the footballer's friends, and if he'd just called one of them then maybe they would have deterred him from the madness. But none of Justin's friend would receive a call. Not that night or ever again.

Back in the car park, Justin grabbed four car wheels that were scattered on the floor and piled them one on top of the other directly under a beam. Picking up an electrical cord that was also lying around, the footballer made a crude noose with one end and then climbed on to the stack of tyres. Once on top, the footballer threw the other end of the cord around the beam and secured it. It was almost time. It seems very likely that Justin said one final prayer before placing his neck inside the noose and tightening it. There was just one more thing to do. To make his plan work he needed to kick off the top tyre he was standing on. The steel rim was heavy, therefore no easy task, but Fashanu always had at excelled at challenges and this one would be no different. As the tyre dropped to the floor seconds later, Justin Fashanu's life came to an abrupt end. It was a tragic and untimely finish to a gregarious but troubled life. Hopefully, the footballer had at last found the peace he was hoping for.

Fashanu's lifeless body was found early the next morning by a man moving his car into the garage. He immediately alerted police. Officers who were first on the scene quickly established the identity of the deceased because Justin had left his passport in his pocket. However, incredibly, police failed to find the footballer's suicide note. Norman Keen would discover it two days later after returning to work following a long weekend. He couldn't believe it had been missed. So much for a thorough investigation. A small bag containing some of Justin's clothing was also in the bathroom. Keen contacted the police who were, naturally, embarrassed and an officer was dispatched to collect the items. Even though Justin's death looked like a suicide the scene was handled with incredible carelessness. This sloppy way police went about things is particularly astounding when you consider that an arrest warrant had been issued for the footballer.

When news of Justin's death was released later that day there was a mixture of shock, sorrow and regret. Only that morning newspapers were still carrying news of the police manhunt with *The Sun* reporting: 'Sex Rap Gay Fash Vanishes.'[54] The *Daily Mail* blared: 'Fashanu Hunted on Assault Charge.'[55] Meanwhile, *The Mirror* ran: 'Fashanu Manhunt Over Boy Sex Claim.'[56] Some tabloids went one step further asking: 'Are you a victim of runaway Fash?' Now everyone knew where the footballer had gone.

May 2nd was a long weekend in England and most people were enjoying the public holiday. Fashanu's death was a huge bombshell and for many the revelry was cut short the moment they heard what had happened. Because his fame as a footballer had been so fleeting, to the majority of the British public he was something of an enigma, but his death was still received with great sadness. It was a heartbreaking end to what had seemed in the sports press and tabloids like an equally tragic life. For those who'd crossed paths with him personally, there was heartache and guilt. What could they have done to save their friend? Why hadn't the footballer reached out to them? They were natural reactions, but Justin had managed to keep his feelings to himself when he was alive and he chose to do the same even as he prepared to die.

Justin's death was almost unbearable for many of his friends and acquaintances who couldn't understand why it had come to this. Fashanu's friend from Norwich City, Dave Bennett, best sums up their collective horror.

'The thought of him walking around with a flex and looking for somewhere to hang himself must have been the loneliest place in the world. He was one of the bubbliest characters I have ever met in my life and to think how low he must have felt to do that in the loneliest and emptiest place in the world. It's a horrendous thought.'

Apart from sorrow, Bennett also felt guilt. The last time the two had met in Nottingham he believed his friend had been trying to reach out to him. Bennett says he had not tuned in and now felt tremendous remorse. Instead of being there for his friend Bennett says he was more interested in going out on the town and having a good time. He also felt bad about making Justin meet him in the players' lounge at Nottingham Forest. Considering the torrid time Justin had faced at the club, Bennett says it was inconsiderate of him. These are things he still thinks about today and wishes he could change. Of course, the truth was far different. Bennett had been a good friend to Justin.

The physiotherapist at Leyton Orient, Bill Songhurst, was beside himself with grief. What made Fashanu's death so hard on him was the footballer had killed himself near to where Songhurst lived. 'I had a flat in east London and you blame yourself. Why? I'm just here. Why didn't you come and talk to me?' Songhurst will always wonder. Coincidentally, the Torquay reporter Dave Thomas was in east London himself when he heard the news, reporting on Torquay United's game against the Orient. Like Songhurst, the reporter felt equally frustrated and upset that the footballer hadn't called someone. Thomas had always felt a special connection to Fashanu and would have dropped everything to help if he'd only asked.

Justin's friend from *Gay Times* Terry Deal also shed some tears. He was shocked that someone who had so much going for him and so full of life had managed to find themselves in such a mess. When Fashanu's friend from Exeter, Alan Quick, found out he was heartbroken. It was only a few years earlier that Justin had been ripping it up on the dance floor at Boxes nightclub dancing to his favourite tune: *A Deeper Love*. Wherever the footballer was now, Quick hoped he'd at least found peace. In the late Nineties, the BBC Radio 1 DJ Dave Pierce hosted a Sunday evening request show for the nation's favourite house music tracks. Quick requested Justin's favourite song and Pierce ended up playing it at the end of his show. Quick was brought to tears. In London, Peter Tatchell was equally disturbed. It had been several years since the two men had last spoken but that didn't make the news any easier to hear. In Tatchell's eyes, as a good looking and charismatic person, Fashanu would never have been short of men to sleep with so the thought of him forcing himself on someone did not sit right with the activist. Tatchell says the sex assault allegation might be true, but he also has some lingering doubts, especially since the accuser's claims were never proven.

It wasn't just in England that tears fell. In New Zealand, Fashanu's former sports agent Nick Mills broke down and says the loss affected him as much as when his own father died. In America Bobby Ammann, John Britton and Neil Slawson were all devastated. Ammann says two days before Justin killed himself he received a missed call from an unknown number. Today, he is still haunted by the thought it could have been Justin trying to reach out. The Maryland Mania president A.J. Ali was in obvious pain too. He was one of the last people to speak to Justin. The footballer had sounded desperate on the phone a few days earlier but Ali never thought for a moment that he would take his own life. Neil Slawson never believed his friend would end it that way either. The police officer believes Fashanu killed himself because he couldn't handle the thought of being locked up.

John Fashanu made his statement through his solicitor: 'John is absolutely distraught at this tragic time. He is truly shocked and distressed by the news of his brother's death. Although there were periods of disagreement between them there were also many occasions when they have enjoyed special times together. John and his family ask that they be allowed to grieve in private.'

Detective Case heard the news of the footballer's death via Interpol and realised the investigation into Fashanu for sexual assault was, effectively, over. He called his counterparts in England, the Metropolitan Police, who confirmed Fashanu's passing and that his death appeared to be the result of hanging. Case was told the investigation was still ongoing. The detective requested a sample of Fashanu's blood to be tested for HIV and then contacted DJ to tell him the news. Nothing in the Harrison County Police Department's report indicates how the alleged victim reacted to the news, but a *Baltimore Sun* journalist claims he broke it to DJ. In his report the journalist said that the youngster lit a cigarette, remained silent for a few seconds before saying: 'I have a lot of mixed feelings. I feel bad that he did it to himself but I'm also disgusted about what he did to me. I'm upset that I didn't get to see him go to trial, to see justice. I didn't get to confront him, ask him why he did it.'[57]

A week after Fashanu's death, the Howard County Police Department was called back to Fashanu's old apartment in Ellicott City after the building manager found it unlocked and trashed. There was glass on the floor from broken picture frames and a message carved on the wall with a kitchen knife: 'I can't help it. I'm gay. I'm sorry.' Despite the prevalence of ghosts in the town, its unlikely Justin's spirit had returned from the dead to carve out the message and police put it down to the work of local kids.

On May 7th a hearing into Fashanu's death was opened at Poplar Coroner's Court in east London. A pathologist said that a post mortem had found some injuries to Fashanu's wrists but that the provisional cause of death was hanging. The coroner said it looked as if Fashanu had hanged himself but he would have to wait for toxicology reports first before recording a verdict. No members of Fashanu's family attended the short hearing and it was quickly adjourned. At the main inquest, many of Fashanu's family and friends turned up at court including Pearl who sobbed quietly. Justin's brother Phillip was the only member of the family to give evidence. When he was asked whether there was ever any hint that Justin might take his own life he replied: 'None whatsoever, none whatsoever.' John Fashanu's former girlfriend Maria Acuna told the court about the dinner she had shared with Justin two days before his death. She said that he appeared like his old self, happy and looking forward to staying in England. Finally, the court heard from the last person who saw Justin alive, the receptionist at Chariots, John Pickford. He stated the footballer did not appear depressed at all when he was in the spa.

In an unbelievable error, a detective constable from Shoreditch Police Station told the court that he'd found no evidence that an arrest warrant had even been issued. 'There was no request from any agency to seek the whereabouts or to seek the arrest of Justin Fashanu at any time. I made immediate inquiries at the time of the incident. I heard from the news Justin was wanted under warrant in the USA for this offence. But he was not wanted and there was no warrant out at all,'[58] he said. He was wrong, and because of his statement many media organisations continue to report today that no arrest warrant had been issued and that Fashanu had killed himself for no apparent reason. The police report containing the three charges filed against the footballer and an arrest warrant issued on April 3rd, 1998 are part of the official file from the Howard County Police Department in Maryland that I received. The charges and arrest warrant were real. At the inquest, coroner Dr Stephen Chan recorded a verdict of suicide.

'He was a man who had achieved success in his life against tremendous odds. He was a man who appeared to have triumphed over his disruptive upbringing, and much difficulty in life, in the face of prejudice against his colour and hostility against his sexual preference. Still in the end he felt overwhelmed by these same pressures, not helped by his worries over an alleged incident in the US against him. Indeed, it is clear from his note that he made a declaration of his innocence and expressed his lack of faith in a fair trial. Clearly, he did not wish to cause more pain or more distress to his family or loved ones. Sadly, he decided that death was the only way out for him,' Chan said.

After the hearing, John Fashanu told reporters: 'We are all very pleased it is over. I beg everybody, especially the media, to look at the coroner's report, listen to what the coroner had to say and I think that says it all.' The matter might have been over for John, but for many people the debate about Justin's untimely death continued. In pubs, cafes and on local radio shows discussions centred on whether Justin really had raped his accuser. Was he really innocent? The fact is we will never know. Although there was evidence that sex between Justin and DJ had taken place, we cannot say whether it was consensual or not. Justin maintained that it was while DJ claimed otherwise. It was a classic case of one man's word against another.

Farewell Fash

THERE WERE tears and smiles from the congregation the day Justin's body was cremated on Saturday May 9th 1998. The tears were for a life cut short, and smiles for the memories of a footballer whose presence had touched many people. The service was held at the City of London Cemetery in east London a week after the footballer's body was discovered. More than 200 people attended the private funeral including Justin's mentor from his Norwich City days, Ronnie Brooks. The chairman of Norwich City had asked him to personally represent the club. When Justin's mother Pearl spotted Brooks she embraced him and thanked him for being such a support to her son. While A.J. Ali was invited to the service some of Justin's other friends like Peter Tatchell were not. A.J. Ali rode in the same car as John to the service and claims John asked him whether Justin had ever forgiven him for not being more of a support. Ali told him that Justin had forgiven him and had been truly saddened that they'd both been at odds.

The service was conducted by a pastor from Justin's former church in Notting Hill, London. Wynne Lewis paid tribute to Justin's kindness, enthusiasm and determination to succeed. Another friend of Justin's, Reverend Andrew Wingfield Digby, also attended. Wingfield Digby was a fellow member of Christians in Sport. As a former professional cricketer, he was familiar with the pressures Justin had faced. At the service he said that everyone shared a great deal of sadness about the premature end to Fashanu's life, but also a great deal of thankfulness that it had touched so many people.

Hundreds of messages were sent from around the world by letters, faxes and telegrams. John Fashanu told reporters that there was even a message from the family of South African president, Nelson Mandela. A photograph of Justin was printed on the front of the order of service sheet, along with an inscription that read: 'Christian, footballer, leader, coach, loved member of our family, and friend.' In the order of service John wrote: 'My tribute - Even though we've had our differences, like all families, I have always loved you and always will. At least I know for sure that you have found your eternal peace. I know that Jesus whom you loved will welcome you home. Free at last! Your loving brother, John.'

Two months later a public memorial service was held for Fashanu in Norfolk. The ceremony was held at St Mary's Church in Attleborough and organised by Edward Jackson and his wife, Rachel. The couple wanted the chance for people who'd grown up with Justin to pay their own respects. Many people who had played football with him when he was young attended as well as friends from school. The memorial book from the service holds many heartfelt messages.

'I have so many memories of Justin as a boy, but one of my lasting memories is one of him as a man. My car tyre had developed a puncture in the middle of Attleborough Town on a very busy day and I was told by a local bobby to move it as quickly as possible. I was feeling quite desperate when this huge figure came towards me with an even larger smile on his face and quickly pushed the car to an appropriate spot and changed my tyre. He left with a quick kiss on the cheek and a cheery goodbye. That was Justin – helpful, kind and always smiling,' wrote H. Friend.

'Fly my friend for now you're free. You tried and tried but they wouldn't see,' wrote Justin's former boxing trainer, Gordon Holmes.

'I used to be a referee when Justin first started playing Sunday League football for Shropham. He soon became a marked man for his outstanding talent... Obviously, word soon spread amongst visiting teams and in one game Justin felt I was not protecting him enough and left the pitch. After a while, he decided to return which meant that I had to have a quiet word with him explaining that he should not leave the pitch without my permission. He responded in his usual jovial way and I had the pleasure of refereeing him on many further occasions,' wrote Malcolm Broom.

The Rector of St Mary's Church, the Reverend John Aves, conducted the service but local Canon Derek Price also addressed the congregation. Price's rhetoric was both poignant and radical. Here are some of his words:

'There was another side to Justin. There is another side to all of us. He had the warmth and humour of the clown and I would remind you that the clown make-up includes a tear on the cheek. Beneath the surface there is often a lonely, anguished heart, self-doubt, confusion and pain. Each of us has a shadow side to our personality, vulnerable spots which others do not normally see and which we choose not to reveal.

'Those who differ from us and whom we find difficult to understand, and whose behaviour we may find offensive we label. Justin attracted labels: "queen", "queer", "poof", and on one occasion, apparently, a "bloody poof." To label a person can be the first stage in their crucifixion, as it was for Justin.

'Whatever the legal verdict on Justin's suicide, I believe the ultimate, original and rock bottom cause was the prejudice and antagonism of the church and society in general towards homosexuals, pushing many of them into a life of excruciating secrecy, deception and despair.

'*Better Dead Than Gay* was a TV documentary shown not very long ago. It explored the suicide of a 26-year-old Ipswich man because he could not reconcile being homosexual with being Christian, part of the predicament, I suspect, Justin found himself in right to the bitter end. Simon Harvey's story concretely expressed the dilemma faced by many homosexual people, especially those who embrace the Christian faith like Justin did. The struggle to find self-esteem and to love themselves amid such negative, rejecting, critical messages, the common use by some Christians of their religion to justify social prejudices, often masked by moral certitude and self-righteousness, together with a one track mind that somehow sees homosexuals as a greater problem to focus on than thousands of fly-blown skeletal men, women and children dying under the Sudan sun or even homelessness.

'I believe that in God's created scheme of things of infinite variety, there are both heterosexuals and homosexuals and every sexual shade in between, and that homosexuality is no more of a deviation, flaw or falling short than being created left-handed, blue eyed or dark haired.

'Only when we can believe that God's created scheme does not exclude, but includes, homosexuality and homosexual love shall we begin to accept and love them and they will begin to accept and love themselves and feel at ease at long last in society. Someday. Someday.

'However, my dear Justin, as we started with a smile so let us end with one. A wry smile at a verse from a song much sung in the very best Victorian drawing room. If only they knew what they were singing!

> _Girls were made to love and kiss_
> _And who am I to interfere with this?_
> _Am I ashamed to follow nature's path?_
> _Can I be blamed if God has made me gay?_
> _Amen.'_

From a man of the cloth it was controversial stuff and the top story in the local news the very next day. Everyone was talking about it with Norwich's _Evening Daily Press_ reporting the cleric's address looked set to fuel controversy. When the paper's reporter asked a representative from Price's church for a response the rep said: 'It would not be appropriate for us to comment on what is essentially an address at a funeral. Mr Price was undoubtedly trying to set this tragic incident in its context and it would not be right for us to take a view and interfere with his pastoral duties.'[59] Price told the reporter that he had never made his views on homosexuality public before then and knew it would cause some controversy. For most people in Norwich they admired Price for being so honest and for having the courage to state his views. When he was alive Justin turned to religion for support and guidance but, ultimately, mostly found discrimination and bigotry. It was impressive for a Christian cleric to acknowledge this fact and even more remarkable that he chose to do so publicly at the footballer's memorial service. Justin would have been proud.

It wasn't long after his funeral that the knives were being sharpened and Fashanu's name was being cut up in the national press. Because Justin's behaviour had sometimes been questionable he was considered fair game. There's no denying that the footballer had lied, schemed and cheated many times in order to make a fast buck and had let himself down on countless occasions. In doing so he'd burned a lot of bridges and just as many friendships. One of the people he treated badly was

Julie Goodyear who said: 'He obviously ran out of lies. He told a lot of lies about me for money. The only relationship I ever had with Justin was one of friendship, but he claimed it was a sexual relationship which wasn't true. I maintained a dignified silence, but I do think these things catch up with you.' The way Fashanu acted was, sometimes, reprehensible as Goodyear can attest. However, one thing that's important to reiterate is that we will never know whether Fashanu did actually attack DJ in Maryland or whether the alleged victim was blackmailing the footballer as Fashanu had stated. Despite this fact, some journalists were happy to call the footballer a rapist. Brian Deer's article for the Mail on Sunday was particularly uncomfortable to read.

Writing about the alleged attack in America Deer wrote: 'Fashanu seized his chance. He would not take rejection a second time. At some dimly-lit level DJ knew what was happening. But his struggle to stop it failed. Fashanu's power was briefly regained. The ex-star raped the boy.'[60] Deer described how Fashanu's hypothetical trial might have panned out if he had lived to be brought back to the US to face his accuser: 'An ageing black sports star, retired with knee trouble. A white victim. An immediate flight. The formula was there: a little OJ II.'

When I asked Deer how he could be so sure that Fashanu was guilty, he said: 'I think he did it. He did exactly what was alleged. I am genuinely convinced that Fashanu was sexually abused as a kid.' Personally, I'm uncomfortable that Fashanu was called a rapist when it was never proven. Another article that called Fashanu a rapist years after his death was written by Tom English for The Scotsman. While investigative articles are to be expected, some reinforce the falsity that Justin Fashanu was guilty of rape. That simply isn't true. While he may indeed have been guilty it can never be proven one way or the other.

Surprisingly, one person who did regret the way things had turned out for the footballer was Brian Clough. In his second autobiography, the Nottingham Forest manager said he was sorry about the way he had treated Fashanu.

'Yes, I dropped a clanger with Fashanu... I didn't treat him with the respect he deserved or give him the help that I gave to a lot of players who were better than him. I should have recognised his problems quicker and not broken ranks. I shouldn't have told people.

'It is dishonest to ignore times you would rather forget - the occasions when you would do things differently if you could do them all over again,

when you look back and think to yourself, 'I wish I hadn't dealt with the situation that way.' I'm thinking of Justin Fashanu.'[61]

While it was big of Clough to write of his regrets, it was far too late. Clough's treatment of Fashanu at Nottingham Forest had been harsh. Justin was barely an adult at the time, and the fact he was forced to endure such public humiliation I believe is a disgrace. No one should ever have to suffer that.

Legacy of a Reluctant Hero

SINCE HIS death in 1998, a great deal has been written about Justin Fashanu and the footballer has been labelled a lot of things. While he's a hero to some people for promoting gay rights, he is a conman to others and an enigma to most. Many say that the footballer didn't even know himself. There's merit in all these viewpoints. One thing is certain: Fashanu lived a gregarious life that was never far from controversy. He was blessed with a propitious upbringing in rural Norfolk by two wonderful foster parents but never managed to get over being abandoned by his biological parents. His inability to deal with that one issue manifested itself in many ways throughout his life. A lack of trust, reluctance to forge close relationships with people and an inability to settle in one place for too long all added to the Fashanu enigma.

The footballer endured many trials and tribulations that caused him great anguish. He was forsaken as a young child, abused because of his sexuality and condemned by the religion he embraced. His own brother's public condemnation, perhaps, cut the deepest. It's not surprising the footballer built what many have described as a 'brick wall' around him. Those few people who were able to penetrate Fashanu's defences found warmth, sensitivity and someone who really only wanted to be loved.

Fashanu was a kind spirit. But as others will attest, there was also another side to the footballer. He had very little self-objectivity and always seemed on the run. He hurt people when he spent their money, yet another contradictory aspect of his character. In short, he could be very selfish.

Fashanu was flawed just like the rest of us. His Achilles heel was money of which he could never seem to get enough. In fairness, a great deal of his cash went towards medical bills as he tried to find a fix for his re-occurring knee injury. Keeping his dream of playing top-flight football alive was expensive, and with so much at stake Fashanu did what he could to fan those flames. But he also lived an extravagant life even when the big money had stopped flowing into his bank account. Attaining the high life sometimes meant cheating people, and he let himself and others down in that regard on more than one occasion. Being in the public spotlight at such a young age didn't help, and whenever he faltered, it was on record for everyone to see. Fashanu never really managed being a celebrity well and learned the hard way that the superficial world of fame and stardom can eat you alive too.

The footballer's friend Terry Deal says Fashanu reminded him a lot of a character in a novel that Deal read in the early Eighties. He can't remember the name of the book but the central character is a closeted gay man who tries to hide his sexuality from the rest of the world. In order to do so he creates a fantasy persona, someone who appears confident and gregarious but, in reality, is far more sensitive and confused because of his sexuality. When the man's two lives finally merge he freaks out and ends up killing himself. The novel has similar themes to Justin's own story. Deal says:

'Gay activists are happy to claim him as one of their own which is great and I'm all for that, but I don't think he really wanted that when he was alive, not for the right reasons anyway. He had a little spell at small-time fame and had to run away from that in the end because he left a lot of shit behind. People like myself and others genuinely warmed to his company and charm and felt miffed by his sudden cutting of apparent friendships, although in hindsight this was a reflection on him not us.'

Deal is right when he says that Justin was hesitant to fly the rainbow flag when he was alive. What he really wanted was to be left alone to his own devices. Of course, that's difficult when you are a celebrity, especially a charismatic and controversial figure such as Fashanu. While he was pulled in one direction, religion was pulling him in another. How easy it is to stand on a pulpit and denounce someone simply for being who they truly are. Everybody struggles with something in their life and it is easy to judge. The pressure he felt from his faith pushed him ever closer towards the precipice from which he eventually fell. How ironic it is that something he looked to for guidance in life turned out to be one of the things that caused his early demise. Its sickening and disturbing that many Christians continue to denounce homosexuals, fellow human beings, today.

One person who does regret what she wrote about Fashanu shortly after he came out in 1990 is Christian writer, Marcia Dixon. If you recall, *The Voice* journalist publicly denounced the footballer as someone who belonged to Satan. Today, Dixon runs a successful public relations firm and when I asked her for a comment she said.

'The article about Justin was written during a time when being black, Christian and publicly admitting you were gay was a definite no-no, and the religious sentiment articulated in the article reflected the prevailing views of the black Pentecostal Christian community of the time. Would I write an article like that now? Not at all. I'm older, more mature and I'd like to think have more empathy and understanding about the human struggle - whatever the area, and recognise that everyone, whether they have faith in God or not, have issues that they grapple with.'

Sadly, as this book went to print, there was no such retraction from Dixon's former colleague at *The Voice*, Tony Sewell. After attempting to contact him several times he never got back to me.

Peter Tatchell ultimately sees Fashanu as a trailblazer. He was a pioneer who beat his own path through life. While Tatchell acknowledges Justin was not a flawless star, he was a bright star nonetheless. Britain's first black million-pound footballer, and the first professional player in the world to come out, Fashanu continues to be an inspiration to millions of people.

Sadly, as of now, Fashanu remains a rare breed. Few other gay professional footballers have followed his lead. In the UK, former Leeds United player Robbie Rogers came out in February 2013 shortly after retiring from the professional game. The 25-year-old American was the first player to do so since Justin did back in 1990. Talking about his decision to reveal all was commendable, and it's truly outrageous that gay footballers feel forced to hide who they are. Rogers says:

'For the past 25 years I have been afraid, afraid to show whom I really was because of fear. Fear that judgment and rejection would hold me back from my dreams and aspirations. Fear that my loved ones would be farthest from me if they knew my secret. Fear that my secret would get in the way of my dreams. Dreams of going to a World Cup, dreams of The Olympics, dreams of making my family proud. What would life be without these dreams? Could I live a life without them?

'Life is only complete when your loved ones know you. When they know your true feelings, when they know who and how you love. Life is simple when your secret is gone. Gone is the pain that lurks in the stomach at work, the pain from avoiding questions, and at last the pain from hiding such a deep secret. Secrets can cause so much internal damage. People love to preach about honesty, how honesty is so plain and simple. Try explaining to your loved ones after 25 years you are gay. Try convincing yourself that your creator has the most wonderful purpose for you even though you were taught differently.

'I always thought I could hide this secret. Football was my escape, my purpose, my identity. Football hid my secret, gave me more joy than I could have ever imagined... I will always be thankful for my career. I will remember Beijing, The MLS Cup, and most of all my teammates. I will never forget the friends I have made along the way and the friends that supported me once they knew my secret.

'Now is my time to step away. It's time to discover myself away from football. It's 1am in London as I write this and I could not be happier with my decision. Life is so full of amazing things. I realised I could only truly enjoy my life once I was honest. Honesty is a bitch but makes life so simple and clear. My secret is gone, I am a free man, I can move on and live my life as my creator intended.'

When Justin was alive, keeping his own sexuality a secret consumed Fashanu with a burning intensity. When the world finally found out he was gay, only then did he feel peace. It's great to hear that Rogers has found his own freedom by being open and, hopefully, it will encourage more gay professional footballers to do the same. And there are lots of them. According to Tatchell, in the early nineties Fashanu knew of 12 other professional footballers in England who were either gay or bisexual and none of them followed Fashanu's example of openness.

Reporter and writer Juliet Jacques has written several insightful articles on Justin Fashanu over the years and describes the player's life as nothing short of astonishing.

'His surprisingly successful spell as English football's only openly gay footballer should not be taken as typical: rather, it was a short, strange interlude in a life that was often complex and extraordinary. His time at Torquay and Airdrie showed that an out gay footballer could be backed by his chairman, teammates and supporters and it was his relationship with the media more than his sexuality which finally derailed him,' Jacques says.

One of the main organisations keeping Fashanu's name and what he stood for alive is The Justin Campaign. Formed on the tenth anniversary of the footballer's death, the campaign has two aims: to show that homophobia is still prevalent in all levels of football and to help create a world where lesbian, gay, bisexual and transgender people in football are accepted. Sadly, there is still some way to go before both dreams are realised. Activist and artist Jason Hall helped kick-start The Justin Campaign alongside Juliet Jacques.

'I had troubles growing up with my own sexuality and so I could relate to Justin Fashanu. I avoided coming out to myself and others and when I played football I disguised the fact I was gay. It was the game for straight people that turned boys into men. The game does not welcome people of my sexuality and that made me want to do something about it,' says Hall.

Since it was launched in 2008, The Justin Campaign has grown into an internationally recognised and acclaimed organisation making waves in the battle against homophobia in football. In 2010, Hall personally met with the British Prime Minister David Cameron to talk about the issue. Hall made the headlines when he presented Cameron with his very own personalised pink football jersey. Another milestone was a successful campaign to have Fashanu inducted into Norwich City FC's Hall of Fame.

The Justin Campaign has its own football team, the 'Justin Fashanu All-Stars', which travels all over the world competing in football matches and spreading the gospel that homophobia should not be tolerated. Whether they win or lose on the pitch is irrelevant, what's important is the message they're kicking around. The Football Association has taken note and joined forces with Hall to tackle what's being called 'football's last taboo'. In 2010, the FA and The Justin Campaign launched 'Football vs Homophobia' a nationally recognised day for people to voice their opposition to homophobia. Hall says the FA has been very supportive and seems to genuinely want to make homophobic behaviour as unacceptable as racism. It's frustrating, then, that for many professional players and managers the message is still not being heard. When the FA and Kick-it-Out (the Football Association's organisation to fight racism in the sport) produced an anti-homophobia video in 2011, professional players and managers refused to take part in it. It seems that no one was willing to put their head above the parapet when it came to fighting such prejudice. It's quite apparent that in the macho culture of professional football many athletes simply aren't accepting of gay men. For Hall, Jacques and others, as it was for Fashanu himself, it's a tough battle to change an entire mindset. The Anti-Homophobia Advisory Group, of which Frank Clark is on the panel, is at least trying. The group works with the FA to deal with homophobia at all levels and that includes players. While Clark admits a lot of ground has been made in stamping out homophobia a lot more needs to be done.

If Brian Clough were alive today it would be interesting to know what he'd make of Ball Bois FC, a Nottingham-based football club of gay and gay-friendly players. Unlike Fashanu during his stint in Nottingham, the players don't have to disguise their sexuality. The team plays in a competitive league organised by the Gay Football Supporters Network, an organisation that promotes the participation of gay men and women. Now in its tenth season, the GFSN is the world's only football league for lesbian, gay, bisexual and transgender teams. Fifteen clubs from all over the UK compete in three divisions.

Scott Lawley, a player with Balls Bois, says the city of Nottingham has been very supportive and Notts County and Nottingham Forest equally so. Both clubs have written positive articles about Balls Bois in their respective match programmes and are happy to promote anti-homophobia events. But many other professional football clubs prefer to ignore the issue. 'I won't mention the name of the club, but when a member of a local gay club contacted them their response was: "We don't have a problem with homophobia in this club because we don't have any gay players." This is what you're up against in some cases, but we're lucky in Nottingham because even the local sheriff supports us,' Lawley says.

While Justin Fashanu remains one of only two professional footballers in the UK to come out, other professional players around the world are finally following his lead. Sweden's Anton Hysén is a notable example. Hysén is the son of former Liverpool great Glenn Hysén and plays for Utsiktens BK in one of Sweden's top divisions. Unlike Fashanu, Hysén's family fully supported his decision to come out.

'I have no regrets about coming out and I don't care what people think. If I hear a negative comment from someone then I just ignore it or laugh. Not everybody is going to love you. I don't see myself as a role model, but if what I have done helps make the world a better place then I'm all for it. My teammates have been very positive about my coming out and all they care about is winning the league,' says Hysén. The footballer occasionally reads negative comments about him that people have posted anonymously on the Internet, but says that they don't bother him. He is surprised that other gay professional footballers have not come forward in Britain, but the UK stands are a far different landscape than Sweden's. While Hysén has openly heard Swedish fans in the stands reprimand someone who's shouting homophobic abuse at him, one wonders if that would happen in England. You'd like to think it would but, sadly, I'm not certain.

Like Hysén, former Welsh rugby international Gareth Thomas is also inspiring change. Before he came out in 2009, Thomas' situation was similar to Fashanu's. His sexuality was the worst kept secret in rugby and it caused the sportsman a great deal of angst.

'It's been really tough for me hiding who I really am and I don't want it to be like that for the next young person who wants to play rugby, or some frightened young kid. I don't know if my life is going to be easier because I'm out, but if it helps someone else then it will have been worth it. I'm not going on a crusade but I'm proud of who I am. I feel I have achieved everything I could ever possibly have hoped to achieve out of rugby and I did it being gay. I want to send a positive message to other gay people that they can do it too,'[62] Thomas said. One theory why more gay professional footballers have not come forward is that they're fearful of losing sponsorship deals and money. If that's the case then Thomas' story demonstrates this may not be true. Since he told the world he was gay endorsements have flooded in.

Unlike Gareth Thomas and Anton Hysén who say they have both received the full support of their families, Justin's own relationship with his family, particularly John, has been well documented. After his brother's death, John seemed to be genuinely heartbroken and sorry for the way he'd treated Justin. A month after the suicide he gave an interview with the TV personality Esther Rantzen and revealed that shortly before Justin's death his brother might have contacted him.

'There was a telephone call to my mobile phone that night and the person wouldn't speak. I could hear breathing. I could feel that it was someone from my family. I could feel that it was Justin, but I didn't reach out. I just put the phone down and thought, "Oh, it's him again." And, of course, the next day he committed suicide,'[63] John said.

John told Rantzen that he would always blame himself and that he could have done more. Former Norwich ace Dave Bennett claims he once asked John whether he regretted the way he'd treated Justin when he was alive. Bennett says he bumped into him at a media event and John could not muster a reply. Bowing his head, he simply walked away. A.J. Ali says he's disappointed at the way John behaved towards Justin.

'My brother Abbey meant everything to me. No matter what he did, I was there for him, even when he was a drug dealer. Even when he went to prison for manslaughter. He paid the price and came out a totally changed person and became a gift to society, always helping people. Whenever I had a problem ever in life, I went to him and he was always there for me, no matter how much I messed up. When my brother died of cancer, his last words to me were "Love is the answer." That's the kind of brother he was. We never had a fight. Even on his deathbed, he was still giving me advice. I can't imagine facing something like Justin was facing while knowing that his own brother had turned his back on him,' Ali says.

John made national headlines again in March 2012 after an interview he gave on the radio show talkSPORT. He sensationally announced that Justin was not gay, rather a publicity-seeker who made up stories to get attention and cash.

'I don't believe he was gay. If you had a brother who came out and said: "Hey listen, I'm gay," we'd welcome you, say: "No problem," but if you had someone who came out and said: "I'm a spaceman," when you're not a spaceman then that's a bit silly. It's a macho man's game and I think there are reasons why we haven't had any gay footballers come out. I don't believe there will be. I'm not saying there aren't some there, but I can tell you in twenty years of playing all my matches I have never come across a gay footballer.

'I'm not someone who says: "I've got black friends, they're all good people." I'm not going to say: "I've got gay friends, who are all good people." It's unfortunate because I don't believe he was, and if he was, who gives a rat's arse? So what? But don't go and sell your stories or make up stories for money for goodness sake. I'm heterosexual; will I make it on to the front page of the newspapers? My daughter was very close to her uncle and it has taken a long time for her to understand that Justin wasn't really gay, he just wanted attention,'[64] John said.

In my opinion, John Fashanu lost his credibility a long time ago and this rant only reinforces this. Despite requests for an interview, John did not get back to me so I was not able to ask him whether he holds the same views today. What's dangerous is his words attempt to place Justin back in the closet and this should never be allowed to happen. Justin was gay, plain and simple, and although not many professional footballers in the UK have followed his example yet, thousands of other people in other sports have. In May 2013, American NBA star Jason Collins made headlines around the world when he announced that he was gay. He received praise for his decision to tell all from teammates, other professional sports people and even President Barack Obama.

Thankfully, there is at least one member of the Fashanu clan who is taking strides to fight homophobia in football. Justin's niece Amal Fashanu was only a little girl when her uncle was alive, but as an adult she refuses to let his death be in vain. Amal openly supports The Justin Campaign, and in 2012 helped produce a documentary for the BBC called *Britain's Gay Footballers*. Her mission in the one-hour film was to try to discover why not one gay professional player has followed her uncle's steps in coming out more than twenty years on. What's most interesting is that Amal calls out her father on the way he treated Justin. Amal was only ten when Justin died, but she was old enough to realise that John didn't approve of Justin's lifestyle. When she grew older she was saddened to learn just how much her father had forsaken Justin.

'The extent of his disloyalty was a shock. Other members of the family have been reticent. It hurts me to think everyone abandoned him. I can't help but think it would have taken just one supportive person to stand up for him. I'm proud Justin was my uncle and that he was brave enough to say what he did. I think my dad now regrets the harsh way he responded. The game needs more people like my uncle if homophobic barriers are to be removed,'[65] Amal told a newspaper reporter.

Justin Fashanu's life and death have not only made an impact in sport, but also made a difference for many individuals. Sure, Justin had his faults, but the following story I found on an Internet site called 'The Tears of a Clown' shows he was clearly a caring, sensitive soul deep down:

'I was an English student living in Atlanta in the US, playing soccer on a scholarship around 1993. Struggling with combining the soccer/football experience with being gay was very difficult. In the college bookstore one day, while passing a section devoted to African Americans, I saw Justin Fashanu's face on the cover of a magazine. I thought it was a football magazine, but on closer inspection it was a black gay magazine. These were days before the Internet and I'd all but lost touch with footballing events in England so I was quite shocked myself to find out Justin was gay, and reading his story that was a couple of years old I was so happy that a player of such high profile had come out. This revelation certainly inspired me and I wrote him a short note of support and sent it off to his Scottish club, Hearts.

'A couple of weeks later, working in a learning lab of the university, my boss told me one of my English friends had been calling to talk to me. I thought it was a mate from Reading, but when he tried again, when I lifted the receiver, he said: "Hi Tony, this is Justin." I was so wonderfully surprised, more because I was talking to a professional footballer who'd played for England! Anyway, we spoke for about twenty minutes and the overriding feeling I got from him was his humility. He told me he was doing things with the BBC, playing for Hearts and in general things were going fine. I was so humbled that he'd taken the time, and he said that the note I'd sent him was one he deeply appreciated.

'Events after that shocked and saddened me and I really did and still do feel for what that man had to go through. I write this as his decision to take his own life made me stronger as a human being and to go about life without stigma. I'm a teacher in London now and while I don't shout about who I am from the rooftops, I tolerate zero discrimination in my teaching, and despite being the wrong side of 40, I still run rings round the kids in football! So, whoever reads this, let the ripple effect of fighting for what is right always win, as there are some who've sacrificed more than we ever can.'[65] Tony

If you scour the Internet looking for articles on Justin Fashanu there are literally thousands to read. The footballer may be dead but his memory lives on. While homophobia didn't kill him, being a gay footballer was incredibly challenging. When the British weekly newspaper The *Pink Paper* asked readers to list their all-time lesbian and gay heroes, Justin ranked at number 99. That speaks volumes. Although he had his faults, it's thanks to Justin Fashanu that as each year passes the world of sport is slowly uniting in its stand against homophobia.

ENDNOTES

[1] *Inside Story: Fallen Hero,* BBC, 1998
[2] *The Pace Setters,* BBC Norwich, 1981
[3] *The Pace Setters,* BBC Norwich, 1981
[4] *Eastern Daily Press,* Ardent, 1977
[5] *Black Sportsmen,* Ernest Cashmore, Routledge, 1982
[6] *Thetford and Brandon Times,* Archant, 1977
[7] *Diss Express,* Johnston Press, 1977
[8] *Diss Express,* Johnston Press, 1977
[9] *Diss Express,* Johnston Press, 1977
[10] *The Pace Setters,* BBC Norwich, 1981
[11] *The Pace Setters,* BBC Norwich, 1981
[12] *The Pace Setters,* BBC Norwich, 1981
[13] *On the Ball,* ITV, Feb, 1981
[14] *Eastern Daily Press,* Archant, 1981
[15] *The Pace Setters,* BBC Norwich, 1981
[16] *Shoot!* Pedigree Group, 1981
[17] *Nottingham Evening Post,* Northcliffe Newspapers Group, 1982
[18] *Nottingham Evening Post,* Northcliffe Newspapers Group, 1982
[19] *Clough, Brian Clough: The Autobiography,* Corgi Adult, 1995
[20] *Clough, Brian Clough: The Autobiography,* Corgi Adult, 1995
[21] *Sunday People,* Trinity Mirror Group, 1982
[22] *Inside Story: Fallen Hero,* BBC, 1998
[23] *Nottingham Evening Post,* Northcliffe Newspapers Group, 1982
[24] *Daily Express,* Northern and Shell Media, 1982
[25] *Nottingham Evening Post,* Northcliffe Newspapers Group, 1982
[26] *Nottingham Evening Post,* Northcliffe Newspapers Group, 1982
[27] Soccer *Match!* Independent Soccer Magazine (U.S.), 1988
[28] *Daily Express,* Northern and Shell Media, 1989
[29] *From Right-Wing to B-Wing,* Football World, 2009
[30] *The Sun,* News Corp Newspapers, Oct 1990
[31] *The Voice,* GV Media Group, 1990
[32] *The Voice,* GV Media Group, 1990
[33] *Football Focus,* BBC, 1990
[34] *Shot Down in Flames,* Transmedia, 1998

[35] *Shot Down in Flames,* Transmedia, 1998
[36] *The Sun,* News Corp Newspapers, 1990
[37] *The Voice,* GV Media Group, 1991
[38] *Sunday People,* Trinity Mirror Group, 1990
[39] *Gay Times,* Millivres, 1991
[40] *Gay Times,* Millivres, 1991
[41] *Tonight With Jonathan Ross,* Channel 4, 1992
[42] *Tonight With Jonathan Ross,* Channel 4, 1992
[43] *Open To Question,* BBC, 1992
[44] *Strong Enough to Survive,* Virago Press, 1994
[45] *The Sun,* News Corp Newspapers, 1992
[46] *Sunday People,* Trinity Mirror Group, 1992
[47] *The Scotsman,* Johnston Publishing, 1998
[48] *The Scotsman,* Johnston Publishing, 1998
[49] *Sunday People,* Trinity Mirror Group, 1994
[50] *Daily Mirror,* MGN Ltd, 1994
[51] *Foul Play,* Bantam Press, 2003
[52] *Press Association,* PA Group, 1998
[53] *Press Association,* PA Group, 1998
[54] *The Sun,* News Corp Newspapers, 1998
[55] *Daily Mail,* Associated Newspapers Ltd, 1998
[56] *Daily Mirror,* MGN Ltd, 1998
[57] *Baltimore Sun,* Tribune Publishing, 1998
[58] *The Birmingham Post,* Trinity Mirror Midlands Ltd, 1998
[59] *Eastern Daily Press,* Archant, 1998
[60] *Mail on Sunday,* Associated Newspapers Ltd, July 1998
[61] *Cloughie: Walking on Water,* Headline Book Publishing, 1992
[62] *Daily Mail,* Associated Newspapers Ltd, 2010
[63] *That's Esther,* ITV, 2000
[64] *talkSPORT,* UTV Media (UK), 2012
[65] *Daily Mail,* Associated Newspapers Ltd, 2011
[65] *The Tears of a Clown,* Stuart Frew, Wordspress, 2007